At Home in the Briar Patch

Mariann S. Regan

Also by Mariann S. Regan:

Love Words: The Self and the Text in Medieval
And Renaissance Literature

Immortality News: A Novel

Gotham Books

30 N Gould St.
Ste. 20820, Sheridan, WY 82801
https://gothambooksinc.com/

Phone: 1 (307) 464-7800

© 2023 Mariann S. Regan. All rights reserved.

No part of this book may be reproduced, stored in a retrieval system, or transmitted by any means without the written permission of the author.

Published by Gotham Books (September 08, 2023)

ISBN: 979-8-88775-285-3 (P)
ISBN: 979-8-88775-286-0 (E)

Because of the dynamic nature of the Internet, any web addresses or links contained in this book may have changed since publication and may no longer be valid.

The views expressed in this work are solely those of the author and do not necessarily reflect the views of the publisher, and the publisher hereby disclaims any responsibility for them.

Praise for Into the Briar Patch

"*Into the Briar Patch* is a richly textured memoir—beautifully conveyed through story, anecdote, dialogue and reminiscence—which brings to life the tangle of relationships binding a strong-minded, yet also deeply loving, Southern farming family from the pre War era to the present. It is also a profound meditation on the mixture of good and evil that we discover in any far-reaching investigation of our personal past.

"First shocked to realize that her 19th century ancestors were slave-holders, Mariann Regan does not flinch from this unwelcome news. Rather, she explores it—not only to understand better the people she came from, but also to reflect on how otherwise hard-working and god-fearing people can not only participate in, but also assent to, such harm. She offers a central story from her family about her mother Maisie, who was saved as an infant from a burning house by her older sister Ansie, to represent the core values of her extended family. Yet the seemingly simple moral of 'saving the baby' could not address the full range of social dilemmas they faced—where being strong, brave, and responsible in family terms could also place one at the center of racial conflict about 'whose baby was to be saved.'

"Taking a deeper step into this morass, Regan traces the relationship between her family's experience of slave-holding and the ways they reared their own children—with an acute sense of care, but also with a belief in the importance of physical discipline—in order to maintain control, not only of unruly others (like slaves or children), but also of their own unruly wishes or desires. Herself a subject of frequent physical discipline at the hands of her well-educated and socially self-conscious mother, Regan has a first-hand understanding of the pain and humiliation of being subjected to the arbitrary will of a more powerful other.

"Yet this is not a memoir of (belatedly recognized) social guilt, nor does it seek to join the contemporary tide of memoirs documenting various forms of child abuse. What is most unusual—and most compelling—about this book is its labor to achieve not only clear-eyed understanding of the past, but also compassion for all of the (living and dead) players involved.

"*Into the Briar* Patch speaks to everyone who seeks to confront his or her immediate past as well as the entangled roots thereof, which necessarily include larger social conflicts, as well as deeper (and sadder) realizations about the fraught and flawed nature of human relationships, not only within individual families but also within the geo-political societies where we all struggle to live and thrive."

—Madelon Sprengnether, author of *Crying at the Movies: A Film Memoir* and *The Spectral Mother: Freud, Feminism and Psychoanalysis*. Dr. Sprengnether is Regents Professor in the Department of English, at the University of Minnesota.

"*Into the Briar Patch* is, first and foremost, the story of a fascinating and quintessentially American family. It's also the work of a gifted and scrupulous historian, a stylist whose warm voice and nuanced prose keeps you turning the page. Mariann Regan is a writer triply blessed and working at the height of her powers."

—Peter Duval, author of *Rear View*, winner of the 2003 Bakeless Prize for Fiction

"Regan recounts her family's history in the South, particularly in relation to slave ownership. In her memoir's introduction, Regan... informs readers that she will present the account of her ancestors—including the period of time in which they and many of their neighbors owned slaves—without judgment. Pulling from an early established metaphor of 'the baby' a family tries to protect and preserve through all trials and transitions, Regan takes us through riveting details of how her relatives 'saved the baby' by physical wherewithal and classically masculine courage.

"With succinct, rich language that rings in one's ear like a wind chime gently stirred by a slow breeze, Regan describes brushes with death, toughening-up scraps among brothers and practical decisions involving life on the farm. She delineates how many of her family's demonstrable characteristics (i.e.; their go-to methods of protecting the baby') were probably hatched, or at least hardened, during the prominent period of slave ownership . . . .

"She shares interesting, well-developed thoughts on how Southern womanhood, particularly inasmuch as it was purported to encompass pitch-perfect purity, was offered as proof that slaveholding was not the barbaric undertaking that Northerners had tagged it. Regan's portrayal of her mother, Maisie, who, as a baby, was saved from a house fire (the event that gave rise to Regan's framing device), is stylistically well-written.... An expansive, accomplished memoir that reverberates with down-home cadence and picturesque rough-and-tumble family memories."

-Kirkus Discoveries, July 1, 2011

Contents

Prologue xv

Chapter One Hold on Tight and Save the Baby 1

Chapter Two Saving the Baby with Strength and Grit 7

    Kirven Family Timeline from the late 1800s through the 1900s 12
    Kirven Family Timeline from the 1700s into the 1900s 20

Chapter Three Ambush 27

Chapter Four Whose Baby Gets Saved? 33

    Interlude: I am born and I am nurtured 50

Chapter Five "A Spotless Reputation" The Baby of Your Good Name 57

Chapter Six "Y'all Be Good, Now!" Slavery, Jim Crow, and the Baby 83

Chapter Seven Baby Paradoxes and Raising the Baby 113

Scenes and Interludes 123

    Towering Uncles 123
    Ecstasy 125
    Not Even My Dogs 127
    Courage in Plastic Bags 128
    Lost and Found 129
    Wanting to Go That Way: Funny No More 130
    Down-Home Recipes 131
    Peacemaker at the Wheel 133

Kiss the Shark... 134
Civil Conversations.. 135
Danny and the Two Mules and the Hat 138
Cathy and the Oyster 139
A Squirt in the Hair.. 140
Ridin' Around Town... 141
Buzz, Buzz... 141
Pink Ladies.. 142
It's Your Father Speaking... 145
Sorry! Sorry!... 146
Special Letter for Tom 147
Up a Tree 149
Fumes of the Patriarchy 150
Why, Indeed?... 152
He Had a Beard 153
What He Offered... 154
Uncle John and the Refrigerator 155
Popping for Peace.. 157

Excerpts from Interviews with Relatives 159

  Beau Kirven Johnson 159
  Cathy Sanders Andrews.. 163
  Julie Kirven Griffin 173
  Diane Williams Yamamoto 180
  Larry Kirven 199
  Anne Kirven... 208
  Laura Ann Kirven Onsrud 211
  Joe Chandler Kirven 213

For Richard, who continues to save me

To all my family in past, present, and future generations

Are you going away with no word of farewell?
Will there be not a trace left behind?
I could have loved you better, didn't mean to be unkind,
You know that was the last thing on my mind.
Tom Paxton, 1964

Prologue

Brer Fox has found Brer Rabbit with his head stuck into the Tar Baby, so that he can't get himself loose. Brer Fox has now caught him at long last, and he wonders how he can free himself of his old frenemy, Brer Rabbit. He calls out, "Brer Rabbit, what am I gonna do with you?"

Now, Brer Rabbit knows what Brer Fox might be thinking, so he pretends to be desperate with this heartfelt plea: "You got me now, Brer Fox, and you can do whatever you want with me. But please, please, *please,* Brer Fox, no matter what you do, please don't throw me into that briar patch right over there."

Of course, Brer Fox winds up and throws Brer Rabbit right into that briar patch, which is what Brer Rabbit, who knows that briar patches are home for rabbits, wanted all along. He drops into the briars and scoots away to be with his whole rabbit family. He calls back, "Halloo, Brer Fox! I was born and bred in that Briar Patch."

The stories of my own ancestors' thoughts and deeds and values during the last few centuries—the history that they made and that made them—these stories can be layered with briars of conflict. If Brer Rabbit can frolic so easily among the briars of his home without getting pierced by them, and if he is so well acquainted with his own family briar patch . . . then maybe my family's briars can brush above me gently as I hop along beneath them.

Of course, briars are the stuff of our all our lives as human beings. Briars were plentiful in the wild blackberry bushes of my childhood, which grew in vacant lots nearby. In May, their white blossoms forecast rich fruit in July. We waited long weeks for the berries to ripen. They began as hard green knots, softened slowly to light red, then turned dark purple and bulged with juice. By the time they were ready, it would be a hot day with sticky air. My sisters and cousins and I would brave the thickets in flannel shirts and sturdy jeans, stomping down thorny just-picked front branches to expose the ready-to-drop berries in the center of the patch, among the fiercest briars.

We endured thorns and sweat and flies and bees and wasps and the constant expectation of snakes. Gloves failed us. With gloves, we couldn't feel the berries. We would fumble and drop them, then lose them in the underbrush, until finally we needed to take off our gloves to hunt for them. That's how we returned with pots full of berries, our unguarded hands and faces thoroughly scratched and smeared. The ripe berries had covered us with red juice indistinguishable from our own trickles of blood. Yet as the adults told us back then, those blackberries made mighty fine pies. We were persuaded that it might be worth getting all bloodied up for a pie that good.

> Men must endure
> Their going hence, even as their coming hither;
> Ripeness is all.
> *King Lear V.ii.3120*

When I first read Edgar's speech to his blinded father in *King Lear*, I connected "ripeness" with the blackberries and thorns of my childhood. A ripe berry and a "ripe" person were both fruits reached by some enduring pain, as I saw it. We all live among metaphorical briars—impediments, hurts, failure, interruptions, delays, insults—and we must move among them.

Chapter One:
Hold on Tight and Save the Baby

Some briars can even be cherished and adopted into family memory. My cousin Diane has shared with me an old family story about my infant mother Maisie and her nine-year-old sister Ansie.

When my mother was an infant, the family home burned to the ground. It was 1915 and early spring in South Carolina. Nine people were asleep inside the farmhouse when the fire started: the husband Tom, the wife Laura, five sons ranging from seventeen to eleven years old, a nine-year-old daughter, and a baby girl. The cause of the fire was unknown—perhaps a single ember had slipped from the fireplace onto the wood floor, or perhaps some malicious person had struck a match in the dark. The family awoke to smoke and flames, yet still in time for everyone to escape alive.

As the flames rose, someone handed the infant Maisie through a first-floor window to her nine-year-old sister, Ansie[1]. She was given a mission:

Ansie! Get a good safe distance away.
Shield Maisie's face with this blanket.
Wait until we come and find you.

Ansie was terrified. Her parents could not help her now, for saving the baby was her task alone. She took the bundled infant and hurried toward the open woods past the garden. As she ran, the voices behind her were unrecognizable—sharp and frantic over the boiling thunder of the fire.

The whole sky glowed red. In that incandescent light, Ansie's own hands flashed red to her, and the baby's howling face lit up like fire. She bent her own face over her sister's, but the baby was not burning. Its skin was cool and smelled like sweet clay. Ansie heard the crack and whine of timber on fire, but

---

[1] Ansie's given name was Laura Ann, to distinguish her from her mother Laura. When the family began to call her "Sis" for "Sister," the two names merged.

she did not turn around to watch the flaming shards explode. She pushed ahead, away from the heat in her wake.

She was far from the house now. Had she run clear of the heat? Would she lose her way in the night woods? Ansie saw a huge fallen tree in the spotted darkness ahead. She stepped around the splintered trunk and crouched behind its mass with the baby. The trunk seemed as wide as Ansie was tall. The fire couldn't reach her here, could it?

Then from her new refuge, Ansie heard a sound she knew well, hooves striking earth, thuds that grew louder, with the grunts and snorts and wheezes of animal panic. The mules were headed her way. They would trample her and baby Maisie, for sure. She pressed up against the fallen tree trunk so that its projecting branches would shield her, blocking the mules. Could they break through thick branches? *Strong as a mule.* Ansie's chest was the size of a mule's hoof. She placed the baby in the small cavity where the trunk curved down and inward. She leaned her body hard into the tree. Her ears filled with hooves, unyielding like the earth they pounded.

Minutes passed. The hoofbeats diminished. The mules must have run off toward the swamp. Ansie peered over the log. Buckets of water were being handed forward near the house. Were those the neighbors from down the road? She looked around and saw that the barn door had swung open. The boys must have let the mules out to save them from being burned alive in the locked barn. Yet the barn and outbuildings were untouched.

The sky was the same, an urgent red, when Ansie heard a sound that was not hooves. She realized it was Maisie, wailing as if her baby heart would break. She placed Maisie across her shoulder, as her mother would have done, and jiggled the baby up and down.

"*Hush* now, *hush* now," she soothed. "It's all *right* now."

Ansie was comforting herself as well. She felt safer because Maisie was safe. She remembered her mother's tuneful voice calling, *Hold on tight now, and don't let go.* Her mother would say that when some precious goodness was at stake.

The house roared and crumbled for a good while that night. Ansie stayed where she was until the water-bearers gave up hope and the flames died down on their own. When the grownups called her back to the house, she returned with a saved baby.

As a child, I heard Mama's version of this story, which was sweet and simple: Someone had handed her out the window of a burning house, and then it was all right. Mama told stories as if through white gauze, purifying them of conflict. Her favorite anecdote was of herself at nine months old being comforted on her mother's shoulder, enveloped by peace and well-being. The more robust version of Ansie's escape from the fire and the mules was told to me years later by Ansie's daughter, Diane.

Ansie is visible in this 1911 photo as the tiny girl in the center row, fourth from left, her hair parted in the middle and pulled back from her ears.

Christmas Day 1911 at the home of James N. Kirven in Darlington, SC. *On porch*: C. Wilson, LaCoste Kirven, Marion Wilson, Simmons Gandy, Ceil Kirven, Noel Kirven, Julian Kirven, Leroy Gandy, Holland Morrow, Bradley Wilson. Short row: Earnest Gandy, Gwaltney Wilson, Mrs. Wyness. Boys: James Wilson, Thomas Kirven, Lawrence Kirven, Willie Coit Kirven, Eugene Kirven, Donnie Kirven. Boys and girls: Marion Kirven, J. Harvey Wilson, Carrie Adele Wilson, Ansie Kirven, Novice Kirven, Adele Kirven, Lois Wilson. Adults: Paul Wilson, Maude Kirven Wilson (holding Coit Wilson), P. D. Wilson, Carrie Kirven, Laura Kirven, Florida Kirven, Emma Kirven, Annie Wilson Morrow, Hallie Kirven Morrow. Standing: Lucia Kirven, May Gandy. Bottom row: Joshua Kirven, Hugh Kirven, James N. Kirven, Robert E. Lee Kirven (holding Eckard Lee Kirven), Thomas Kirven, Luke Kirven, Mary Kirven Baskervill

This story of saving the baby from a house on fire could be a parable of our family's efforts to take care of one another—a parable that may hold true for many families.

Everyone can empathize with the urgent impulse to save a baby. It's an entrenched goal that we each know in our gut. People tend to perceive babies as if they were life itself and all that makes life worth living. An unharmed and innocent baby is a mystery of rejuvenated life, a creation that is "germinated out of the invisible" and "animated by invisible forces" (Becker 1975, 21). In ancient societies, ancestors re-entered the world through babies, and today we all can see dead relatives in each baby's face, alive once more in the living sparkle of each baby's eye.

Even when no actual babies are involved, and even in the absence of physical danger, people can be hit by this same visceral feeling, this sense of emergency that something precious must be preserved, and with care. Saving the baby is a story for everyone, if we extend our idea of Baby to any living, vulnerable being who is as dear to someone as the infant Maisie was to her family. A conceptual Baby can carry a world of meanings. Any perceived good that serves to validate the family's life and all life—that can serve as a symbolic Baby.

A divine Baby inhabits the world's religions as a sign of promised life and ineffable truth. To us, our beliefs and causes are fragile Babies, which we leap to protect. They are steadily on our minds, and Saving the Baby is always an emergency. Babies are the eternity we mortals cannot imagine living our brief lives without. Who is *not* compelled to Save the Baby, and *hold on tight?* Here is my uncle Marion as an infant, standing in for the Baby we each need to save. By contemporary custom, he's dressed as a girl with a bow. This tiny wide-eyed boy-girl can seem radiant with our own feelings about those presences we most cherish and yearn to protect, like the fragile Hope at the bottom of Pandora's box.

Joseph Marion Kirven, c. 1905

This aspirational Baby is a fundamental concept that religion shares with other disciplines. Some psychologists believe this Baby is in essence a caring relationship, two beings in one, deep in the memory. "This vital spark must be conferred on [the newborn] through exchanges with another human being, a partner" (Spitz 1965, 95). Infants deprived of this necessary presence will die by failing to thrive, despite enough food and physical care. This "vital spark," this absolutely protected state of identification with a loving parent, is preserved as a deep longing within all adults. Their rooted sense of self is a "basic good self-object constellation" (Kernberg 1976, 60). That is, the Saved Baby is the central tube of our adult tree, the innermost ring of each person's concentric circles. The "basic mechanism by which our genes control us is the deep, often unspoken (even unthought) conviction that our happiness is special" (Wright 336), no doubt as special as the bond between infant and loving parent. In this sense, to Save the Baby is to save ourselves.

At the same time, a symbolic Baby is our connection with a felt sense of immortality in others. "From the very beginning, the child experiences the awesomeness of life and his problems of survival and well-being in other people." This link provides the foundation of a social contract. Our reciprocal-altruism genes are designed to save both our Baby and the Babies of others, in fellow-feeling. People project their needs "in the form of intense mana onto certain figures to [whom] they defer. They follow these figures with passion and with a trembling heart" (Becker 47, 51). To one cultural anthropologist, "the force of intense emotions" spurs us to "cultural expectations and social norms" that we improvise through our "crucial relationships" (Rosaldo 1958, 92). We confer urgent value upon this self-and-other Baby, this magical well-loved child that lives within us all.

Chapter Two:
Saving the Baby with Strength and Grit

Nine-year-old Ansie was not the only Kirven who showed amazing qualities of courage and protectiveness, while rescuing at night the infant girl who would become my mother. All the Kirvens could be strong, bold, and determined, whether male or female. Physical strength and outspoken courage were qualities they learned to cherish.

Grandfather Tom (1868-1921) was known for his strength. Here he is late in his life, discussing the next move with his son, the second Thomas Jackson Kirven, my uncle. Even at age 51 and in poor health, he is set on being involved in decisions about the family farm. His eyes scrutinize the landscape and the future for whatever trouble is on the way, as if he is planning his next move. His narrow-eyed, strategizing look is a familiar family expression. You didn't cross him. He was strong, and he had the sharp Kirven temper.

Tom carried a gun, and he would use it. Once in 1913 or 1914, a year or two before the house fire, Grandfather Tom and his wife Laura and their daughter Ansie were traveling northeast on Highway 76, then a two-lane unpaved road. Tom's wife and daughter sat behind him in the buggy, while he drove the horses. Ansie was about seven years old at the time. They had been riding from Sumter to Florence and beyond, to visit some of Tom's childhood family.

Grandfather Tom, c. 1919

They arrived at the Big Pee Dee, a formidable river in Low-Country South Carolina, hundreds of yards across with dense, tall growth on either side. In those days it was spanned by a metal truss bridge. On one side of the river, an earthen highway rose to meet the plank deck of the bridge, which joined the descending earth bank at the far side. Waters that rose above the flood level would be channeled over the two ends of the roadway.[2] In the Big Pee Dee—and in its floodwaters—alligators and cottonmouths lived.

On the day of this family journey, the weather was calm and sunny. The waterline was low, and the heat had warmed the bridge planks. Tom, Laura, and Ansie started across in the buggy.

In the middle of the bridge, Tom stopped the horses.

Laura shushed Ansie and pointed out the buggy window to signal "Look there." Two cottonmouths were sunning themselves on the planks, side by side, a few yards ahead. They had crawled there, or swum there, from the Big Pee Dee waters. Mother and daughter tried to breathe silently.

Cottonmouths are large, fanged, strong-venomed snakes, three to four feet long. They are aggressive and ferocious. They are named for the white lining of their mouths that hang open in a visual battle cry.

Tom did not hesitate for a second. Either he felt no fear or considered it his duty to reveal none. Wordless, he slipped out of the buggy, drew his pistol, and fired one shot into each gaping cottonmouth head. Both snakes died on the instant.

Tom returned to the buggy. He said nothing.

Laura and Ansie replied in kind. Silence.

Tom's action was a given, with no need to elaborate on his role as the ultimate protector. He acted with no more ceremony than if he were opening a door. He just remounted, clucked the horses, and drove on past those two cottonmouth corpses.

My cousin Diane, Ansie's daughter, was driven at fearsome speed over this same Big Pee Dee bridge more than a quarter of a century later, in 1941. Our uncle Marion crouched at the wheel of a maroon Pontiac, while four-year-old Diane gritted her teeth in the back seat. *Chunk-a-chunk.* The planks rattled and clattered. Ansie was there, too. The family was rushing Uncle Donnie to report for World War II duty, this time with Marion "Barney

---

[2] My cousin Perry Williams, Ansie's son, explains that these bridges were built so high that flooding water would spill over the road before it could surge into the metal structure of the bridge.

Oldfield" Kirven as the fearless protector. He took the short cut over the old, nearly deserted Big Pee Dee bridge, hurtling them all toward Columbia.

Today a massive turnpike rises far above Big Pee Dee.

Tom dispatched those cottonmouths just as Marion floored that Pontiac, pursuing the family's belief that it takes confident strength to face down danger.

The South Carolina of my ancestors was a quasi-frontier of woods and open farmland, without today's easy call to 911. Along with venomous snakes there were rabid animals, cows and horses with lashing hooves, mean bulls, lunatics with guns, swamps with gators, and treacherous farm machines. My great-uncle Joseph, one of Tom's nine brothers, was killed as a child in a cotton gin accident. Those were times when whooping cough, tuberculosis, polio, tetanus, smallpox, or swamp fever could kill you right quick. Even in the 1950s our young heads spun with fierce warnings to stay away from other children in case there was—or could be—a new danger of polio, or tetanus, or rabies. I was yelled at never to cross State Highway 130 alone, lest some speeding truck squish me into a little grease spot.

Even these days, I've heard of local rainstorms so fierce that their swirling waters could wrap around a dog, suck him into a culvert, and cast him across the road, drowned. Of fire ants so hungry that they would fill one cousin's workboots in two minutes straight, and land him fainting in the hospital. Toxic mosquitoes blown in by Hurricane Hugo, and enough of them to turn another cousin yellow up to the eyeballs and make his skin slough off like a rattlesnake's until it was a wonder he survived.

In the South of my relatives, boys were given guns early and taught to shoot. My cousin Joe Kirven's first gun was a .410 gauge single-barrel shotgun. He practiced on squirrels for quite a while, until by 1939 when he was nine years old, he had sharpened his aim.

One afternoon that year, Joe and his father Tom were walking toward the back porch of their house in Eastover, a simple dwelling raised on brick pillars. They were used to being alert for whatever came along. That day, what came along was a mad dog.

Uncle Thomas J. Kirven, c. 1939, wearing his snake-protection boots

Joseph Chandler Kirven, c. 1939

They knew at first sight that the dog was rabid. In Joe's words, a mad dog "ran at an even gait, looking neither to the left nor to the right," with "eyes glassy and froth falling from its mouth." One nip would infect you with rabies.

The frantic cry of "Mad dog!" would send everyone scrambling. Joe writes in his book of stories that people were seized with the uncanny ability to bolt up tall trees or leap impassable ditches whenever they heard that cry.

This time, the dog was loping straight for them, with barely enough seconds for Joe to slip his hand onto the back porch and grab his .410 King Nitro shotgun. He and his daddy stood fixed to the spot. Retreat was not an option. They made a quick plan.

Wait till he's bout thirty feet away, Tom said.

Yessir. Joe positioned his hands on the gun.

Aim for the head, Tom said.

Yup. Joe admits he was scared. He thought his hands would shake.

Right at the forehead, boy, said Tom.

Blam! The buckshot drilled the dog between the eyes, and it crumpled. People emerged from their hiding places, breathing and grateful. They steered clear of that rabies-filled carcass.

Joe kept the shotgun. He would always have that memory of saving the family and the neighborhood. Not that Joe was a "boy scout," he insisted, meaning that he wasn't the type of child we would have called a "goody-goody." His younger brother Larry remembers Joe as a mischievous older brother who tossed chunks of watermelon rind at Larry's head.

Years later, Joe was able to show his strength and courage again when he became a football hero at Presbyterian College. Here is his photo.

Joe Chandler Kirven at Presbyterian College, c 1952

Kirven Family Timeline from the late 1800s through the 1900s

Thomas Jackson Kirven (1868-1921) and Laura Fraser (1871-1935) married in 1897. They bought farmland near Sumter, SC.
They had seven children:
Thomas Jackson Kirven, (1898-1975), the author's uncle
Lawrence Kirven (1900-1980)
Donald Kirven (1901-1981)
Coit Kirven (1903-1971) and daughter Sarah Harriett "Beau" Kirven (1927-2020)
Marion Kirven (1904-1973) and three daughters: Winkie, Anne, and Jo
Laura Ann "Ansie" Kirven (1906-1981) who married George Williams of Mullins, SC. They had two children, Perry and Diane
Mary "Maisie" Kirven (1915-1992) who married William Sanders, Jr. of Summerville, SC. They had three daughters: Mariann (the author), Catherine, and Laura Beth
1909: Thomas Jackson Kirven, the author's grandfather, was shot and wounded. He never regained his health and died in 1921.
1915: Ansie saved Maisie, as an infant, from their burning home.
1921: Thomas Jackson Kirven, the author's grandfather, died.
1932: Mary "Maisie" Kirven began to attend Coker College in Hartsville, SC.
1933: Thomas Jackson Kirven, the author's uncle, lost the farm in Sumter, SC, and moved with his family to Eastover, SC, where they worked the land.
1935: Estimated year of Laura Fraser's death
1944: The family of Thomas Jackson Kirven (1898-1975) returned to Sumter and reclaimed their farm. He and his wife Eva Chandler Kirven (1901-1977) had eight children:
    Ophelia Kirven (1925-1962)
    Thomas Jackson Kirven (1927-2011), the author's cousin
    Joe Chandler Kirven (1930-2011)
    Laura Ann Kirven
    Daniel "Danny" Kirven (1936-1962)
    Lawrence "Larry" Kirven (1938-2020)
    Julie Kirven
    Russell "Rusty" Kirven (1942-2014)

Five years before Joe shot the mad dog, my uncle Coit Kirven and his 357 Magnum met three human varmints, upon whom Coit was able to demonstrate extreme strength.

It was 3 a.m. and freezing, one morning in November of 1934. A young motorcycle officer named Coit Kirven was doing his rounds in downtown Sumter, and his police dog Ted was riding with him.

From half a block away, Coit spotted a black Ford V-8 coupe easing down Main Street, with several figures inside. Nearby, at the corner of Bartlett and Main, was the Claremont Hotel. The police report had described a hotel robbery ten days earlier, in a nearby city.

Coit walked into the Claremont and sat quietly in the lobby, telling the night clerk Coleman Crabtree that he was there just to warm himself at the radiator. He quieted his German shepherd Ted at his feet, then put his own cocked pistol in his lap. Man and dog tucked themselves near a potted fern in the lobby, all but hidden.

Time passed. Crabtree lay down on a couch in the lobby. James Little, the sleepy bellboy, sat by the elevator. In the shadows, they forgot Coit was even there.

Then all at once, two of the robbers charged through the Bartlett Street door, leveling pistols at Crabtree and Little. The older robber, Weger, shouted "This is a stick-up!"

Unseen, Coit slid to the floor in a dark corner, kept his dog quiet, sized up the field of battle, and bided his time.

Weger forced the bellboy face down, and he made Crabtree kneel to open the safe.

Turner, the other robber, swiveled his gun between the Bartlett and Main Street exits, ready to shoot. He threatened Crabtree, who was fumbling with the combination lock: "If he passes that number again, I'll blow his brains out!"

Coit waited until the safe was opened and emptied, Crabtree and Little were riding the elevator to the top, and the robbers themselves, Weger and Turner, were running for different doors. Coit, in the crossfire between the two, was "about at my wit's end."

Even though Ted the police dog caught Turner by the ankle, Turner managed to escape by Main Street.

But Coit loaded his gun, unaware that the older robber, Weger, was waiting for him on Bartlett Street. On the other hand, Weger didn't realize that Coit had had military training at Fort McClellan.

The newspapers relate the climax:

> Following Weger closely, Officer Kirven went through the inner door and started onto the street when he noticed a split-second flash of light from the right side of the outside doorway. Acting from instinctive reflex he sprang, catlike, flat against the right wall and began to inch his way to what he now knew was the older bandit's hand and gun, just barely visible through the early morning darkness.
>
> [*Coit*] grabbed the gun and hand, twisting at the same time. This move wrenched the gun from the wounded man's hand and with it, Kirven smashed the left side of Weger's head, immediately dropping him to the ground. [*Weger*] died a few minutes later.

The newspaper photo shows Weger's body, disfigured because his jawbone had been ripped out in a former attempted prison escape.

Turner was caught and arrested the next year.

Uncle Coit was unhurt. One of the 13 shots fired by the two robbers had made a hole in his leather coat, and another had pierced his hat. Coit was a hero for life, in Sumter and throughout the Carolinas. This audacious shooting capped his resume. He had already graduated from the National Policy Academy in Washington and been awarded best all-around soldier and marksman at Camp McClellan in Alabama. In 1940 he was made Chief of Police.

Mama whispered to me as a wide-eyed child, "Your *uncle* is *Chief of Police.*"

Coit slept close to his 357 Magnum pistol, and in the daytime it never left his side.

Sarah Heriot "Beau" Kirven, Coit's daughter and my cousin, thought of herself as her father's "son" because he had wanted a son, and she was his only child. Coit taught Beau how to shoot. She was the perfect student. At thirteen years old, she was a better marksman than any member of the Sumter police force. The local paper featured her firearms test:

> *"Beau" has been target practicing with her father and members of the Sumter force for a little over a year and has shown a remarkable aptitude for firearms. In the test recently "Beau" made the remarkable score of 191 out of a possible 200 with her father's .38 Smith & Wesson revolver, shooting target ammunition.*

Harriet "Beau" Kirven at 17.

At 17, Beau set another shooting record, 196 out of 200 with a 357 Magnum at 25 yards. The article describes her as "vivacious" and a "very lovely young lady." Coit and Beau are pictured on either side of the target, with Coit smiling broadly. Beau has also set marks shooting from the hip and holding the gun upside-down. "She never loses her composure, her father states proudly" (*The Carolina Sheriff* 1945).

Throughout her life, Beau continued to show bravery, as her father's "son." She earned her commercial pilot's license in order to ride in one of the South Carolina Air National Guard's new F-104 Star Fighters, which can go twice the speed of sound. Her husband Bob Johnson, a pioneering aviator and then a Brigadier General, took himself and Beau to Mach 2. In a DVD explaining the history of the McEntire Air National Guard Base, there is a family picture of Beau, dismounting from this flight.

Beau after her flight in an F-104 Star Fighter at Mach 2

My first younger sister, Cathy Andrews, has always been equal to a physical challenge. Not usually including combat skills . . . and yet I do recall a time when Cathy and I visited Anna Louise Kirven Booker—my great uncle Bob's daughter-in-law—when she lived near Atlanta. We had lunch and a long, animated talk. As we were departing, Anna Louise made an offer to Cathy: "Wanna arm-wrestle?" Anna Louise had been good at college sports. In contrast, the family she married into, the Bookers, were quiet and studious, as their last name implied.

So Cathy and Anna Louise arm-wrestled right there on the glass coffee table. Maybe she thought that as a Kirven among Kirvens, she needed to be tough. Later, Cathy told me "She's a strong woman, and she knows it." We will miss Anna Louise and her brother, Eckard Lee.

Anna Louise Kirven Booker, c. 2000, with her son Henry Booker, Jr., and her daughter Cecilia Booker

Cathy grew in physical confidence during the summers she spent at the farm in Sumter with our uncle Tom Kirven—son of our Grandfather Tom—and his family, including his five sons who worked the farm: Tom, Joe, Danny, Larry, and Rusty. Cathy was strong-minded and tough, and she liked a challenge. In her words,

I don't remember whether it was 1963 or 1964. I had proven I was responsible enough to take Joker, the horse, out by myself any time I wanted. I don't believe it was as late as 1965 because that was the year I met my husband Mike, and I went to the farm after Christmas that year. I am certain I didn't go at Thanksgiving too that year because I was ambivalent enough about leaving my new boyfriend once.

So I suppose it was '63 or '64. I had been spending summers and Thanksgiving holidays at the farm since 1961. I'm not sure why my normally restrictive mother allowed me that freedom. On reflection, I was the most rebellious child—the middle one. It was probably self-defense.

Getting to the farm meant I got to ride horses, work alongside my older cousins and generally do things I knew would make my mother cringe. I rode a Greyhound bus from Winston-Salem to Sumter. Usually my uncle Donnie picked me up and drove me to the farm. I knew my mother trusted him to look out for me, but what does a bachelor know about keeping a determined adolescent reined-in?

Joker was 15 hands when he was fully grown, a surprise to everyone who didn't know his mother was going to foal. He became my horse because, at not much more than 5 feet tall, I could easily mount him without a saddle. He would allow me to ride him without saddle or bridle. The only problem was that unless I had a stick in my hand, size was irrelevant. He was the one in control, as I learned the hard way more than once.

I arrived at the farm quite proud of my new leather jacket that I had saved the enormous sum of $40 to purchase. The corn had been harvested some time ago, and the hay fields had given up their last crop for baling. I was eager to ride Joker whom I hadn't seen in several months. The air was crisp and cool, a good excuse to show off my new jacket. I did put a saddle and bridle on Joker but eschewed the stick, figuring that I could control him.

We started off at a slow canter. After all, it had been several months since I had ridden him and I wanted to get the feel again. On the way to the swamp I did remember to close all the gates I opened. Not closing gates on a dairy farm is a serious offense for obvious reasons. At the time they were heavy iron gates. The fencing was a wire weave with barbed wire on top.

On the way back from the swamp, both of us were ready for an all-out run, a 15-year-old and a horse headed back to the barn and feed, the faster the better. As we approached that gate, I realized that he had no intention of stopping, despite my vigorous pulling on the reins and verbal commands. Fortunately, I did have the common sense to turn him into the field, so that when I was thrown into the fence, most of the damage was done to my pride and my jacket. The proudly purchased jacket was in shreds, but I was not left paraplegic and had only a stellate laceration on my right leg, which after more than 40 years has faded completely. Today, I would have insisted that such a laceration required stitches. Then it was treated with turpentine. Worked.

Cathy is now a retired family physician from Marietta, Georgia, who has treated a host of appreciative patients. She's proud of that visible, self-defining scar, a sign of her boldness.

Cathy Sanders at The Farm in the early 1960s. The boy on the horse is Daniel, a second cousin twice removed, descended from Great Uncle Joshua Pollard

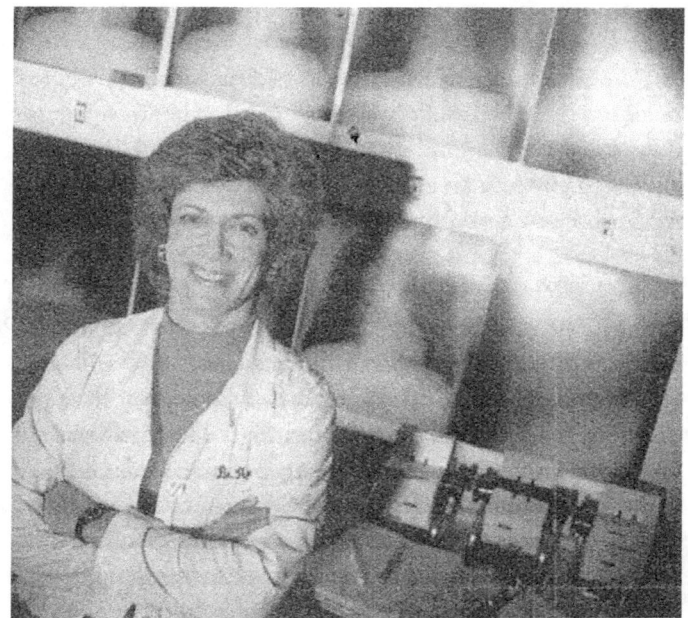

Cathy Andrews, M.D, in Atlanta Magazine, 1992, in an article on doctor-recommended physicians

My second younger sister, Laura Beth, was physically strong and daring to an extreme degree, in the Kirven style—even though she knew virtually nothing about her ancestors. L. B. ran marathons, went to Princeton on a ROTC scholarship, and was the first woman East Wing Chief Surgical Resident at Massachusetts General Hospital. She was tall, lean, an exerciser and no smoker. She radiated health and energy. She had an astonishing sense of humor, cutting through all varieties of nonsense. She chose the abbreviation L. B. to avoid what she considered the too-sweet and icky tradition of her Southern-style and girly double name, Laura Elisabeth.

When my cousin Perry, who had never met her, saw a photo of L. B., he stared at her confident face for a moment and then made a simple declaration: "She's a Kirven."

Contests of strength have a long history in our family. My grandfather, the first Thomas Jackson Kirven (1868-1921), was one of the sons of Erasmus Goodson Kirven (1817-1897), who were infants or young boys during the pre-war years.

Kirven Family Timeline from the 1700s into the 1900s

1 Morris Kirven, perhaps "Maurice Kerrivan" lived in Maryland (1700-1755)
  2 Thomas Kirven (1740-1830) moved from Cumberland, NC to Darlington, SC
    3 Caid Kirven (1761-1829) moved from Cumberland, NC to Darlington, SC
      4 John Kirven (1791-1878) lived in Darlington, SC
        5 Erasmus Goodson Kirven (1817-1897) and Mary Caroline King lived in Darlington, SC. Erasmus served in the Confederate Army during the War. Mary Caroline Kirven secretly reclaimed their farm's mules from Sherman's troops during Sherman's march through South Carolina. They had 14 children, 9 boys and 5 girls
        6 Joshua Pollard (1855-1938)
        6 Erasmus Eugene "Hugh" (1858-1933)
        6 Mary Caroline "Carrie" (1859-1924)
        6 Leila (1861-1894)
        6 James Noel (1863-1956)
        6 Robert E. Lee (1865-1941), Eckard Lee's father
        6 Thomas Jackson (1868-1921), the author's grandfather
        6 Augusta Viola (1869-1956)
        6 Luther Cade (1872-1935)
        6 Joseph (1872 -) died young in a cotton gin accident
        6 Maude (1875-1963)
        6 Edward (1876-1938)
        6 Kate (1882-1966)

Great Aunts and Uncles
Front row: *Hugh, Jim, Bob, and Luke*
Second row: *Josh, Maude, Carrie, and Tom*

Bob's living son, Eckard Lee Kirven, who agreed to talk to me, said that his father Bob was a best friend to my grandfather Tom. He told me that Tom was named for Stonewall Jackson, and Bob was named for Robert E. Lee. So as fate would have it, Eckard Lee and I are both descendants of the Confederacy. When Eckard Lee announces, "We rode with the Red Shirts," my emotions scatter like a flock of birds, unmoored for a time.

In Eckard Lee's voice, I hear his pride in being a treasure chest of family stories. With phenomenal recall, he lists Kirven siblings and calls up stories to define their personalities. The Kirven family has survived, with all those babies moving forward in history. Eckard Lee is plainly glad. He is a confident and unabashed narrator. Whenever he slips into the harsh race and class words that I heard in my childhood, his daughter Debbie is with us to steer him back: "Dad, that's not how we say things now."

Eckard Lee as a young man, born in 1910   *Eckard Lee and Maelese Keown Kirven, c. 1995*

Eckard Lee tells me that the six men in the photograph—unsmiling, solemn, and tough—tested their prowess against each other as young men. They would challenge each other to a "throwdown" to try their strength and burnish their reputations in family legend, and sometimes they even took in outside challengers with the prompt, "Let's see what you can do, brother." Eckard Lee told me this about my grandfather Tom:

> Uncle Tom was a wrassler—he threw some man that was such-and-such a wrassler up at school there where he went [to college], and the man told everybody that Uncle Tom threw him.
>
> [Afterwards] Papa and them told Tom that Hugh is gone throw you and hurt you, but don't let him *hurt* you. Hugh jumped in there and thought he was gonna throw Uncle Tom, and somehow or other Uncle Tom whipped him down and throwed *him* down. His father and him were ragging Uncle Jim and saying let's do that again! But Uncle Jim said no, that's enough.

I was relieved to learn from Eckard Lee that an end could be called to one of the "throwdown" fights.

In at least one throwdown, someone had a firearm. Eckard Lee related that Great-Uncle Luke "once advanced, without firing, on a man who was shooting at him. The man shot Luke in the arm. Then he shot Luke in the chest. Luke kept coming. The man panicked too late, because Luke finally shot at him and wounded him right before he turned to run. And Luke? He was just fine." This is the only instance I've heard of guns being involved in the "throwdown" games among my great uncles.

But then Eckard Lee asks me, "You want to hear one more story?"

Sure. Now I learn about the oldest brother, Josh. The brothers, lined up in the photo as a family of strongmen farmers, were too young to fight in The War. [Let's use that name for the long conflict called The Civil War by the North and the War Between the States by the South.] However, Josh Pollard did manage to fight during Reconstruction. This violent and chaotic time lasted for a decade after The War. Near Darlington where the Kirvens lived, many poor and frantic people lived near farms that had been laid waste or abandoned. Marauding bands of men would attack anyone making a living, Eckard Lee recounted. They stole bales of cotton or machinery or mules or livestock, grabbing at whatever might keep them alive.

"Were these men white or colored?" I asked.

"Both," he said. "All kinds. Everybody was poor."

Erasmus Kirven would usually fight these roving thieves himself. He believed the law was too weak or corrupt to rein them in.

Great-Uncle Josh Pollard, Erasmus' oldest son born in 1855, grew to manhood under Reconstruction. He is the first one on the left, front row. A wry grimace is visible beneath his mustache.

One day during Reconstruction, Josh left the farmhouse with his rifle to defend the family's land against plunder. He took cover as if on a battlefield, among trees behind a rise, to hold off predators with his ammunition.

His mother, Mary Caroline, waited at home, uneasy. Was Pollard all right? Finally, she sent a boy to ask after her eldest son. The boy popped right back with his message:

"Pollard says, 'Mama, send more ammunition! I'm still shootin!'"

Eckard Lee laughed and laughed when he told me this story. Those uncles of his! They kept fightin' no matter what! They were probably still fightin' in the next world! This zeal for combat was so far gone that it was hilarious to Eckard Lee.

From another relative I was told Pollard's fate later in life. He had two wives—in fact, two separate families, neither of which knew about the other until the Kirven reunion in the 1990s, or so it was said. Whether he had money problems or fell ill, Pollard as an old man walked off into the woods and ate his shotgun. Maybe he wanted to die while he could still imagine himself protecting his family from bad guys. Still shootin' at the very end.

Eckard Lee mentions that his own nickname as a boy was "Bully."

"Why?" I ask. "Why Bully?" I recall the great uncles, each a bull of a man.

Eckard Lee chuckles. "Well, 'spect I'd better not tell you till we're in the next world." He recounts his stories with unfailing good humor, having enjoyed a long life in a family whose adventures fascinate him. He seems to resent no one, to regret nothing. He has a big smile.

Eckard Lee's kind daughter, Debbie Kirven Sanders, sits down with us for our sessions. Afterwards, Debbie sent me a version of her own story that is often told by her father with a certain perspective on "Bully."

> Sometimes the simplest things can lead to a fight with the Kirvens, especially the men. As my father talked about his childhood he never had any problems with his sisters, either Novice Rivers Kirven, the oldest, or Anna Louise Kirven Booker, the youngest. However, he did have trouble with Robert LaCoste Kirven, my older brother. My father, Eckard Lee, told me this story:
>
> One spring day while I (age 8) was roaming around outside, I found a new ripe strawberry on the vine. Instead of eating it myself, I decided I would surprise Louise (age 4) with it. As I was walking to find her and trying to hide the strawberry, my brother LaCoste (maybe age 14-16, but my father did not say) came up and asked me what I had, and I told him that it was none of his business. LaCoste started coming toward me and trying to get the strawberry out of my hand. That's when I hit him and the fight began. We started fighting, each other and rolling around on the ground. Papa came and got me off of La Coste, and I asked La Coste, "Do you want some more?"

Do temperaments run in families? My maternal ancestors are both Scots (Frasers) and Irish (Kirvens). I'm familiar with descriptions of the hot tempers that can belong to those of both Scots and Irish ancestry. In the 1544 Battle of the Shirts in Scotland, including the Fraser clan, "it is said that large bands of men from the opposed clans of Donald and Fraser threw off their plaids and fought in their shirts, all day, to the finish. At sundown, eight Macdonalds were left, but only five Frasers. For days after, the Loch is said to have been red with blood" (wikipedia). As for possible combative traits inherited from the

Irish, we can now remember the TV series that was popular in the first decades of the 2000s, *Peaky Blinders.*

As for me, born Mariann Kirven Sanders, I value stories and poems. I never was much attracted to fights, or group sports, or even jogging. I like reading books. I hope that our universities keep teaching all of us more about the humanities.

There was at least one time when my mother, Maisie, took exception to her brothers' fascination with fights. She wrote a story in college that describes her father (our grandfather) Tom bringing home a little brown puppy when she was four years old. And "bless goodness," as they say in South Carolina, that puppy was for her! He was her very own puppy to cherish, or so she thought.

Yet before Maisie could turn around, the puppy had disappeared.

What had happened?

Unhappy answer. Her older brothers had "borrowed" the puppy for a dogfight in progress at the next farm. They would have been in their teens then. A fight was fun! They placed a bet on Maisie's puppy—to be a more "manly" dog than the other dogs, perhaps. Maisie wrote that she would never forgive them. Even when the puppy was returned, scarred and scared but not fatally harmed, Maisie said she would never trust her brothers again. Violence could creep into their play.

My grandfather Tom had five sons in chronological order: Thomas, Lawrence, Donald, Coit, and Marion. A family story describes one of the older brothers chasing one of the younger ones across the roof with a brick, ready to throw. Maybe Kirvens expected each other to play rough.

Chapter Three:

Ambush

Once upon a time it is a December afternoon in South Carolina, a Wednesday in 1909. Sunlight flows between the tree trunks and warms the cold air.

Behind the farmhouse where Tom and Laura live with their children, a hard-sand trail leads back through pines, live oaks, hickory, and sweet gum. Down the trail half a mile away, there are a dozen box-shaped wooden tenant cabins, each with a door and two windows in front, an angled roof, and a chimney. Winter has browned the grass and erased the wildflowers. The soil in the cabin gardens is bare now. Pigs snuffle and chickens *ku-dat* from homebuilt sheds.

A rider approaches down the path. He clicks his horse to a walk as he nears the semicircle of cabins. He is a white man, sturdy and medium tall. There are a few gray strands in his brown hair thatch, but he seems young in strength. His mustache is well defined, his jaw set.

My cousin Joe Kirven has pictured this place for me. "The twelve-horse farm had at least eight tenant houses on it, all occupied by tenant farm families. The crops planted were cotton, corn, and tobacco, as well as cane for syrup, wheat for flour, and oats to feed farm animals. All tenant families planted gardens, and most of them raised hogs, cows, and chickens. These families were paid a daily wage for their work, and they collected it every Saturday." Cotton was the money crop, according to Eckard Lee.

The rider, Thomas Kirven, is going towards the tenant cabins. He has been figuring out how much he owes his tenants and how much they owe him, under a sharecropping arrangement. Today is reckoning day. He tells himself that he is a fair man, like his father was in Darlington, and yet he must be paid. He has six children.

A thick memo pad and pencil are in his left jacket pocket, with additions and subtractions in fair columns for all to see. He checks the pad to see the debt of the family in the second cabin.

There, the woman. The two boys, why . . . I know that rattle sound.

Tom pulls on the reins.

A door bangs shut. Someone is hollering. He hears footfalls on packed earth. His side is numb. Can't he even sit up straight?

There is yelling. "Run to the farmhouse!"

Sweat? Blood? Sticky. Tom holds onto the horse's neck. The sunshine is warm behind the trees. Laura is there. Tom feels her hand on his cheek. Buddy DuBose is there. Laura is whispering.

"Tom? Don't distress yourself. We'll take you to Willie Shaw's. Tom, we've got you."

Tom is eased from the horse and held upright by Buddy, a family friend. Tom's legs strain to move him forward. Pain swells inside his body.

The Watchman and Southron of Sumter reports on December 11, 1909:

> Mr. T. J. Kirven, of Providence, one of the best known and most progressive farmers of Sumter county, was shot Wednesday afternoon and severely wounded by Wash Williams, a negro share-cropper on a farm owned by Mr. Kirven, four miles east of this city. The shooting was done with a shot gun, loaded with small shot. The load took effect in Mr. Kirven's left hand, arm and side, and but for the deflection of the shot by a heavy overcoat worn by him and a memorandum book and papers in his pocket, he would probably have been killed, as a large part of the load lodged in the side and muscles of the chest directly over the heart. As it is Mr. Kirven is quite seriously wounded and will be confined to his bed at the Sumter Hospital, where he is being treated for some time.
>
> The shooting occurred between 4 and 5 o'clock Wednesday afternoon. Mr. Kirven went to the farm to seize the crop to which he had an interest under a warrant of attachment. It was alleged that Williams had been disposing of the crop and had not made proper returns to Mr. Kirven who had a claim on it for rent and supplies advanced under a share-crop agreement. When he entered the yard he was received in a threatening manner by the wife and sons of Williams, woman threatening him with a pitch fork and

one of the boys with an ax. While his attention was attracted by the woman and boy and their impending assaults, a gun was fired through a crack in the house near where he was standing, the load taking effect as above described. Mr. Kirven made his way with assistance to the house of Mr. Willie Shaw near the scene of the shooting and physicians were summoned by telephone and Sheriff Epperson notified. Mr. Kirven's wounds were dressed and he was brought to the Hospital.

Sheriff Epperson sent his deputy to arrest Williams but he could not be found, although diligent search was made for him that night and Thursday morning. Williams' wife and two sons were arrested and committed to jail. They have employed counsel and will apply for bail.

Wash Williams is said to be a bad negro and a warrant was issued for his arrest on another charge only a few days ago by Magistrate Harby. When the Magistrate's Constable went to make the arrest on Tuesday Williams took leg ball.

Mr. Kirven is suffering considerable pain, but is doing as well as could be expected. Unless there are unforeseen complications he will recover within a few days.

Grandfather Tom did not recover within a few days. He never did recover. His strength did not return. Maisie confided to me that she did not really know her father, because he was always sick or in bed. He died when she was five years old. She never mentioned this confrontation with a tenant who seriously wounded her father.

There are rumors within our family that some unnamed friends of Grandfather got together after a while to hunt down and "lynch" his shooter, who was identified in the newspaper article as Wash Williams. In the parlance of those days, "lynch" did not always mean hanging—it referred to any kind of violent retribution against a man described as a "bad negro," in the familiar terms of the newspaper article. There are no particulars known about any retribution. It is pointless to write down rumors.

I have my own question, though, arising simply from my own efforts to figure out the entire story. If any friends and relatives of Wash Williams *did* suspect he was lynched, or *did* for whatever reason hold some grudge against my grandfather, might they have conspired six years later, in 1915, to light the fire that burned down the family's house, when the family—with Ansie and Maisie—had to flee? Might that fire have been "payback"?

The shooting of Grandfather Tom calls up other historical questions. Was sharecropping itself, set up during Reconstruction, a means of further exploiting blacks even after slavery was outlawed? The sharecropper might pay rent to the landowner, and the sharecropper would work to plant and grow the crop, but the sharecropper would typically own only half the harvest. The other half belonged to the landowner. This arrangement suggests to some people that sharecropping was a legacy of slavery—in other words, it may have been one further way to exploit the labor of black people.

History can be argued and discussed. But the event of Grandfather Tom's shooting required further emotional catharsis within my family. My uncle Tom, the son of the victim, himself called a family meeting in 1972, to tape a family conversation about the shooting of his father. The audiotape is garbled and full of static, so I asked technicians to clean it up and preserve it on a CD, decades ago.

Then I sat at my computer and hit the tape "replay" again and again. By then, the actual shooting was 63 years earlier—past history—but the voices of the listeners were keening, lamenting, grieving, preserving, extending their sorrow to the future. I hear my cousins Julie and Laura Ann, my aunt Eva, Laura Ann's friend Tona, and others I do not know. My uncle's voice itself rasps from laryngeal cancer.

The women linger over details that carry meaning for them all. The shooter stayed inside and "shot him through a V in the window," a hole for the villain's gun barrel to poke through while the attacker himself stayed hidden. Grandfather's coat was "all bunched up with paper stuffed in his pocket," so maybe it was the memo pad that saved his life? Or perhaps "the shot stayed at the watch," so maybe his wristwatch saved him? Maybe "he had his arm up, holding the gun, and that's how the gun saved his life." They pause at gritty particulars: "both barrels at one time, number 6 and number 4 shot . . . He passed a hundred and twenty-two shot on the johnny" that day. Oh yes, they reassure one another, it was all but a miracle that Grandfather Tom even survived.

Ummm, the women say, *ummm*. They are keening. The sound is a tribute, an honor, a recognition. The grief is equal to the love. More than equal.

Concentrating on physical strength will not Save the Baby, not in the way we are incanting that phrase in this book. It will not support our desire to assume the presence of fellow-feeling within other people, or our deep need to preserve the lives of human beings we truly love, or our heartfelt wish to embrace and preserve the goodness in humanity.

No matter how many victorious "throwdowns" Grandfather Tom Kirven had so earnestly practiced and performed in his youth, his vaunted physical strength could not secure a good life path for himself or his babies. His manly prowess could not win meaning, protection, and fulfillment for himself and his loved ones.

Chapter Four:
Whose Baby Gets Saved?

When I first had a real conversation with my cousin Thomas Kirven in Sumter, it was already 2004. He was fifteen years older than me, and I was then past sixty. With the nurturing company of my husband Richard, I was on a quest to meet my South Carolina family once again, after half a lifetime out of touch.

I knew that this Thomas was the son of my uncle and the grandson of my grandfather—three Thomas Kirvens in three successive generations. In my childhood I had been far too scared and shy, not to mention too absent, to get to know all my cousins especially well. Yet as Tom and I sat down across the big table in Joe Chandler Kirven's house, Tom started right away to heap spontaneous praise upon Grandmother Laura.

He was overflowing with compliments, punctuated with enthusiastic gestures. "Laura," he enthused, was "the kindest, sweetest woman ever." She had a special cure for wounds and cuts brought on by farm work. She would take a container of kerosene, distill it with a wick, and make up a good supply to have on hand for any child who was kicked or gored or bitten or slashed by wire or punctured by a rusty nail. She would apply her purified liquid to a child's wound. To her oldest child, Tom, this magical talent personified Grandmother Laura. His eyes flared with excitement. Distilled kerosene cleanses the wounds and starts the healing process, he explained to me, just as well as antibiotics. All our other cousins at the table were murmuring in agreement. Laura Fraser Kirven was a family icon of kindness, or to use a Southern expression, she was just as sweet as she could *be*. She was always ready to Save the Baby.

In response to my cousin Tom, I remembered my sister Cathy's earlier story, when during a visit to The Farm she sustained a "stellate laceration" from a horse-riding accident, and her wound was treated with turpentine. "Worked," Cathy proclaimed.

These thoughts bring me into a new dimension, where I can consider nurture and care as companion forces for Saving the Baby. Persistent nurture and care could resemble another version of strength.

Women among my ancestors specialized in endurance. They were "little round women," as Kirven men say teasingly, "but they were brave." My cousin Joe Chandler Kirven has repeated that generic compliment more than once. Nurturing is a brave project. In the huge group photo from 1911, the first in this book, two of my Great Aunts—Maude and Carrie—stand beside each other, both holding sturdy babies. They are center left, and then far left near the bottom row is Great-Uncle Hugh's daughter Lucia. These three women were especially well known by their descendants to be tough and strong-minded about caring for their families. Fraser women, as well, were tireless and reliable in caring for relatives and helping children who became ill.

The family women whom I have known were intense about their nurturing. They would see every illness through to its cure, if humanly possible. Women in our family, a family with a history of slaveholding, may belong to a tradition of extreme nurturing—a determination that spreads throughout the generations from the frustration and guilt that Southern white women felt during slavery. Slaveholders' wives would often need to care for both white and black children, along with adult slaves—all the while sharing their nurturing strategies with the white male slaveholders. My great-grandfather Erasmus owned dozens of slaves, and his wife Caroline was his partner in communicating with them and caring for them.

Perhaps Grandmother Laura's version of nurture that has impressed my cousin Tom has been imitated by others in my family. It's a practice with its own kind of toughness.

My cousin Larry has wanted to save baby animals since he was a child. When he was a boy, he caught sight of a newborn pig that his father, my uncle Tom, found one day down at the branch. The baby pig was all but frozen.

"Don't take that pig," said my uncle Tom. "He's going to die, anyway."

Larry took that little animal, though. He named him Billy the Pig. Billy thawed slowly in the kitchen and soon was able to drink my aunt Eva's all-purpose milk and egg mix for baby animals. Billy grew large and fat. The family finally sold him to another farm, because they couldn't bear to kill him.

As an adult, Larry lost his baby son Tommy. The son was named Thomas Jackson III, after Larry's father, Tom. Years later, as if in response, Larry and his second wife Carol began to save baby animals. They have nurtured groups of baby ducks and owls over the years. In 1998 they raised a baby deer, Buttons, in their home. Buttons became friends with a black Labrador. Neighbors would rub their eyes whenever they spotted that dog-and-deer pair walking through the fields. Buttons was finally returned to the wild. Larry and Carol's tagged ducks have been sighted as far away as Pennsylvania.

Saving baby animals is constant work, sometimes as teeth-gritting as raising children. Carol told me that she had to let Buttons go when time approached for the rutting season. Carol and Larry have had sharp discussions about their ducks, owls, and deer, almost as parents discuss children. At one point, they found a baby deer apparently abandoned in the grass behind their house. The deer was almost invisible. They almost tripped over it.

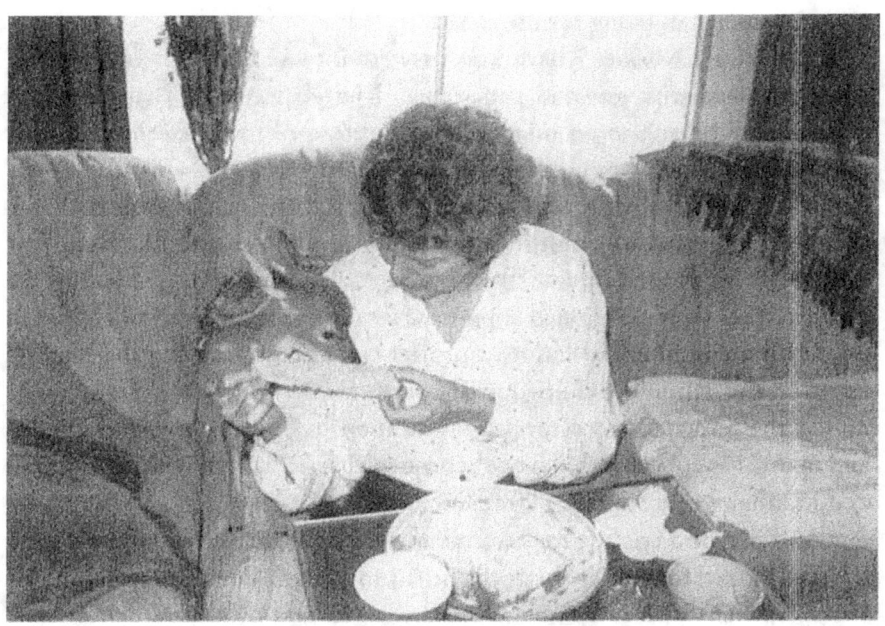

Carol Kirven, feeding corn-on-the-cob to Buttons

They cared for that baby deer for a while, and after a long stretch they took the deer into the forest and set it into a bed of leaves, hoping that the mother would find it. When they returned the next day, the baby deer was gone.

Now they worry.

Worry belongs to the work of nurture. A friend of mine says, *When you have a child, a part of you deep inside starts to weep, and it never, never stops.*

Genuine care can draw out any person's energy, and the more so when the need is urgent. My cousin Julie Kirven Griffin bravely nurtured herself through a long and debilitating attack of Guillain-Barré when she was in her fifties. That's the disease Joseph Heller made unhappily famous, in which after weeks of paralysis you either gradually recover or you die.

In Julie's darkest days, locked in her own paralyzed and sleepless body, she held on. She told me she couldn't find a name for the reality she was clutching with all her might as she lay there in bed. It was like memory, or like sayings from the past, or like God, or like images of her family's faces, or like blind determination. Through it all coursed a sensation of *holding-on-tight*. Maybe her survival was natural, and maybe it was an extreme example of heroic care against the odds. In some ways it reminds me of the personalities of Julie's family members.

While she was *holding on*, Julie's husband, her three daughters, her grandchildren, and her patients were steadily depending on her to pull through. They needed her to keep nurturing them. Perhaps by nurturing herself, she helped Save the Baby of their well-being, as well. Julie's daughter Leigh Chandler Griffin is now a nurse, a buoyant woman who helps her patients keep their sanity at the end of their lives, even while facing death.

My second sister, L. B., spent seven years of heroic nurturing for the benefit of her son Luke—and for herself as well. She saw the two as one.

In her mid-30s, L. B. was without any warning struck with esophageal cancer and was sure she would die. Yet she lived through a nine-hour Ivor-Lewis esophago-gastrectomy and four rounds of chemo.

Julie Kirven Griffin with her daughters Julie Lynn Born, Leigh Chandler Griffin and Jackie Dawn Griffin

Afterwards, she was to all appearances cured. I visited L. B. and her husband in Maine. I wept when I saw that she was well, even buoyant. She was learning to water-ski on one foot.

Two years later, L. B. phoned me to announce, "I'm a little pregnant."
"What?" I gasped, "Have you considered . . . ?"
"Life is risk," she retorted in her brisk voice, before I could even utter the question.

That was how she embraced a Kirven-Fraser nurturing style to a typical extreme, as her temperament directed her. When her son Luke was born in 1995, he rocketed to the center of her universe. She lived for him. Whenever I saw them laughing, I thought of her undergraduate thesis on Henry James: "One small light can carry all the flame." She thought that James might have had in mind the spark of "light," or moral clarity, that could be passed from women to their children.

Before Luke's third birthday party, L. B. was struck by another, different cancer: stage IV ovarian. She was sure she would die, and this time she was right. It was a four-year progress to death. L. B. sought out all treatments, many of them excruciating, that might give Luke more time to be nurtured by her. Cisplatinum, gemcitabine, a stem-cell transplant. She got near-fatal sepsis and fought back.

"You're a brave person," I told her every chance I got. I had the notion that all my family members tried hard to be "brave"—and besides, she was.

"What am I gonna do?" she always retorted. "Hide under the couch?"

L. B. and Luke lived in the celebration of each other's company. They went deep-sea fishing, partied with each other while riding in her green convertible, tasted art in museums, spent time cuddling and reading on their huge couch, played with their golden retriever, joined friends in dances through the house, and enjoyed Luke's quest for a TaeKwonDo belt. When she could manage to sit at the computer, L. B. wrote a voluminous book, *Letter to Luke*. Brave, quick, and spirited, this book is the story of both L. B.'s life and her life with Luke, intended as a guide to Luke by means of the seeing-glass of her own memory. She was eager to leave her writing, in good faith, to her son.

After this intense, more-than-heroic, and blessed pilgrimage to Save the Baby, L. B. passed away on the evening of her spirited 46th birthday party— held right there the hospital—just weeks before Luke's seventh birthday.

I have never seen—and may never see again—a more energetic or fuller or more tragic and more joyous, good-faith, and celebratory pilgrimage to Save the Baby.

The nurturing quest to Save the Baby can take even more concentration and more raw courage than the physical bravery shown by Tom Kirven and his muscular brothers in their "throwdown" games.

My great-great grandmother Mary Caroline King Kirven stands out to me among those Kirven nurturers who would go to all lengths to Save the Baby of her family's well-being.

During The War, General William T. Sherman was a threat to Caroline's family, right in there with cottonmouths and mad dogs and ruthless criminals. William Tecumseh Sherman treated South Carolina with special ferocity because it had been the first state to secede, and so the devastation of that state might break the enemy's morale. Sherman's theory of *total warfare* drove him to lay waste not only soldiers, but buildings, farmlands, and civilians.

L.B. Sanders, as pictured on a memorial wall at the Lahey Clinic in Massachusetts.

He didn't sow salt into the fields as the Romans did at Carthage—but then, he was in a hurry. After the burning of Atlanta, Sherman's army marched to the sea at Savannah, turned, headed northward through South Carolina, and took Columbia. The city caught fire—perhaps an accident, but as Sherman often said, "War is cruel." On February 20, 1865, his troops moved through Camden, Chesterfield, and Cheraw—northeast toward the Big Pee Dee River.

Caroline and her husband Erasmus Kirven lived on a farm not far south of Chesterfield. Looking at a South Carolina map and several maps that show the path of the Union army under Sherman during the War, I would guess that the Kirven farm at Dovesville was perhaps a dozen miles south of the 15th and 17th Corps of traveling Union troops. Here is an account by an army commander who crossed South Carolina with Sherman, Major General O. O. Howard:

> March 1, marched ten miles, crossing Big Lynch Creek; camped on Brewer's Farm. On the Right Wing, refugees from Charleston and Columbia crossed the line of march and fifty wagons were captured. March 2, made a forced march of some twenty miles to Chesterfield Court House, hoping to secure the bridge over Thompson's Creek, but it was burned. Next day remained in Chesterfeld waiting for the Fourteenth Core to close up. March 4, moved twelve miles to Cheraw.

March 3, 1865, the day the army stayed at Chesterfield, may have been the day when Sherman's men rode down to the Kirven farm at Dovesville and stole the mules. For who could stop them? My great-grandmother Mary Caroline King Kirven would have been alone at home with four young children and several slaves. Her husband, Erasmus, was off fighting with the Confederate Army.

That evening as darkness approached, or so says the family story, Mary Caroline and a male slave rode away on two horses, somewhat northward, to Sherman's camp. I picture this precarious expedition, an act of nurture at the risk of death.

The two may have ridden long hours and into the night, wary of every sound. Mary Caroline could have known the region around Dovesville and Chesterfield and Cheraw from visits to relatives. The pair of them would have skirted crop fields, passed beneath thin-trunk pines, and crossed patches of sand deposited in prehistoric times along the eastern border of what is now Sand Hills State Forest.

When I first saw the old site of Great-Grandfather Erasmus's farm in Dovesville, in July of 2005, the land was sun-drenched and flat, divided into big plots for soybeans and cotton. The fields lay exposed, flanked with woods. The Dovesville area resembled the early 1865 *Harpers* sketches of the same countryside under Union siege, with its half-denuded pines and spare underbrush. Such thin trees would have allowed room for cannons to roll through, but they would barely have provided cover for stealthy riders.

I imagine Scipio and Mary Caroline at last making out the camp ahead, seeing its red fires, and hearing the brash voices of battle-weary men.

Scipio the slave whispers, gestures: "Miz Mary, you be behind this brush?"

Mary Caroline nods. "Right here is where I'll be."

Scipio signals, "They not gone care 'bout me. Them mules can smell me."

The mules would have been tethered at the edge of the camp, and Scipio would have zigzagged, just a harmless no-account black person to any enemy white soldiers looking out for Confederate white men with firearms. These events happened during the last throes of a winding-down war. The surrender at Appomattox would come about a month later, on April 9, 1865.

Eckard Lee passed on this story to me as it was told to him:

> Grandaddy [Erasmus was] was off with the southern part fightin' and she [Mary Caroline] was there by herself. She had to take the mules into the woods and hide 'em so that they [Union troops] wouldn't find 'em. And the po crackers [poor white neighbors] told 'em where [the mules] was, and they *stole* 'em.

> And the slave in charge of it went up there and told grandmother about the mules, and she said saddle up two horses and we'll go *get 'em,* and she rode up in the [*inaudible*] somewhere at night and he [the slave] said he could recognize the mules and turn 'em loose. They'll all go and we can *have 'em.* And she [*Mary Caroline*] told the colored fellow to ride off and all the mules . . . and she got 'em back.

Mary Caroline and Erasmus Kirven, c. 1850

At times, nurture might hang onto one simple act of courage.

Mary Caroline acted to nurture her family by helping Save the Baby that was the family's livelihood. Those reclaimed mules might have helped save the Kirvens from financial ruin, which did threaten many Southerners after The War.

Mary Caroline happened also to be the mother of Great Uncle Josh Pollard Kirven who one day during Reconstruction took a gun and left the house to defend the family home from marauders—and later sent a message back to his mother that he needed more bullets! He was "still shootin'!"

Erasmus did have to sell the farm, but then the wealthy buyer hired him to cultivate the land for re-purchase in seven years. The family worked the land, and then three years after the The War, their new son Thomas Jackson was born.

The care of children and loved ones—Saving the Baby within a nurturing family—may seem simple, natural, easy, or automatic. It is not. Nurture can be a grueling battle against fierce threats like fire, snakes, mad dogs, murderers, General Sherman, thieves, cancer, outrage, illness, debilitating toil—and even wrenching internal conflicts within the family itself.

What forces could have worked against the nurturing capabilities of Grandfather Tom and Grandmother Laura Kirven? Several.

By the act of marrying, Tom and Laura may have distanced themselves from the whole-hearted and enthusiastic support of Tom's family. Both he and Laura, in their private correspondence, refer to an unspoken and regrettable alienation between Tom and his father Erasmus—forever unresolved, because Erasmus' death occurs the same year as Tom and Laura's marriage: 1897. In those days, the Kirvens in Dovesville were several hours away.

In moving to Sumter, Tom took out a mortgage on his own farmland. In contrast to the scene in Dovesville, the sharecropper-tenant system that Tom chose for farming was thought to be unkind to both blacks and whites. Tom does declare himself a "Tillmanite," meaning he is opposed to the black vote. There is no record of farming advice by Tom's brothers, and scant worry about his eventually fatal buckshot wound—although two of Tom's sisters, Carrie and Maude, do express their concern.

What about nurturing in Laura's family? Ladson Lawrence Fraser and Hannah Atkinson Boone themselves were a model of nurture at the Booneland Plantation in Sumter, well-known for treating slaves and children with particular care. But Laura writes that she felt inferior in caring for servants as "children," in the way that her mother and grandmother did in Boonesville. As a staunch Presbyterian, Laura thought she was responsible for her own children's moral improvements and was known to focus on making her children "do right." If her "dear ones" did not "do right," she would pass them on to their father for physical punishment.

The struggle to nurture their children faced more obstacles. Tom and Laura had health challenges, not even counting the time that Tom was shot in 1909. Years before that, in 1901, an abdominal operation hospitalized Tom for a week. He was "greatly reduced in flesh," in his own words. Laura describes the pain of a father's separation from his babies, writing to Tom:

> Every now and then they think they recognize your familiar step, or mistake someone at a distance for you, and it would do you good to see their faces.

Tom writes back: "Kiss and hug the dear ones for me while I am delayed."

In 1910 Laura caught tuberculosis, and that fall she stayed at the Charlotte Sanatorium in North Carolina. Tom writes to cheer Laura, the absent nurturer of the family, by describing his own plans to gather the cotton crop whenever the rain lets up. He adds up both the earnings of "my two bales" and "your first picking, which made a light bale."

Sheer toil can deplete the energy available for nurturing. Tom and Laura had to alternate their care of children with the hard work of growing their crops for a living. On September 26, 1910, the year after he is ambushed and shot with buckshot, Tom describes his own labor to Laura while she lies in the hospital, recovering from tuberculosis.

> P. S. Have just finished picking the big front field and weighed up and commenced in your cotton. Will finish it today and probably pick all at the Manigault place tomorrow. You can see why all this hurry. I have no help am getting on all OK. All are well.

While harvesting cotton and managing a corn-picking contest for the boys, Tom also tends to the young ones at home. Coit is seven years old, and Marion is five. Coit, or "poor little Beetle," has a toothache, and Tom administers a warm-water cure.

Another child was born, and then two children were conceived who could not be born. After mother-to-be Laura was healed from tuberculosis, Maisie was born in 1915. Two more children are recorded in a distant family document, probably denoting two later miscarriages or deaths in infancy.

Maybe Tom and Laura tried to convince themselves, and each other, that they each had a store of nurturing abilities, and they wanted to reassure each other that they would not become too sick, or too tired, to nurture their children.

I wonder whether there is now one last item on the family list that they hoped could be combined with nurturing—that is, rebuilding their house after it was burned to the ground in that frightening and mysterious fire. I don't know when that task happened. But it cannot have been easy or automatic.

Although Tom's health continued to deteriorate, it may be that they came to believe, as a family, that they should concentrate on the many successes of their family life. Perhaps they simply decided to "declare victory" over all their hard times by arranging a photograph of themselves as a handsome and impressive family. So they posed around a photographer's prop and boosted Maisie onto the table. Although Tom was suffering from the long-term effects of buckshot wounds and revealing only his right arm, he and his family did look good together.

The Kirven family in 1920. From left: Thomas Sr., Lawrence, Ansie, Thomas Jr., Laura, Maisie, Donnie, Coit, and Marion.

This successful photo was treasured by the Kirven family. Even so, it was clear to everyone that Grandfather Tom was failing. He had finally lost the use of his left arm.

In 1921, Tom's brother Bob (Robert E. Lee Kirven) came down from Dovesville to perform a last favor for his dying brother. Eckard Lee remembers the occasion: "I remember the last time I saw him (Tom Kirven), Papa (Eckard Lee's father) took him in the buggy, and he went out and looked over the crops." Tom was all but paralyzed then. He died on October 11, 1921 at age 53.

After Tom's death, the family struggled financially while his five sons were in the process of getting jobs and wondering how to pay for all the college educations that the family wanted and needed.

The Kirven Family Timeline in the 1900s will help with this next paragraph:

It is now the 1920s and 30s. Whereas in 1919 Lawrence had boasted to his father that he is "set to dig $300 out of the soil" at home that summer, four years later in the summer of 1923 both Lawrence and Marion are working on an Ohio farm and trying to find another job for Donnie. Donnie is writing to Laura from college, protesting that he counts every penny and resents paying five dollars for a "sheepskin." Coit, next in line, writes from college in 1921 with the message "so far so good," and later he chooses military training and the Police Academy. Donnie gives up his dream to study medicine, so that he can join Investors Syndicate and help with college expenses for his three youngest siblings: Marion, Ansie, and Maisie. Donnie graduates the year that Marion begins college, in 1923. Marion graduates in 1927 and becomes an insurance salesman. Ansie's college costs at Winthrop last from 1925 to 1929. It is quite a pileup of expenses.

Meanwhile, Grandfather Tom has asked his oldest son, the second Thomas Jackson Kirven, to take over the family farm. Tom has married Eva Chandler, and they already have four children: Ophelia, Thomas Jackson, Joe Chandler, and Laura Ann. This new family lives at The Farm in Sumter.

In the fall of 1932, Maisie begins to attend Coker College at Hartsville, S.C. Her tuition is due.

Then in the spring of 1933, the Depression comes to The Farm.

As my cousin Joe Chandler writes in his book of stories, "Cotton that should have brought over 40 cents a pound was sold in 1933 for 3 cents a pound."

Whose Baby Gets Saved?

One day the bankers' agents show up at the front door of The Farm in Sumter. The second Thomas Jackson Kirven, heir apparent, strides around the side of the house and meets them with a gun.

"Get your hands off those machines! You can damn well *wait* before you take more of our money! Who says you can starve out a family?" His voice rasps.

The bank agents would have shuddered. "There's no help for it, Big Red."

And there was no help for it, in the end.

Grandmother Laura, who herself had been educated in the humanities and languages by the prosperous Frasers of Sumter, was convinced that a college education—which all her other children have received—was also required nurture for her youngest daughter, Maisie.

In fact, both Kirvens and Frasers revered education. Anna Louise Kirven Booker told me that once when she labored over a Latin assignment, her uncle (my Great Uncle) Hugh said, "Give it here, girl" and then translated the lines on the spot with no dictionary—just as a well-educated and Latin-loving strongman farmer should.

In the end, it was decided that the family had the right to make the final call, even though some long and painful conversations were needed. Maisie did attend Coker, and she continued for her Masters Degree.

It was a throwdown. Competitive nurture. For better or worse, Laura and her daughter Maisie won. It was just as agonizing for the losers as a "throwdown" competition among Tom and his brothers. There was grumbling at the referee's call, and lingering resentment. When I asked how the family felt, at least one relative referred obliquely to "our grandmother's bad decision."

Nurturing can be a tough wrestling match.

It is not clear today whether saving the tuition costs for Coker College could possibly have kept The Farm from going bankrupt. It may not have been clear even then. But what was the price of losing this one metaphorical "throwdown"? It was suffering and struggle for my uncle Tom, his wife Eva, and all their children. It was a journey into the wilderness, almost biblical in its level of hardship.

It was eviction.

The family left The Farm in 1933. The travelers included my uncle Tom, Eva, nephew Buddy DuBose, and the children Ophelia, Tom, Joe, and Laura Ann. Four more children—Danny, Larry, Julie, and Rusty—would be born at the family's destination. They were moving to Eastover, thirty miles west of Sumter. They had signed on to farm another man's land and supervise five other families. This exodus meant both a loss of material comforts and a lower status in the planter-and-tenant hierarchy. My cousin Joe Chandler put the scene in concrete terms:

> We moved to a 300-acre farm about two miles from Eastover, situated a hundred yards from the railroad track between Eastover and Columbia. The land had not been cultivated in several years. Weeds and grass made it almost impossible to plant a crop the first year. Alfred Scarborough, who owned the land, was pleased to find somebody willing to tackle such a formidable task. The contract, sealed with a handshake, was five dollars rent per acre for as long as we wanted to stay.
>
> We lived in a simple frame house, with wood siding and inside walls of plaster. Most walls had missing patches of plaster, and you could see from one room to the next. The house sat on brick pillars three feet from the ground. In many places you could see the ground through cracks in the floor.
>
> The roof was made of well-worn shingles. One rainy night, I counted thirteen pots and pans necessary to catch leaking rainwater.
>
> My father's farm equipment consisted of two 2-horse wagons, one 1-horse wagon, an assortment of plows and harrows, and a reaping binder. There were also cotton planters, fertilizer distributors, and eight mules. There was no time to waste in getting a crop planted in three months.

Joe's sister Laura Ann also recalls those times:

> We cooked on a wood-burning stove and had kerosene lamps for light, until years later when the house was wired for electricity. There were no fences on the property, so posts had to be put into the ground and the wires stretched and secured to make fences to keep the animals in. This work was laborious, difficult, and backbreaking, but very necessary. All the plowing and planting was done with mules. It was quite a few years before the tractors were used.
>
> On one occasion as he was breaking corn [breaking ears off stalks], a rattlesnake struck one of Daddy's boots, a frightening thing to have happen. During those long, hot South Carolina summertime days, there would be a period when many animals all over Richland County became rabid—foxes, cats, raccoons, opossums, squirrels, and dogs. One afternoon Danny, Pansie Mae [the black cook's daughter] and I were under a huge mulberry tree in the side yard playing. A cat leaped up and bit Pansie Mae on the arm. Danny and I rushed over to the nearby spigot to wash the blood away. The cat was rabid, and our efforts had put all of us in danger. All three of us had to have shots for rabies, every day for twenty-one days.
>
> Keeping a large family in clothes was always a concern. Hand-me-downs were a must. Clothes for the younger children were made at home, and we were lucky our mama knew how to sew. She bought her material from the only merchandise store in Eastover. Clothes washing was all done in the yard with a large black pot in which water was heated. There was no washing machine. Clothes were washed in one tub with a scrub board, rinsed in another tub, and hung on a line to dry. We always hired colored women to do the washing.
>
> Years later we had a hot-water tank, heated by the wood stove. When we finally returned to Sumter, we had a washing machine.

The family of my uncle Tom lived for years without the basics of electricity or a washing machine or a tractor. This was subsistence living. The family braved out this life for eleven years.

What about Grandmother Laura, who had compelled this harsh change? After 1933, she virtually disappears from family memory. There is a "Club Market" book of accounts by Laura with entries labeled "Eastover" under July and August of 1933, then one entry under "Fall." It could be that Laura tried to move with her family to Eastover but could not endure the hardship.

My mother Maisie told me, years later, that when she visited her mother Laura, on a break from college at Coker, she was aggrieved to see Laura's situation. She described Laura as old and sick, miserable, having been placed in a wretched, mean room rather than allowed her *own* room. On the other hand, my cousin Laura Ann told me that Eva and Tom definitely took better care of Grandmother Laura than did any of Laura's other children— Lawrence, Donnie, Coit, Marion, or Ansie, who were all out of college by then.

Others have suggested that Laura may have wanted to stay in the front room at Eastover with her son's two youngest children, then toddlers. Still others have lamented that Laura may have been assigned this room when she was too old to care for young children around the clock.

Briars in our family cluster next to stories about Laura Fraser, and special thorns linger on these briars. The gaps in family memory are painfully sharp. What really happened to Laura? Was she resented, or treated with tenderness and care? Did she soon flee from Eastover to her sister Harriet's big two-story house in Sumter? Well, how long was she actually in Eastover? Answers twist and curl: A day. Several months. Two years. Was Laura's health failing? Not at all. Definitely. Um, perhaps.

My cousin Beau told me that she was present at Laura's death. She says it was 1933, and Beau and her parents, Coit and Doll, were renting an apartment at Aunt Harriet's house in Sumter, a big old humongous house with many rooms. Beau told me that Laura had heart problems and often asked her brother Donnie to bring her to Sumter for a doctor's appointment. This time, Laura arrived the night before the appointment and went to sleep in one of Harriet's double beds.

When Beau walked to Laura's bed and tried to wake her, there was no response. In this telling, Laura dies peacefully in her sleep, near people who loved her.

And then? It has been within the last few years now, maybe a hundred years later, that the Kirven family has decided officially to name the year Laura died. They got together and chose 1935, and they put that year on record. But no one actually does remember. No one could provide anything like proof or evidence.

But what is this I see, on this sunny day in 1944 in Sumter? Someone is driving a tractor? On the highway? Let me ask. Oh, they tell me it is Joe Kirven, from that old Kirven family who used to live on that old farm? He looks mighty young, that's for sure. What, you tell me he's fourteen? Lord have mercy, how can he be driving? And who is that policeman fellow, waving his arms and clearing the way? You say Coit Kirven? Didn't he win some prize or other for police work? And that young man is steering that tractor and combine toward the old Kirven farm? The old Kirven farm? Gracious, it's been years since anyone was out there. They what? The whole family, you say? But I thought they had gone. To where it was, I can't rightly remember.

I will choose to remember Grandmother Laura, who died before I was born, with the insistent words of my cousin Tom, the third Thomas Kirven and the oldest child present during the exodus to Eastover, who spoke to me the moment I arrived in 2004 at Joe Chandler's home in Sumter, for my long-delayed family visit.

Tom said this to me: "Laura was the kindest, sweetest woman ever."

Laura Fraser Kirven as a young woman, before 1900

Laura Kirven and her sister Harriet displaying their hats, c. 1930

Interlude: I am born and I am nurtured

Yes, it is certainly strange that I am able to remember the moment I learned to walk. I am with Diane and Perry at the large open door of a big room. Diane and Perry are cheering me on. I manage to stay upright for a few steps through that open door. I remember thinking a good thought that felt like, *Oh, things are going to be different now!*

That big room is Ansie's living room, which will soon become The Town and Country Shop in Fairmont, North Carolina. I am living at this house with my mother because—as I will learn much later—my father is overseas as a soldier in World War II. Ansie has rescued both my mother and me by inviting us to live with her family. Hm. Today I can reflect that Ansie is Saving the Baby once more.

I have no memory of Ansie's kind husband, George Williams. That is because he is usually at Duke Hospital, sick with a heart condition. George will die tragically when Perry and Diane are young, and his death will become the reason that Ansie will need to create The Town and Country Shop in her big living room, which will become a store famous for selling stylish clothes for women.

I also can remember the day I met my father, when I was three years old. We are at the train station, and he climbs into the back seat of a car where I am sitting by myself. I have a stick of fancy wrapped chewing gum to give him. Aha, I see that he has a stick of the same fancy wrapped chewing gum to give me. We trade chewing gums. This man does not say much, but he smiles.

This man and my mother and I, all three of us, will leave Ansie's house, even though I don't want to. We will drive to a town called Winston-Salem. Maybe the town is named for cigarettes.

When I am older, the grownups let me visit Ansie's house by myself. I remember being there as a child, visit after visit, when I am feeling just fine.

At Ansie's house we are sitting in a small and peaceful human circle, out of harm's way. We are at a plain, everyday supper where we sit around a table that has room for six people. Ansie and Diane are there, and often Perry too, and Ansie's brother, my Uncle Donnie. I am a young child getting bigger. We are having a plain everyday supper.

For a whole hour we have shelled butter beans, and now a bowl of those tiny half-moons, hot and light green, sits on a trivet before us. There is sweet corn from the market, picked that day. A kind neighbor has left homegrown tomatoes on Ansie's front step, and we've sliced them for the table. There is a plate of chicken pieces, dipped in egg and rolled in corn meal and fried in oil. Hot biscuits are in a basket covered by a small towel. Could you please pass the butter? The strawberry jam? Dessert smells float in from the kitchen: peach cobbler.

We sit and eat. Diane says, "It's mighty quiet—people must be enjoying themselves."

No mad dogs tear at the screen door, no snakes curl up the chair legs. We are at peace. We share the plain joy of being alive.

In this particular scene, our family's ways of Saving the Baby have worked well. We *keep body and soul together,* as the saying goes. In a while, someone asks Donnie if he wants more biscuits, and he answers Donnie style, *Thank you ma'am, I have reached my sufficiency.*

Ansie Kirven Williams in the 1920s

Donald Fraser Kirven, c. 1950

Mariann and Perry reading, c. 1944

Mariann, Perry, and Diane in the 1940s

Interlude

Another time, I am in the back seat of a car, driving down Highway 76 in South Carolina. Mama and Daddy are in the front seat, and sometimes my younger sister Cathy is in the back seat with me. We are on the lookout for the house. Have we missed it? Should we turn around? We are six hours away from our home in Winston-Salem, and it is early afternoon.

The pine trees have thickened and grown so that I have to scrunch down in the back seat to see the tops. Now all at once you can see a house beyond them, a two-story wooden house, plain and unornamented and circled by a porch. It is set among enormous oak trees that vie with the pines for height. The Farm lives in the woods, it seems.

We turn into the sandy driveway scattered with pinecones and extract ourselves from our airless car ride. Now I can leave behind my parents' worries that I might lose a shirt button, go barefoot, start eating dinner before the hostess (Mama) raises her fork, wander off and get lost, eat spoiled food (unrefrigerated mayonnaise is certain death), behave like a ragamuffin, or touch the woodwork with dirty fingers. The Farm is parole from home. Here I won't have to hide in my bedroom with my books, nibbling torn bits of paper from the page margins.

"Hold still while I fix your collar," Mama says to me after we step out of the car. Mama is forever nervous that she might appear at a disadvantage before her oldest brother, my Uncle Tom. I want to kick off my shoes and feel the sand move under my feet.

A few of my uncle's eight children stroll up to our car and lead us back to the kitchen steps, where folks always gather. My cousins have tanned faces and strong limbs, and they are beautiful creatures like athletes, completely at ease with their own bodies. We look at each other while the grownups sing out greetings, and yet "the cat has my tongue" and I can't think of a thing to say. My cousins are bigger and brimming with confidence. The oldest ones—Ophelia and Tom and Joe Chandler and Laura Ann—are 16, 14, 12, and 10 years older than me. They would have been adult-sized when I was six years old. I remember once Joe stooping down to show me something, maybe a bird's nest with an open shell, maybe a fishing lure. It doesn't matter what he holds, because his smile calms my shyness.

I like how my cousins talk. It is musical. It is liquid and sensual. They savor their own voices, pulling their vowels out like taffy. They say *ain't* with pleasure, the way Elvis will later sing it. Larry tells his stories with pell-mell tumbling inflections.

That rooster? He won't bother you none if you don't bother him. He moves that redcomb head like a hammer, kerchunk-a-chunk. Don' you worry, we gone find us some eggs in the henhouse. Law, they make a noise, all that kut-kut-kut-kut-ka-DAAT. See, I scootch this chicken aside right quick, take up the egg.

You never milk a cow? Well, now. Sit right down here on this stool, grab one of these things here and pull. That's right, ain't gonna hurt you. Now squeeze down at the same time. Oh, lawsy mercy, don' point it at yo face! Yeah, it's warm, that's how it come out the cow! Now be sure to jerk yo head back if you see that cow foot move.

I hang on my cousins' every word.

Julie is the most confidential. Her steady blue-gray eyes wonder what she can safely share with me. She is perfect, with curly windswept hair, and she will probably become a model or go to Hollywood.

One summer when I am twelve, Julie and I walk in our bathing suits to the homemade swimming pool that is past the cow fence, all by ourselves. It is filled by an Artesian well and drained through a pipe at the top. The water is brownish and the bricks slippery, and it smells healthy like water and grass and clean dirt. It is good for cooling off.

We splash around for a while and then Julie says, "Let's take off our suits," and I don't want to be the squeamish city cousin. Then we are even cooler. Insects buzz, going nowhere. We grab our suits and hold them below the surface against our bodies, while we tread water.

Larry arrives on a horse. He stops.

"How y'all doin'?"

"We're doing just *fine*," Julie says, serenely.

Larry salutes and rides off.

My cousins caution me, dare me, chuckle at my efforts, and teach me.

Being at The Farm scares me, too. One oak that charges into the sky bears a huge tire swing. Who has put that rope so skyscraper high? Is some cousin going to lift me onto that tire and push, just for a joke? That bull is rumored to be harmless behind his fence, but I have my doubts. I would never dare to ride the horses, but my sister Cathy grows up and then learns to ride bareback.

As a child, I learn that rounding up supper at The Farm is a group sport, with everyone hauling bowls from the icebox, tending the fry pan, shucking corn, locating another plate when one more person drops by. Once I help

Interlude

cousin Danny mix his famous blueberry muffins, with his speedy hands and his infectious laugh, and then he and I drive on a mercy mission to deliver some to a friend. Family friends multiply at The Farm.

Supper might be corn bread, green beans, fried chicken, potatoes, a pitcher of fresh milk, peaches, and ice cream. Salt and pepper are the spices. Cleanup is an assembly line. One person sponges off the dishes in the soapy-water bucket, another dunks them with tongs in a tray of scalding hot water, a third piles them into dishracks to air-dry. Laura Ann, my teenage cousin with cascading brunette curls, warns me not to burn my hands in the rinse water. This dishwashing routine drives Mama bats. She stage-whispers, "Have they *scrubbed?* Are those dishes *clean?*"

On one carefree summer night, we children are allowed a drive-in movie. I scramble with a passel of cousins into the bed of a pickup. Mama doesn't protest or else doesn't know I am going. An old-enough male cousin takes the wheel as we drive into the dark alongside some cotton fields.

"Hold on tight," Julie tells me. "Don't fall out of the truck, or we'll have to come back and fetch you and we'll miss the start of the movie."

"I'm not scared," I lie.

At bedtime, places to sleep materialize either on the porch or in the house. One time they line five or six of us children side by side upstairs beneath tall windows. The boards underfoot have a soft, worn surface. We are exhausted, and we sleep as companions beside the angled moonlight and the long shadows.

I wake the next morning alone, for the others have left to do their farm jobs. There are no weekends or holidays for the animals and the crops.

Staying at the Farm relieves me from my usual parched and anxious thoughts. I feel renewed, and I revel hanging out with my confident and supple cousins. I like the easy grace of their generosity: You're welcome to share what we have. Just put another pallet on the porch.

One time in later years, when I came home to Winston-Salem on a college break, Cathy and I drove by ourselves to The Farm for a day or two in 1961.

I found my uncle Tom leaning on a post in the back yard, like a skeptical giant. He said this to me: "Are you down here for the *experience?*"

"What?" I asked. "What do you mean?" Was he being sarcastic? He was not accustomed to explaining himself, so I never found out.

Inside the house, I talked with his wife, my Aunt Eva. She was a commanding presence with a peaceful smile. Eva's royal blue eyes watched me, their judgment suspended. "Do you like it down here?"

"Yes, ma'am," I answered, "I like it fine."

"Will you come back to see us?" Eva asked. "We're your family. It's important."

"Yes, well, I *hope* I can." By then I had fully taken in the emotional reality that Mama resisted visits to The Farm. I think this conversation with Eva was about family loyalty.

But in 1964, I moved to Connecticut for graduate school. A few years later, my youngest sister L. B. arrived in Boston for medical school. We two were the apparent defectors—"Yankees" by location.

So in 2003, forty years after my relocation to the North and one year after the tragic death of L. B., my heroic youngest sister, I reached out again to my Southern family. I wrote a letter to Joe Chandler Kirven:

> *Are you the one I knew as Joe Chandler when I was a little girl? I remember mama taking us to visit the house at Sumter, which was an exciting place to me, and I always wished she would take us there more often...*

Joe wrote me back, in a letter that begins, "I am indeed the Joe Chandler who is your cousin. I am 73 years old."

In the summer of 2004, for the first time, I walk into Joe and Sallie's house in Sumter. My husband Richard is with me. Many of my cousins are there, too. Here is Beau, putting her arm on my shoulder. "Mariann? It's Beau." She doubts I can remember her after all that time.

Tears come to my eyes. Silly me.

This book is the result of many more journeys South.

Chapter Five:
"A Spotless Reputation"
The Baby of Your Good Name

The Baby is rescued from the fire. Yet the Baby must still be Saved.

People can see the Baby as a symbol of extended life and even immortality. Since actual babies are finite—they grow up, they grow old, they die, they are only us—we sometimes replace them with symbolic Babies, even better suited to our innate need to save. The Baby in the abstract can theoretically be saved completely. The further we move from physical danger, the more ideal the concept of the Baby, and the more intense and conflicted our saving efforts must be. The moral rectitude and Good Name of the family is one of these extremes. In trying to preserve a Good Name, our family has sometimes tripped over this metaphor and fallen into mistrust and hard feelings.

> Good name in man and woman, dear my lord,
> Is the immediate jewel of their souls
> *Othello III. 3*

Here Shakespeare reveals a human predicament: that a Good Name feels infinite and pure, even though it is tied to finite or "immediate" matters. Anyone is susceptible to the wish for a spotless reputation, as pure as a newborn. A Good Name can imply a life on another plane, high above any insinuations of scandal or ridicule. Reputation can be indefinitely long. A person's "good name" could feel as if it might be alive forever.

In the South of my ancestors, a Good Name usually meant a *white* Good Name for white people. And it seemed to depend in some way on the sexual purity of white women. This family ideal, at least for white Southerners, may have come into being partly through the outrageous circumstances of slavery, when white slaveholders could intimidate black women into having sex. The resulting large numbers of mulattoes gave rise to the widespread crime—as white Southerners called it—of miscegenation, which was often perpetuated by white men themselves. On the other hand, white Southern Womanhood was a concept that could help affirm moral dignity.

Protecting the family's Good Name can feel like an urgent mission.

The 1800s brought escalating debates about the evils of slavery, from the North and from the South. The vaunted inviolate purity of Southern women may even have acted as a counterpoint to abolitionist outrage. If the true Southern woman was as unstained as an angel, how could white people be anything but good? Never mind what the abolitionists or the Yankees said about the South—behind the skirts of unblemished white women, no moral flaws could be seen. White women still carried the public weight of extreme goodness when I was a child in the mid-twentieth century. This ideal was sustained in our family by exhortation, as if our very lives depended on it.

My sister Cathy and I are being driven on a momentous trip in Winston-Salem. It is 1951. I am nine years old and Cathy is three. Our customary grumbling disrupts the back seat, while in the front seat Mama stubs out a butt in the ash tray and lights another cigarette. My head hurts. I roll down the window a crack, and Cathy slides over to breathe the fresh air with me.

"You two keep still! Don't you dare crease those dresses!"

On the familiar hill into town, we turn left and stop at a dark red house, with white posts supporting the porch roof. Mama's upheld finger keeps us still until she opens the Ford's back door and slides us out, gingerly, from toe to top: patent leather shoes, white curly-edged socks, pastel organdy dresses with chiffon tops and lace collars. I itch all over. Cathy scratches her tummy through her dress. To stop her, Mama takes Cathy's two hands into one of hers.

"Both of you, keep your hands off those outfits."

We pick our way up the porch steps. The grown-ups greet each other with sliding high notes, as nice as pie. We are led into a bare room curtained to darkness, with an awkward metal contraption that I recognize by now as a professional camera. And there is the bench, draped.

Cathy is arranged beside me on the bench. Our feet are placed. Our skirts are fluffed to seem natural, our chiffon sleeves pinched upward on our arms, the straps of our pastel under-dresses straightened, our lace collars flattened, our hair re-brushed and re-barretted to reveal foreheads equally as clear as the forehead of the Brittany doll that Daddy brought back from France in World War II. Cathy holds that doll on her lap. If a hair escapes, or if one part of the composition goes askew, we start over. The preparation takes a long time. The photographer waits for Mama.

Mama's hand is anxious and hard on my shoulders, chin, waist. She pulls until I sit up straighter. She brushes my ears, re-parts my hair with the comb teeth, tightens my crescent barrette. I try not to move. I feel her conviction that in this project everything is expected, no mistakes tolerated.

At Mama's touch my body remembers years of being handled and worried about. The long, hot, anxious car trips along the back roads of Winston-Salem in search of houses where sufficiently delicate lace was sold in the parlors. My complaining, and Mama's explaining. The hair-washing ritual, my body laid out flat on the metal countertop, my dangling head scrubbed with stiff fingers and rinsed too hot with the sprayer. Double shampoo, double rinse. Urgent trips to another photographer. My fingers tugged into tiny string-lace gloves, the rest of me fastened with collar, belt, hair clips, shoes. Ow, ow, ow. Wait now, Mama says, can't we pull this darling little string purse handle over Mariann's arm? It's not too tight, is it? Let's do it one more time and make her perfect for Daddy. It is 1944, and I am sitting on Mama's lap.

Maisie and Mariann in 1944

Now in 1951, when Cathy and I have been completely readied for the shot, we are told next to arrange our mouths in the right way. No, don't grin, and don't show your teeth. In fact, don't smile. The photographer takes another shot, and another. Cramped and edgy, I arrange my mouth as I must do, in order to leave this place. Feelings well behind my eyes, feelings assuring me that I am still myself. They are forbidden feelings. Will the camera see the NO in my eyes and betray me? It is bad of me to feel this way.

The original black-and-white photograph is then hand-painted, a technique that Mama seeks out, worried about finding the right artist. Color is added, and lingering flaws brushed over. In the carefully re-done picture, I see two young child virgins as eternal as the lovers on Keats' Grecian Urn, not counting the love. We are pure, scrubbed, well-bred white children. No spot is visible.

Those barely detectable curves on our under-dresses seem an asexual and empty hint of future breasts. Mama has had those pastel dresses made to order, with a child's version of the "sweetheart neckline" that has been re-tailored to be high-cut, as another layer in the protection of our family's Good Name.

In my childhood "impeccable" meant a perfect appearance, and the root of the word also means "without sin." Becker alleges the *"sacredness of class distinctions"* because "all [class] power is sacred power . . . it begins in the hunger for immortality" (49). The Baby is both material and spiritual, the center of everyone's natural "conviction that our happiness is special" (Wright, 336). Safe from all social infamy.

The Brittany doll, Cathy, and Mariann in 1951

Two ways of protecting a Good Name stood out in our family. One was static—a perfect appearance that bespoke "good breeding." The other was dynamic—virtuous and honorable behavior that attested to religious faith. A spotless appearance, impeccable behavior, and a good record of churchgoing were all joined like chain mail to make a perfect shield for the Good Name Baby. Our family tried to *hold on tight* to a good reputation behind this armor.

The prized formal photograph was a family tradition that Mama, in her fervor, may have taken to an extreme. Others in the family followed the same tradition. Three of my cousins were dressed up and photographed by Mama's brother Marion and his wife Mabel. These cousins showed dignified deportment, restrained smiles, and purity, with long skirts added and hair pulled safely away from their foreheads.

Anne, Mabel Winifred "Winkie," and Josephine "Jo" Kirven, in the 1940s

A photograph was taken of my mother when she was a child of nine or ten.

This photo could belong in the dictionary under "Good Name." The child seems to embody perfection and strength, as a virgin and a warrior. James Kincaid suggests that as twin figures "the child and the lady were eroticized precisely because of their innocence" in these times, especially if they were white and middle class (Essig). The child Maisie has an air of defending herself against the world in this photo. I will always wonder what demeaning or insulting language Maisie perceives herself to be guarding against, with this valiant pose.

Maisie Kirven as a child, in the 1920s

Throughout my childhood, Mama and I recycled this conversation:

"You know what my brothers used to tell me?" Mama would frown.

"No, what, Mama?" I would respond, though I knew already.

"They used to say to me, *Maisie, you ain't worth a poop. You ain't worth a damned poop.*"

"Oh, no, Mama, that's not true. You're worth a lot."

"Well, I've learned to hold my head up high. You just be sure to hold your head up high, no matter what happens. Don't you reflect badly on the family." (This casual and repeated insult by the brothers may sound ridiculous, but in time it would have tragic consequences.)

Photographs like these become links in the family Good Name Armor. The photos help to refute any possible scurrilous defamers of the Kirven or Fraser families. Photographs like these would challenge any outside forces that might impugn the family name. They reveal a family that will value "Good name in man and woman" just as much as they value strength and nurture.

In graduate school, I found the same advice that high-born ladies should "feign ignorance" of curses or improper words in Castiglione's *Book of the Courtier* (1528). That's what Mama insisted: If we acted like ladies, we

A Spotless Reputation

could *hold our heads up high* even though we were not wealthy enough for her daughters to join the high-class Winston-Salem debutantes (who ironically, rumor suggested, did have some famously raunchy parties). Mama warned us that if we stumbled in our ladylike behavior, people would think we were *po'buckers* who couldn't *do right* because no one had taught us any better. Our pure behavior was proof that we belonged to a higher class of people. With Good Names.

There is one large drawback to the concept of the Good Name Baby—namely, that anyone who really wants to cultivate the vaunted necessity of a "good reputation" could need constant work—and steady attention—to keep this "immediate jewel of the soul" alive and well, safe from all possible defamers. Even the term "Good Name" suggests work: an ongoing, painful conflict against all imaginable insults.

The insistence on *having* a Good Name can be treacherous, though. A Good Name is a potential defense. Trying to assure the utter safety of the Good Name Baby can be a painful and endless enterprise. Real and imagine attacks can persist.

Once when I was visiting Mama and Daddy at their home in Roanoke, Virginia, L. B. returned from a date with a high-school boyfriend.

Mama confronted her, asking this question in a caustic voice: "Have you been necking? How far did you go? Are you a lady of the evening, these days?"

L. B. stayed quiet, knowing there was no safe reply to these words.

In the late 1960s, Mama and L. B. kindly visited me in Connecticut, where I was enduring a short (not short enough) first marriage in which my husband was becoming abusive. Rattled, I mentioned this problem to Mama.

She simply shook her head resignedly. "Oh, yes," she said. "I know *all about* those notions. When I grew up, it was common knowledge that some men considered women to be worthless, good only for doing whatever menfolk wanted. To prop up the men."

Mama could give me no practical advice. Soon afterward, I summoned the good sense to flee from my disturbed husband when he purchased a gun. Perhaps he thought I was a cottonmouth or a mad dog? I might have been idealistic, but I wasn't stupid.

The trouble with the Good Name Baby is that this baby can take perpetual upkeep and polishing. There are always forces in the world trying to wound or destroy the vaunted ideal of a family's "good name," even when a family feels that its reputation is safe. Constant work is required to keep it safe enough.

I can remember the first time I watched Aunt Ansie open a thick mailing envelope and pull out legal-sized pages of handwritten charts from Uncle Lawrence. Frequent family trees for both Kirvens and Frasers were assembled by Lawrence with genealogical enthusiasm. The trees grew backwards through older branches, in smaller and smaller handwriting.

In the tradition pioneered by Lawrence, other family members have found versions of the Kirven (Kirwan) crest and a picture of Kirwan castle in Galway, Ireland. The Fraser crest was established as well, and a Fraser tartan scarf was given to me one Christmas. These vaunted ancestries seem somewhat questionable to me. Still, the two crests were framed in my parents' old house in Virginia, and I've noticed them in other relatives' houses as well.

High-class ancestors can be nourishment for the Good Name Baby. There's a taste of eternity in this claim. My cousin Joe lent me a copy of Alexander MacKenzie's *History of the Frasers of Lovat with Genealogies of the Principal Families of the Name (1896)*.

Sitting in Joe's house in the summer of 2005, cooled by the ceiling fan, I worked on digesting that tome along with Lawrence's notes and markings. I think I found the source of Lawrence's theory. In the line of Lovat there was a John Fraser in the 1700s, reported dead, yet rumored to have faked his death and sailed from the Old World to America. Lawrence stretched out that rumor a bit to suggest that this same John Fraser, of the noble Lovat line, may have sired children in America who descend from that Lovat family. We do indeed have one ancestor, most likely a different John Fraser, who was a South Carolina cotton farmer in the early 1800s. But Lawrence preferred the theory that would put our family in the direct line of Fraser nobility—in other words, to make us the lost and unacknowledged descendants of the Lords of Lovat.

So I went to ancestry.com, today's provider of family lines, which stipulates that our Frasers belong to a "cadet" family of Frasers, descended from a "natural" (illegitimate) son of the fourth Lord Lovat. So sorry, Lawrence! Yet aren't we relieved that we don't descend from Simon Fraser, Lord Lovat, that infamous scoundrel who kidnapped his wife and eventually was beheaded in 1745 on Tower Hill in London? Well, perhaps some of my relatives might even admire an ancestor with enough "spirit" to get himself beheaded—a tale that could be proof of dauntless courage.

By contrast, the many sons of Erasmus Kirven seemed to be carefree and spontaneous in the face of any Good Name pressures. To Eckard Lee, these sons were just high-spirited *characters* who made better stories than tame, model citizens would. All their *fussin 'n fightin* plots were so tangled that I couldn't catch every detail Eckard Lee told me, but the theme was clear. One brother stormed upstairs to find his woman in bed with another brother. The two "got in a fuss and they had a lawsuit." Then one time Great-Uncle Ed, a dentist, told the police to arrest his brother for debt. "Lock him up!" Great-Uncle Ed shouted to the police.

I couldn't keep straight whether it was Bob or Luke or Hugh that Great-Uncle Ed demanded should be locked up, maybe all three, but whoever it was, they wriggled free on bail, then bided their time until the trial, and finally drove to town for court—all without any of their wives learning about this little adventure. Maybe they felt riled up, or maybe they were exuberant, but these brothers could work the Good Name system to their own satisfaction.

My impression was that Erasmus' sons rather enjoyed batting around one another's Good Names, just to see which one was batted the furthest. It was like a Good Name game of throwdown. When they weren't playing pranks on each other, they were disputing points of honor and fairness. They had more fun competing, I'll bet, than they ever did in any Good-Name-inspecting church. Eventually, they went their own ways. Tom and Bob moved further south near Sumter. Ed moved to Florida. Luke set up his own homestead. Pollard had two wives. James began to raise horses. Hugh lived near his father. John lost a leg and grew so cranky that the others tried to stay out of his way, with little success.

My father let me know, in his gradual way, that the Good Name baby might be more about church etiquette than about any religious theories.

The Episcopal Church was a pleasant haven. I got to sing in the choir. The prayers were encouraging, and worshipping? That was what good people did. Sitting in that church pew, I could imagine the possibility of my own goodness. We dressed up in frilly dresses, patent leather shoes, and sizeable hats. The main issue seemed to be whom or what to Save. Would it be the family member who might burden the family financially or emotionally, yet who is a flesh-and-blood person, or would it be the immediate jewel of the collective family soul, which needs the secure walls of convention to thrive?

People can sometimes imagine that they hear the family's Good Name crying to be saved—a phantom cry so distressed, and in such dread of fiery infamy, that its cries block out the needs of actual family members. No family dares risk being shunned by the community, nor does any one person want to be cast overboard by the family. Whenever I sat in the church pew as a child, my mind would swing between inward pleas for good thoughts and a practical-pig oversight of my outfit and gestures, which were supposed to be "outward and visible signs of an inward and spiritual grace." We always put on special outfits for church.

Mariann and Diane dressed for church

On the day of my first communion, when I was twelve years old, Daddy and I went to church by ourselves. Months before that, I had attended communion classes with other twelve-year-olds to practice communion etiquette and to be catechized about Christian doctrine. In those classes, I had dared to ask *what* we were being saved *from,* and learned that it was not proper to mention Hell in the Episcopal Church.

As Daddy and I sat together in the pew, I felt a touch of awe. I wondered, strangely and for the first time, whether Daddy was a true believer. Could it be? His conversations with my sister and me had always been spare, leaving us to guess the shape of his thoughts. Behind his near-silence, did he embrace deep beliefs, or private aspirations to holiness and sanctity? This first communion of mine could be my first chance to commune with Daddy, in a real bond. Maybe Daddy and I could *share* religious feelings, beginning *now.*

We were both quiet. We both wore glasses. Maybe our spirits were alike. We had come by ourselves, on our own. Was this setting Daddy's way of inviting me to join him as an adult in his faith? If so, I should be super-vigilant. I reviewed the program for the sit-stand-kneel instructions. My first goal was *not* to embarrass Daddy, so that he might share his genuine religious feelings with me.

The service transpired as planned. We new communicants had all worn our neatest dresses and suits. My dress was a linen hand-me-down which had been "in the family," earning an extra layer of sanctity. We stood to take communion along with the congregation, as we had been schooled step-by-meticulous-step to do.

Pairs of ushers posted themselves at the front of the nave and moved back in regular stages, to signal which rows should walk to the chancel for communion.

"We wait until they stand one row *behind* us," Daddy whispered to me.

"Yes, I know."

Didn't Daddy believe I had learned how to act?

St. Paul's Episcopal Church in Winston-Salem, North Carolina, 2011

The ushers cleared us for walking up. Daddy moved into the center aisle and let me pass in front of him, as men were supposed to do. Correct so far. I walked up to the altar, knelt on the maroon cushion and turned my palms up, right hand over left, in the position to receive the wafer. Daddy knelt beside me. This was good. It was holy. I lifted the waver unobtrusively to my mouth, licked it in, and dissolved it with my tongue, careful not to let it stick to the roof of my mouth like peanut butter.

Now the chalice. "The blood of our Lord." I steadied its base with my left hand, barely touched its bowl with my right, took the slightest sip of wine, did not gulp, and swallowed in silence. Did Daddy notice how well I was doing? I knelt the obligatory two seconds more for solitary contemplation, then rose without putting any downward pressure on the altar rail. I exited to the *right,* because we were sitting in a *right-hand* pew. I headed for the *side* aisle to re-enter our pew from the *far* side, just as the teachers had said.

"Down *this* aisle," Daddy murmured, behind me.

"I *know.*" Had I not yet proved trustworthy?

As we slipped back into our pew, Daddy leaned toward me.

I hoped he would say *Good job,* or maybe even, *Would you like to have some serious talks with me about religion, sometime?*

But what Daddy whispered in my ear was: "Your slip is showing."

Ah. I had been hoping for a Daddy who would be bold and deep. But this was the Daddy I had—one who treasured the Good Name Baby. A truly good Southern woman would never prance about with her slip showing.

When Mama died, Daddy was 80, and he and I began to talk a bit more freely on the phone. One day, soon before he expected to die, he blurted out these words to me: "I fooled them all."

"Who, Daddy?" I asked amiably, cherishing any confidence from him. "Who did you fool?"

"Everybody," Daddy replied, happily. "*All* of them."

No details were forthcoming. Since then, I have determined at least one overriding meaning from his words, or his lack of words. Daddy was happy that he would be dying with his Good Name Baby well saved.

I asked some questions, trying to fathom what "fooling" them all could possibly mean. He answered that he had pretended not to be angry when the neighbors had returned our sled in a broken condition—which was then decades ago. And that he had concealed his annoyance at me, long ago, when at six years old I spilled my milkshake at the Toddle House. Maybe the "fooling" he meant consisted of hiding his genuine emotions.

I'll never know his exact meaning. Maybe he was saying that now, close to death, he could realize that he had Saved the Baby of his Good Name completely, to his own satisfaction. He had hidden all his "ungentlemanly" feelings, and his reputation would now be forever safe. He sounded victorious.

My mother pursued her own definition of victory as she worked to shield her own Good Name Baby once and for all. First, she acted to establish to her personal satisfaction that she would no longer be ridiculed by her brothers. She had a plan. When L. B. left home for college, Maisie commuted from Winston-Salem to Chapel Hill to win her doctorate in English literature from the University of North Carolina. Now, late in her life, she could announce her victory to her own satisfaction: "My brothers used to laugh and laugh at me. *There's little Maisie with her nose stuck in a book again.* Well, now I'm a Ph.D."

To Maisie, her Good Name Baby had become a reality, for all to praise. Even those mocking brothers could disparage her no longer. She had reached her ultimate goal.

She was old. She was determined to avoid any further humiliation. and circumstances favored her in an upside-down and unfortunate way. She contracted an illness she could not name or explain. She developed episodes of excruciating pain below her stomach, and she chose to bear down bravely through them, again and again. The pain became a war of her own choosing, and she waged it time after time. In her own mind, standing the pain meant refusing to put up with the indignity of some high and mighty male doctor—who might very well be just as judgmental and dismissive of her as her brothers were, when they kept telling her that she "wasn't worth a poop," for heaven's sake—and that doctor man, so proud and self-important, would be fooling around with her body and making pronouncements. *No thank you.*

It took many months for Maisie to ask her own physician daughter, L. B., if she could get the advice of doctors from the Lahey Clinic in Boston, where L. B. worked. Those doctors found her hard to diagnose, because they believed that no one could keep enduring actual gall bladder attacks. They were far too painful.

"Oh, yes," I answered the doctor when I sat in on of Mama's interviews. "She is saying it is a *sharp* pain, not a *dull* pain."

"But *how* sharp?" he challenged.

Maisie had bravely, even heroically, endured the attacks. And it turned out to be cancer, as eventual tests showed months later.

Maisie had held on tight to her own self-respect—the Good Name Baby most crucial, even vital, to her—and the cost may have been her own life.

Our family has several examples of possible sacrifices to the Good-Name Baby. Some sacrifices were carried out, while others ended in rescue. Some relatives cared greatly for the Good Name of the Family, some cared much less.

> A gay man who died of AIDS in a distant city, with the cause of his death never mentioned by the family.

> A young woman pregnant before marriage and disowned by her parents, not even allowed to hold her newborn baby in the hospital. Ansie—so often a saver—had later challenged the parents: "Well, do you love her?"

> Another pregnant young woman welcomed immediately into the family and then married with full ceremony by the father of her child.

> A young gay man gradually re-building the connection with his father who was at first devastated by that news.

> A middle-aged man who slowly drank himself to death as his wife and children watched sadly. They all "kept up appearances," because the Good Name Baby can be ruthless.

> A father excommunicated from the Church for drinking to excess.

> A young mother who suffered deep, crippling anxieties without daring to tell anyone but her husband.

> A woman depressed by her illness and called "just hysterical" by some family members, who nevertheless acted against stigma and got helpful medication.

In the 1800s, the family church might have taken over the job of policing Good Names. They may have partly believed in Luther's cry, "By faith alone!" Even so, the church kept track of parishioners' deeds and made decisions based on those deeds.

When I first began reading the microfilmed minutes of the Black Creek Baptist Church in Darlington County, it was possible to find the moment on July 3 1803, when my 3 x Great Grandfather Cade and my 4 x Great Grandfather Thomas joined the church community:

> . . . a door was opened there came forward Cade Kirven and Thomas Kirven and was Received by Experience and initiated into the church by assertion by the Rev. James Coleman Dismist by singing and prayer. [The phrase "a door was opened" means a door of reception, meaning that the person was received into the Church.]

The Black Creek Church in Darlington, South Carolina, before it burned down on Easter Sunday in 1922

Reading further, I discovered that in this church, the congregation was put in charge of Good Names. Everyone's weekly conduct was generally known, and on Sunday flawed behavior was ruled upon. Ungodly conduct included cursing, excessive drinking, hitting one's wife, fathering a bastard, cheating, striking one's neighbor, and disagreeing with Church decisions. After discussion, some members would be "warned," which meant admonished or censured. Brothers of the Church would visit their wayward fellows during the week to "labor and pray" for them. On later Sundays, the members would be tried by the Church and judged on improvement. They would repent and be restored to the church, or they would be excluded or excommunicated.

This discussion affirms that "a man's whole lineage" was implicated in honor or shame. This tradition may explain why I heard so many times as a child, "Don't disgrace the family."

Churches in the Dovesville and Society Hill area were populated by Welsh Neck Baptists, who had traveled South from Pennsylvania and earned their living as farmers. These people resisted the traffic in slaves for a while, but as the 1800s continued, many of them bought more slaves to work their land. Their "former anti-slavery convictions fell away, and many joined the slaveholding ranks" (Wyatt-Brown 2001, 107). Slaves were admitted as members of the Black Creek Church, with such names as Mingo, Plato, Damian, and Leannah taken from the Bible or classical times. Yet slavery did not have to impugn the white people's Good Name, or so the community tried to believe, for they meant to be *good* to the slaves. In 1861, in Great-Grandfather Erasmus's day, the Black Creek Church had 125 whites and 52 blacks.

The Black Creek Church may have been the official regulator of Good Names for the Kirven family in Dovesville. I have no record of what the Kirvens thought of this church, but I do find a record of how the church dealt with my Great Grandfather Erasmus. He would have been 32 years old then, six years before the birth of his oldest son Josh Pollard. The Church first charged him and then gave its verdict on June 30, 1849:

> The committee appointed to investigate the charge of bastardy alleged against Brother E. G. Kirven reported that the evidence before them was insufficient to convict him, but enough, in their judgment, was elicited to satisfy them that he was obnoxious to the charge of fornication, for which offence we recommend his exclusion from the Church.

Therefore, Erasmus Kirven was not excommunicated, but he was excluded. However, Erasmus later joined the Swift Creek Baptist Church and lived until 1897. Here is a newspaper obituary for him, from the Darlington Library:

> For thirty years previous to his death it was my good fortune to be personally acquainted with Mr. E. G. Kirven and I must say that I never knew a Kinder or more benevolent man than he was. He was a friend indeed to the poor and, in all the walks of life, he dealt honestly with his fellow men . . . . If there was one trait about Mr. Kirven more prominent than another it was his frankness. His faults and his virtues were alike known to the world; no deception and nothing hidden about him.

People may ascribe different levels of importance to the reputation a given person may be cultivating for the sake of a precious Good Name. A person's particular Good Name Baby may be strict or lenient, imagined or seriously credited.

Thomas Jackson Kirven and Laura Fraser, who would become my grandparents, carried on a five-year courtship from 1892 through 1897 though their letters. They lived thirty long miles apart, Tom in Dovesville and Laura in Sumter. They wrote several hundred letters then, about 62,000 words. These letters were found by L. B. and me in my mother's attic, after her death.

The letters reveal a man and a woman struggling towards intimacy through the thick protective armor of each one's Good Name. They write these letters privately, yet they do seem to believe that their behavior and their words exist under communal scrutiny. To hold on to their good names, Tom must be the soul of honor and Laura the soul of virtue—the ideal Southern Woman. The silent community that oversees appearance, behavior, class, and religious faith is always present in their minds, prepared to assign a Good Name or take it away.

Heavy social criteria weigh upon their love. Tom and Laura raise Bad Name ghosts out of words and then put them to rest with more words. The pressure of a Good Name can bring discord and misunderstanding. Words can ambush and hurt them, with no intent to hurt. Only in marriage will their words pose no further threat to their spotless reputations, those jewels of their souls.

Tom's letters idealize Laura for her virtue. Men have been writing such words to women at least since the 1100s, the dawn of Provençal poetry and *fin' amor,* which is the forerunner of what we still call "true love." Dante's words about Beatrice and Petrarch's poems about *his* Laura have modeled for centuries how men should write to their beloveds. In them, love is a heaven and the angelic lady inhabits an almost unreachable height. Ideal Southern Womanhood is one descendant of this literary line.

Tom's words create Laura as a semi-divine presence. He speaks of her spirit, rarely of her body, simply complimenting her "beautiful brilliant" eyes and "the girl of my soul" and his "immaculate and angelic friend." She is his "dear, pure, sweet, & immaculate Darling" who is a *paragon of All* that is commendable in woman." He exults, "I have the *honor* to be engaged to the *peerless &* immaculate Laura A. Fraser!" (11/17/1896).

The idealization goes both ways. Tom's names for Laura reflect back upon himself as a perfectly honorable lover. He longs for Laura, but not insistently. He keeps his distance to protect their ideal reputations. There are 30 miles between them, even though she is his "All in All" who makes his life worth living.

> You have the purest of pure minds, the gentlest of gentle spirits, The most loving of devoted hearts & the very sweetest of dispositions. (9/6/1896)

> So, in spirit, pressing your dear little head nearer, if it be possible for me to press it nearer, to the heart that has been and is still full to overflowing with the very purest love for you . . . (5/15/1895)

> Had I a perfect mastery of all the languages in the world and were to select from them all the most expressive words, and use them in an attempt to tell you how much I love you & how much I wish to be with you at all times, my feelings would be but feebly and very feebly expressed even then. (11/15/1896)

Like a poet of true love, Tom laments that it is "a cruelty and a hardship to be kept away" from Laura. He invokes constancy, eternity, absolute truth, enduring life, and divine loving kindness.

Tom 's unstinting words take up many times the volume of Laura's. His penciled script is open and flowing, between three and six words to the line, in

A Spotless Reputation

long letters that repeat his most passionate phrases. He doesn't stop to edit his spelling. He is sincere and unselfconscious. Anyone who utters so much as one critical word about Laura will have Tom to reckon with, as the loyal protector of her Good Name.

My relatives have one composite observation of Grandfather Tom: *He sure did have a temper.* Says Eckard Lee, "He didn't take nothing off nobody." One Sunday morning, Tom was at the Black Creek Church service while Laura was attending the Presbyterian Church thirty miles southwest. An anonymous man behind Tom whispered something about Laura. What he said is not known. But Tom found the remark insulting to Laura's virtue. He writes:

> My own & only Dear, I have often told you that I would risk my life in the most hazardous place for you or in defense of you or your good name; and if you had been at church today you would have seen the same demonstrated. . . . I heard a mean slander of you, whereupon I called him a *lying puppy,* which he resented by trying to shoot me with his pistol, but failed so utterly till I am now in possession of his pistol, which I took from him. I would have hurt him after I got the pistol had I not been prevented by 20 or 30 men. I guess the dirty rascal will have to account for such conduct in church; but while I deplore that it should have been necessary, I do not regret, *one bit,* that I gave him the lie; for if I had done differently, I should have always considered myself unworthy of *you.* (9/27/1896)

Tom is worried that the news of a fight might reach Laura before he does, portraying him as a "brawler" and staining his image in the community's eyes and hers. Yet he is proud to be a hero in attacking Laura's reputation. Eckard Lee emphasized to me that it did take thirty men to pull Tom off of that lying puppy. Tom was on a sacred mission to defend Laura's Good Name. He was a rough-and-tough Kirven with a visceral need to Save the Baby.

How could two such perfect lovers fall into discord? Well, how could they *not?* Two people who embody the Good Name Baby for each other are destined for conflict.

One early letter from Laura apparently made Tom feel that she had impugned his honor. This letter has been lost. But Tom's reply defends his

Good Name at length, using that formidable temper of his. He says that Laura has heaped ridicule upon him, and he demands an apology:

> My unspeakable disappointment at yours of the 11 inst. finds its equal only in my surprise at the same. It appears to me that for some reason, best known to yourself, you have labored very arduously, ransacking more than one language, for adequate words in setting forth the false premise, upon which, you have so sarcastically drawn your insinuating and insulting conclusion.
>
> Your letter bears upon its very face the undisguised intention to sarcastically criticize and ridicule, and to severely insult me . . . . So, as a matter of justice, I demand an apology of you for the *unfounded* sarcasm, the false charge, the *bitter* ridicule, the *vile insinuations* so *ruthlessly* and so *unjustly* heaped upon me in your last. (2/28/1895)

All of Laura's early letters have disappeared. Because Tom died first, she may have burned her own letters from this difficult early period. Or perhaps Tom threw all her letters away the moment he received her (alleged) insulting letter.

But did Laura apologize? No. An apology would have put *her* honor into question. To his hot indignation, she replies that *his* letter, charging her with sarcasm, contaminates *her* Good Name. Her honor, her character, and even her womanliness, she feels, have been sullied by Tom's angry words. In his ensuing

Thomas Jackson Kirven in the 1890s

letters, Tom gradually backs away from his position. He stops asking for an apology. Finally, *he* apologizes to Laura.

During this fragile period, Laura officially breaks up with Tom, yet they continue to write. In late April he visits her. They reach an accord. It is an interlude that they don't have to put into words.

The first of Laura's letters preserved in that attic box is the one right after this reconciliation, on May 12, 1895. On this day she begins, "Tom, 'my dear heart's *dearer* heart.'"

Months later, Tom and Laura still refer to this deep "misunderstanding" of early 1895, which almost caused them to part forever. She asks whether Tom *meant* to hurt her feelings with his indignant and self-protective words. He protests that he was just defending his honor.

Through their courtship, Laura is careful to distinguish human love from divine love. Her views can deflate the idealism that Tom likes to express, but that same idealism can imprison Laura. Once Tom has called her "the *paragon of All* that is commendable in Woman," how can she take up her pen and write what she feels? She appears to believe that she must be cooler, more skeptical, and more guarded than Tom, for society and Tom have cast her in the part of the idealized, distant Southern lady. Her letters are shorter than Tom's and perfect in grammar. She hints and implies, rather than expressing. She displays her learning, with occasional phrases in French. She quotes Shakespeare and Lydia Sigourney—there was a small volume of Sigourney's poems in that attic box. Among Mama's memorabilia was a lock of light brown hair, braided and encased in glass like a relic. It is Laura's.

Once Laura worries that she may be answering Tom's letters too soon, too eagerly. (Even today, singles are warned about seeming "desperate.") In another letter she says, "I dare not give my pen freedom; for you would surely think me crazy" (7/2/1895). Her words, her behavior, and her faith all constrict her here, for Laura was a devout Presbyterian. She invites Tom to attend church with her at Hebron to hear Dr. James Woodrow. Her father, Lawrence Ladson Fraser, has written a history of the Hebron church. She calls Tom's protests of love extravagant. It takes Laura a year even to admit that she misses Tom, and much longer to express stronger emotions.

The Frasers, so proud of their Good Name, may have been rather closely buttoned. Laura in her twenties is not allowed to drive a carriage alone. In one letter Laura's grandfather, also Lawrence Ladson Fraser, warned his son at the University of South Carolina to "trust no one," especially those companions who might induce him to carouse.

Only in the last few months of their long courtship does Laura permit herself to be more direct:

> My heart is aching for you, not only in loving sympathy and anxiety, but for your dear presence! (6/25/1896)

> The truth is this—I have been so *lonely* since you left, until this evening. (10/12/1896)

Once when Tom cannot come to visit her as promised, Laura even exclaims, "Oh! Tom, how could you disappoint me so?" Her protective Good Name defense has yielded, this once, to emotional reality.

The one unbridled emotion Laura feels free to express to Tom is her sympathy for the ill and the dying—her corporal acts of mercy. Sick children exhaust her, until she is not herself when Tom comes calling. "Little Janie is, we hope, out of danger, her recovery from the jaws of Death the Dr. regards as almost miraculous. . . . I wonder if you had any idea how utterly weary your poor little sweetheart [Laura] was that night!" My own mother, Laura's daughter, may have been taught Laura's extreme compassion for a sick person, especially a child. When I was ill with measles, mumps, chicken pox, or poison ivy around my eyes, Mama cared for me with unusual gentleness and even brought me homemade custard from Laura's own recipe.

Even a generation later, my niece Amy Holland, who is my sister Cathy's daughter, remembers the tender care she received from her grandmother Maisie:

> She doted over me and my brother and took care of us for a whole month while my dad was hospitalized after his motorcycle accident. When I couldn't sleep because I was worried about my dad, she rubbed my back until I fell asleep (I will never forget that gentle touch) . . . When I was 8 and Michael was 6, we both came down with chicken pox. That meant two weeks out of school and a lot of itchy misery. Mama [Maisie] and Bill took care of us during our illness, so Mom and Dad could continue their duties at school/work. It was always, for me, a smooth transition.

> It felt completely natural to be at Mama and Bill's house. I particularly remember the itchy red oozy welts that were all over my body. Michael got a mild case, but I got a full-blown case! I itched and itched! Mama put me in a nice bath, then one by one, dabbed calamine lotion on each of my spots. I didn't want the lotion, so she encouraged me by giving me a penny for each spot I allowed the lotion to be applied. I made $11.62 in one sitting! She did the same for my brother (who only made around $6.00 because he had a lot fewer spots).

In letters written almost a hundred years before the scene Amy describes, Laura, who would be Maisie's mother, shows complete sympathy when Tom's father may be dying, even though Tom and his parents are estranged.

> My own sorrowing Boy,
>
> How my poor heart *aches* for my sorrowing loved one! Dearest, you can never know. I have never ceased, remembering your dear one [his late sister Leila] at a throne of grace, since first you asked— and told me, of the necessity. Today your letter was handed me; and my heart is poured out to God for his salvation and restoration if it be God's will.
>
> Do not think I speak lightly, when I say, would God it *were* my *privilege* to be around your Father's bed, he would have no nurse more prayerful, more kind and loving. This could not be, you know, but, I only wish to show you, how entirely my heart is with you. Pray *for* him; and *with* him, Sweetheart, if he will allow it. (9/19, 1896)

When two women of the Church pass away, Laura writes, "It was a sight to touch my heart to see those poor, motherless babes and children and hear their pitiful sobs at the open grave. May I never witness a sadder!"

During these courtship years, Tom is sick more than once—with flu, a slashed foot, nervous prostration, boils, even bilious attacks that are life-threatening. Laura is openly sympathetic then. She lets down her guard. When no one is sick or dying, though, Laura can be intimidating and peremptory.

Once late in their courtship, Tom spends several sleepless nights in a tobacco barn, to cure his crop and save a little money in a "distressingly low" market. He and Laura have been discussing whether to live near her family in Sumter or his family in Darlington, and whether they can even afford to marry. Tom is tired and low-spirited, in what he calls "a semi-unconscious stupor," and he pleads with Laura to soothe his "bleeding heart":

> In fact I am so much absorbed in my cares for you and what you care for me till I guess I care very little for anyone or anything around me. "Lost"! Have I any conception of the sensation? Indeed, my dear Laura, I am "lost," if not "ruined." (10/17/1896)

In his letter the very next day (10/18/1896), Tom mentions that "it is now 10 o'clock at night, & I am smoking my second cigar." He continues, "Can you imagine your boy's trouble? And can you sympathize with him?"

Oh, dear. Laura has no patience with Tom's lack of "manliness":

> Oh! Tom! Is it *true*? Can it be *possible*?
>
> You can never know the pain, verging on disgust, your [letter] carried to my heart! Yes, Sweetheart, I do know your "trouble"! Are you, indeed, bereft of *manhood* to stem the tide of trial and disappointment?
>
> And sympathize? No! Thank Heaven, I have never yet been so weak that I could "sympathize" with those who cringe and whine at Misfortune's lash. But I do *pity* you, from the depths of my soul. Our estate is indeed pitiable (if not worse) when the fumes of a noxious weed are more potent to sooth, encourage, and sustain, than the pledged and plighted word of a *true* woman! A fitting lesson!
>
> My disappointment is great—my humiliation complete. Long may its potent influence assuage thy burdened soul. (10/25/1896)

As we might say today, that's harsh. She fears that Tom's weakness for tobacco puts his manly honor and her feminine virtue ("a true woman") at risk! But no! Theirs must be the story of an honorable, courageous man and a peerless, true woman, or there will be no story at all.

Tom must have been seriously pained by her words. He writes back simply,

> Can it be that *you* refuse me sympathy, when I apply to you for it? . . . Can it be true that the only one who *can* comfort refuses? And not only refuses but thrusts the *cruel* dagger of sarcasm deep into the *already bleeding and aching heart?* Surely it must have been someone else, and *not my Laura* that wrote those words! (10/28/1896)

There's another story of Tom and Laura, during their marriage, that reveals Tom's temper at work. Laura had barely recovered from tuberculosis, as the story goes, and Tom was driving her to town in the buggy, to visit the doctor.

Another man's carriage was parked in the middle of the street. Tom had to ease his buggy around the right-hand edge of the carriage, slanting it onto the sidewalk and crowding the storefronts. He and Laura continued to the doctor's office and at last returned by the same route. The man's carriage was still there, in the same spot, blocking the road. The man himself stood beside it, chatting idly with a friend.

Tom stopped the buggy. He climbed down, walked up to the man, grabbed him by the shirtfront, and flung him through a nearby plate-glass window with one wordless motion. The man was not hurt, as it turned out. Yet Tom must have deemed him a clear and present danger to Laura's well-being.

Chapter Six:
"Y'all Be Good, Now!"
Slavery, Jim Crow, and the Baby

In Edward Jones's rich novel *The Known World,* a black couple in the antebellum South, Augustus and Mildred, buy their freedom and later manage to buy the freedom of their son, Henry. As an adult, Henry aspires to own a plantation and tells Augustus he has bought his first "man."

> Augustus stood up so quickly his chair tilted back and he reached around to catch it without taking his eyes from Henry. "You mean to tell me you bought a man and he yours now? You done bought a man and you didn't free that man? You *own* a man, Henry?"
>
> "Yes. Well, yes, Papa." Henry looked from his father to his mother.
>
> "Don't you know the wrong of that, Henry?" Augustus said.
>
> "Nobody ever told me the wrong of that."
>
> "Why should anybody haveta teach you the wrong, son?" Augustus said. "Ain't you got eyes to see it without me telling you?" (p. 137)

Augustus is saying that by nature, a person recoils from the very idea of owning another person. Chattel slavery is wrong, and that truth should be self-evident.

The Declaration of Independence stands on self-evident truths, among them the inalienable right to liberty. Yet in 1776, half a million slaves lived in the colonies. Neither slaves nor slavery were directly mentioned in the

Constitution in 1787, although that document held a promise not to prohibit the slave trade until 1808. That promise was worded in euphemisms.[3]

What's the story here? Were the authors loathe to write the word "slavery" into our founding documents because they knew it was a self-evident evil, and it violated the core principles of our new nation? Why did our founders not confront this contradiction and resolve it? Their avoidance, many say, led ultimately to The War in 1861.

Joseph Ellis, in *Founding Brothers*, tells the story of Congress's failure in 1790 to eradicate slavery in a free society. This story reveals important paradoxes. In homage to Ellis, here is a précis of his chapter "The Silence," explaining the Congressional debate in 1790. At issue was whether Congress then had the power, or the will, to abolish the slave trade and free all the slaves in the states. (81-119).

Quaker Delegations. We call on the House to end the slave trade right now, and restore liberty to all Negroes. Benjamin Franklin has signed our petitions, which uphold the values of the American Revolution.

James Jackson of Georgia: Slavery is God's will. Besides, our citizens' livelihood depends on slave labor.

William Loughton Smith of South Carolina: Southern states would not have joined the union, or ratified the Constitution, without assurance that northern states wouldn't interfere with their property rights to hold slaves.

Abraham Baldwin of Georgia: Remember the pain inside that closed-door Constitutional Convention in 1787? If Congress tries to re-negotiate the slavery issue now, our nation could disintegrate.

John Laurance of New York: We thought slavery was becoming extinct. Under our Declaration of Independence, one man cannot own another.

Elbridge Gerry of Massachusetts: You Southerners have been betrayed into the slave trade by the first settlers. We can rescue you from that fate. We can compensate you with money to replace your slaves.

John Page of Virginia: If we don't consider improving the lot of the slaves. there will be slave insurrections.

Jackson of Georgia: Don't you remember the Sectional Compromise at the 1787 Constitutional Convention? The South conceded the federal regulation of commerce so they could keep the slave trade until 1808. Slavery has been grafted onto the character of the Southern states, as a habit

---

[3] The euphemism for the slave trade was "The Migration or Importation of such Persons as any of the States now existing shall think proper to admit."

established long before the Constitution. If it's a crime, the British did it. It's a self-evident reality now, and a necessary evil. If the slaves are freed, how can black and white possibly live together? If you know where to put freed slaves, tell me.

Smith of South Carolina: Any attempt to re-work the Sectional Compromise, which recognized slavery, would dissolve the union. If slaves are freed and intermarry with whites, the white race will become extinct.

Petitions were referred to committee, whose March report included words by Jackson and Smith giving "virtually every argument that southern defenders of slavery would mount during the next seventy years . . . right up to the eve of the War (97)."

Benjamin Franklin published a parody of Jackson's speech, under the name "Historicus," as a fictional African argument to enslave Christians. It used Jackson's same reasoning. Afterwards, northern representatives in Congress criticized Southern positions and questioned the very existence of a Sectional Compromise. James Madison later called proslavery arguments "shamefully indecent."

Nevertheless, debate was finally silenced. With Madison's help, the report of the committee was edited. It was resolved that Congress had no authority to interfere in the emancipation or treatment of slaves. The 1790 resolution passed by 29 to 25.

It was a crucial debate about which precious Baby should be saved: the Baby Liberty or the Baby Union. The Baby Union was chosen.

This is how the 1790 Congress left the new nation struggling between incompatible Baby ideals—until finally, after seven decades, The War broke out in 1861. The original Baby Union lost six hundred thousand of its citizens to violence or disease in the nation's bloodiest war. All of the combatants, whether they fought for the Union or the Confederacy, may have believed that they were genuinely fighting to Save the Baby Liberty—everyone in their own sense of the word.

During the conflicted seventy-year extension of legal slavery in our new nation, many people, both black and white, lamented the ruling that slavery would continue. From the beginnings of slavery in America, many had believed that slavery was wrong. Almost a century earlier, in 1772, John Newton had written "Amazing Grace" after his ship, on a slave-trading journey, barely survived a deadly storm at sea. In The War, slavery played out as a moral catastrophe for this country.

It is Martin Luther King Day in 2009. I am reading an editorial by Henry Louis Gates, Jr. and John Stauffer about Abraham Lincoln, who once made an interesting effort to prevent The War. Lincoln, according to the writers, "harbored fixed and unfortunate ideas about race." They explain Lincoln's doubts about whether blacks could ever be equal to whites, especially in intelligence. In 1862, they relate, Lincoln "invited five black men to the white house to convince them to become the founders of a new nation in Panama consisting of those slaves he was about to free." He supported black emigration to Liberia or Haiti. As President he very much respected Frederick Douglas. Still, this pre-white-house Lincoln, say the authors, was a "recovering racist." This classification is entirely understandable.

Lincoln's idea gives us one example—though impractical and possibly racist—of someone trying to solve a potentially combative situation by simply placing the combatants far apart. But his suggestion does sidestep what the combat was *about*, because in one sense it was clearly about the nuts and bolts of earning a living. Ever since the late 18th century, when the slave trade had started to grow in the United States, those people who bought slaves in the South were much better able to make a living in the market—in cotton, tobacco, corn, vegetables, fruits, or other products that could be farmed. Those who refused to buy slaves, or could not afford them, would be less able to make a living—unless perhaps they had many children and relatives who could help with the labor. And supposing you were born into a family who owned slaves and depended on them to earn a living—then what could you do if you believed that slavery was morally wrong? Leave home?

My ancestors, like most Southerners, tried to adapt their minds to the prevailing culture of slavery. Many Kirvens were born into families who owned slaves, as were Frasers. We remember that the character Augustus in *The Known World* believed that everyone should renounce all owner-slave arrangements at once. But for a child born, say, between 1800 and 1861, when could this "at once" happen? During the 17th and 18th centuries, slavery was a plain reality in the nation and in the South, and the nation still struggles to acknowledge the continuing effects of slavery.

Responses to our history of slavery have been and still are intense, throughout the country. People idealized, raged, denied, rationalized, and despaired about the situation as it was happening. Some people tried to make the reality of slavery *better* in some way, or *less inhumane*. Martin Luther King had a Dream that we could all be born into a new day. Even while slavery was taking place in the South, there were efforts to create owner-slave relationships that would allow the people involved to feel, at least in some ways, Good at Heart.

The history of importing Africans to this country was no help in this effort. The journey from Africa on slave ships had savaged the humanity of those who would become slaves. The middle passage killed multitudes, and the survivors arrived weak, sick, terrified, deaf to the language, and bewildered by the customs and the religion of a strange world. They were treated barbarously by being put on the block and sold—not just their labor, but their whole selves sold. They became agricultural commodities in a prospective list of equipment: a horse, a mule, a plow, a cow that could calve, and a black woman who could become pregnant with more slaves.

The presence of a large and dehumanized black population was an everyday reality in South Carolina, where by 1860 almost 60% of the people were black, more in the coastal areas. We have slowly learned—and probably we should have always known—how soul-crushing slavery and its aftermath have been to blacks, and we continue to learn the harmful effects, even generations later. We have been more reluctant to imagine what the chattel slavery of blacks did to the minds and hearts of whites. What effects have come from living among dehumanized Africans, owning and using them, pitying and fearing them, theorizing about them and trying to put these theories into practice?

Jefferson thought that the institution of slavery would "corrupt" white people, making them cruel and tyrannical over their fellow man. President Jimmy Carter referred to the historical treatment of blacks by whites as our country's "abominable circumstances," when he said that "racism" prevented whites in general from believing that Barack Obama, as a black man, was qualified to be President. Can people ever outlive the effects of chattel slavery?

It is the summer of 2004. My husband Richard and I are driving along South Carolina state highway 52/401 north of Darlington, looking for the road that will take us to William Wilson (Bubba) Kirven II. Bubba Kirven is my second cousin, for his grandfather is Joshua Pollard, brother of my grandfather Thomas J. Kirven.

"Take the first left past the railroad track," we've been told.

Darlington, which we are seeing for the first time, appears to be a city of railroad tracks. Every half-mile we bump across steel rails and ballast.

We take a left. Futility. We return to 52/401 and try again.

Darlington is a sleepy, well-groomed city in July. We've heard of the Darlington Raceway, but there is no party in this city now. Few people are around. We see a drugstore, the Darlington Library, tall pines, flat stretches, storage units, cotton, soybeans, and soybeans. We see no trains, just tracks.

I call Bubba Kirven's phone. His wife Betty answers.

"Hey, we're headed north on 52 . . ." I call out.

"Have you passed the Nucor plant yet?"

Finally, we are seated in the comfortable living room of Bubba and Betty Kirven. Another second cousin has driven from Kingstree to join us: James N. Kirven, the grandson of my Grandfather Tom's brother, Jim.

Hello, hello. I've never met any of these people. We are all grandchildren of the Great Uncles, the strongman farmers, but I don't have each single one of those relationships in my head yet. I want to learn what my Kirven relatives—the ones who lived during slavery and owned slaves—knew about the morality and the politics of those times. What were their lives like during slavery, The War, and Reconstruction?

My second cousins are extremely polite to me. I'm family. So I simply ask, "What was it like to own slaves back before The War? Have your relatives told you about those days?"

One of them answers, "Wellsir, I believe it was hard, like everything else. Hard work." This surprises me a bit. Not that I expected them to describe resting in the shade with mint juleps, but . . . I suppose that owning slaves would probably take planning and organizing and supervising and traversing the fields in the hot sun most of the day. I wouldn't like to do that.

I ask whether the crops were destroyed by The War, making the people poor? They reply that Sherman left Darlington alone, because when he stormed by, it was a ways north of here.

I ask, what about our grandfathers and all the others in the family? Did they combine their land and have a plantation?

No, they didn't get on so well. There were disputes about property. Oh yes, that's what I've heard.

James N. Kirven asks me, "Have you heard of the Reverend John Leighton Wilson?"

I admit I have not.

"You haven't? Let me show you. He's famous. We've got one of his books. See this one here?" James Kirven has the book ready. His smile is wide and proud. His face is lit up like a kid's at Sunday school.

"We claim him as family," my second cousin James continues, "because there were so many marriages between Wilsons and Kirvens in the 1800s." When he tells me this, I happen to have already seen the Christmas Day 1911 photo that is placed at the beginning of this book, with a dozen or so Wilsons and maybe twice as many Kirvens.

My second cousin continues, "We've got one of his books. See this one here? He was a good man, a smart man, the first Christian missionary to Africa. He wrote several books and won awards. He's like a brother-in-law or a cousin-in-law of the Kirven family. You could look up exactly what relation."

Later I find that John Leighton Wilson is related to Eckard Lee's mother, Florida Wilson Kirven, who I suppose is my first-cousin-once-removed-in-law, and then . . . ah, those family tree mazes!

"Missionary to Africa," the group echoes. "Before anyone else. He was the first."

John Leighton Wilson is my relatives' favorite topic. They revere his memory. He was a Presbyterian minister who spent eighteen years on missions to Africa, especially among the Mpongwe people of Cape Palmas. He wrote against resuming the British slave-trade, and his words helped bring illegal slave traffic to an end. One is his pamphlets is called *The foreign slave trade: Can it be revived without violating the most sacred principles of honor, humanity, and religion?* His answer was a resounding No.

The Reverend John Leighton Wilson, 1809-1886

The slave trade had been officially abolished in 1808, but some Southerners were arguing that it should be revived. In 1859, Wilson crafts a prophetic story with a plot and characters designed to prevent that revival:

> There has been no little discussion in the South, for some time past, about reopening the African slave trade; and, if we may judge from the earnestness and vehemence with which it is pressed upon public attention by its advocates, we may expect still more serious agitation of the subject. There is every reason to believe that the great majority of the more intelligent classes are very decidedly opposed to it, and no doubt this will continue to be the case . . . We have too high an estimate of the good sense, the Christian moderation, and the honorable bearing of the Southern people, to believe that they ever will, from either motives of retaliation or the hope of gain, lend their countenance knowingly to the revival of a traffic which, in its progress, must necessarily trample in the dust every sentiment of honor, humanity, and religion.

He describes white people as honorable, Christian, sensible Southerners who never would revive the slave trade through "hope of gain." By complimenting their characters, he is telling them that they are Good at Heart, and he is evoking the Baby of their Good Name.

Eckard Lee's sister, Anna Louise Kirven Booker, proudly showed us a commemorative plate awarded to John Leighton Wilson for his achievements.

Wilson's prophetic story in 1859 may have helped somewhat to change the plot of history, for the slave trade was not revived. Then The War broke out just two years later. Might Wilson's arguments have averted The War? Not likely. In the debates of that time, Wilson occupied a no-man's land. Some Southerners called him an abolitionist because he and his wife freed their thirty slaves before they went to Africa, while Northerners called him a slaveholder because he could not persuade two of his slaves to take their freedom.[4]

John Leighton Wilson freed his slaves, while at the same time arguing that Southerners are too Good at Heart to repeat the evils of the slave trade. The question left unanswered was how to incorporate blacks into the hopefully Good-at-Heart nation, now that blacks had originally arrived as slaves—and they were not going to emigrate to Liberia or Haiti, as Lincoln had suggested.

In daily life, it was individual Americans—and especially Southerners—who were the ones positioned to respond to the new black population, most of them slaves. Then as now, perceptions of white people about black people, and black people about white people, continue to evolve. Even today, we have vastly different responses to the slogan *Black Lives Matter*. This simple phrase, welcomed as common sense to some, has become to others an incitement to debate—even a sort of war cry. Sometimes we worry about our national character, while at other times we can hope for amazing victories over people's most troubling tendencies.

Among both Kirvens (my grandfather's family) and Frasers (my grandmother's family), I have found relationships between whites and blacks that variously suggest love, care, respect, trust, even carefree companionship, and often a determination to be honorable. Of course, virtues like these might be mixed with racist feelings and thoughts.

In the South, land of former slave masters, there are varying opinions about the ethics of slavery. My late second cousin James N. Kirven, a gentle

---

[4] *The Daily Item* of Sumter, August 13, 1970. Besides, Southerners said the Civil war was about the right of states to secede from the Union.

man with a kind smile, explained his thoughts about owning slaves. His branch of the Kirvens raised horses, and they were known for treating those horses very well indeed.

On a trip South in 2005, my husband Richard and I were invited to supper at the house of James Kirven and his wife Harriet, in Kingstree, South Carolina. Before us lay dishes filled with squash casserole, butterbeans, biscuits, ham, okra, and sweet tea. I ventured a question that seemed to me somewhat risky: "Jim, do you think that our relatives in the 1800s felt conflicted about owning slaves? Was it a hard period to live through?"

Jim's answer was slow and peaceful. He seemed untroubled by the question. He held a calm view of blacks as fellow members of the animal kingdom, like horses or perhaps even like white people. Cruelty was lamentable. His words suggested a vast human-and-animal tapestry.

He answered, "I imagine it was just like anything else. You have all kinds of owners. I know some men who treat their horses badly, while others treat their horses kindly. Slavery was pretty much like that, I imagine." He may have been suggesting that a good slave owner should know by heart the responses of his slaves, in order to empathize with their needs, and that kindness can be instinctual. I chose not to argue the comparison of human beings to animals, not only because I don't like to pick fights but also because I enjoyed the emphasis on *caring*.

My uncle Tom Kirven and his family at The Farm had a black maid whom they named "Sing" because she always sang in the kitchen while she cooked. Sing would often stay with her white employer overnight, to be safe from her abusive husband who lived out back. Family stories describe my uncle bearing down upon Sing's angry and drunk husband at the kitchen steps.

Several summers ago, we were at my cousin Larry's house, eating butterbeans, biscuits, corn on the cob, and fried chicken, and we were hard on our way to the peach cobbler. My cousin Julie had recovered enough from Guillain-Barré to drive down from Fayetteville and join us. She and I sat side by side.

Julie is a strong woman, and generous. When she looks at you, then you know you've been looked at. The subject of Sing came up. Julie fixed her eye on me, the cousin who had traveled to her home from the North.

"We loved *her*," Julie began.

I nodded in assent.

"And *she* loved *us*," Julie finished. There was no more to say.

Analyses of Southern paternalism aside, how can anyone measure the quality of another person's relationship? In that area, I accept what people tell me.

Great-Uncle Hugh lived in Dovesville near his father, Erasmus. His daughter Lucia Kirven was especially close to the cook, Big Mary, who lived down a dirt road at the bottom of the hill. In 1918, Lucia got married, moved north, and did not return for a visit until 1964.

Lucia and Big Mary had their own special reunion. Lucia's son Dave, who saw them meet again, told me that they knew each other as if no years had passed. They were both weeping.

"Big Mary" and Lucia in 1964, at Great-Uncle Hugh's place in Darlington, South Carolina

Great-Uncle Luke was the seventh of Erasmus's nine sons, born in 1872. He's the one who resembles a hefty fox with a widow's peak, sitting front row right in the 1911 photograph. Luke lived by himself at Homestead, a distance from his brothers' places, and he ignored social constraints whenever he chose. He didn't believe in marriage. He had children with black women and white women. Some relatives believe that Luke married a white woman later in life, but those records are lost.

One time, Eckard Lee told me, Papa [Bob Kirven] went over to Luke's house. He had heard Luke was sick, and he thought he should pay him a visit. In the front yard were some children, playing in the mud. Eckard Lee said, "They had got themselves so muddied up, Papa couldn't tell *what* color they were to start with."

So Bob Kirven went to the back of the house, opened a door, and there Luke was. He lay under the covers in his big old bed, sick as a dog. All around him, babies were jumping up and down, little black babies and little white babies.

"Come on in!" says Luke to Bob. "Come on in!"

All those babies were crawling over his sickbed, and Luke didn't mind a bit. The babies were happy—or so said Eckard Lee, with a large helping of glee.

This story of happy and perhaps uncomplicated love reminds me of the "hippie" culture of the sixties . . . minus the music. The scene also reminds me of "*Hop on Pop,*" by Dr. Seuss. A Kirven cousin once murmured to me, half in jest, "Don't look too deep. You might find some black babies."

Here's one thing I do know, though. Of all the Kirven tombstones in the Darlington Cemetry near the old Black Creek Church, the most elaborate one is Luke's. Somebody or bodies loved Luke enough to pay him this great big tribute. I'll probably never learn who that somebody was.[5]

Tombstone of Luther Kade Kirven, July 26, 1872–March 12. 1936

Our family also has stories that combine respect and genuine love with a motive that seems to me like Southern "propriety"—a word that I was taught to believe signifies what *isn't done* as opposed to what *is done* in civilized or polite society. For example, in days far past this kind of comment could be heard: "Oh my dear, dating without a chaperone just *isn't done!*"

My aunt Ansie Williams, after she settled down to live with her family in Fairmont, North Carolina, supported the family by transforming her own living room into a store for stylish women's clothes. She called that store The Town and Country Shop. Whenever women heard of its reputation, they came to Fairmont from near and far to purchase their best clothes there.

---

[5] *Luke's tombstone was probably set up years after his death. His body is buried down the road and across the bridge, in the deeper woods of the Old Black Creek cemetery. Or so they tell me.*

In the 1950s I am visiting my favorite aunt Ansie and my favorite cousin Diane in Fairmont, North Carolina. Ansie's black maid Josephine, her cook, is tall, upright, and deep black, and she wears an imposing bandana. A smile from Josephine is a rare gift. I can never tell what Josephine is thinking, or whether she approves of what I am saying at the moment. My diffuse fear is that Josephine will think I am selfish, deceitful, and stupid. Josephine has a "lazy eye" that veers off at an angle, and I never know which eye is seeing me. I suspect—I am almost sure, most of the time—that Josephine disapproves of me deeply.

"Josephine," I quake, hoping that my smile is friendly instead of timid, "Ansie would like to know how many potatoes you plan to peel."

Diane has often explained to me her mother's lasting esteem for Josephine. Ansie admired Josephine's intelligence, her fierce independence, and her confidence in her own self-worth. Josephine was a proud woman. You didn't have to tell Josephine what to do, said Ansie. Josephine *knew* what to do.

For supper, we form the same dining group as usual: Ansie, Donnie, Perry, Diane, and me. One other person is *almost* with us—Josephine, in the next room, eating her supper on the kitchen counter while sitting on the kitchen stool.

"Thank you, Josephine. It was delicious."

That is what we would have said. Anything more, either syrupy or fawning, would have been patronizing to Josephine. She took no guff from anyone. She didn't even accept teasing. People treated Josephine with respect.

When we finished supper, some of us washed and dried the dishes while others of us piled into the Chevy and took Josephine back to her house in a different district of Fairmont.

Josephine did not sit down to eat with us. It just wasn't done. Diane would eat with Josephine in the kitchen from time to time, but when company came, Josephine ate in the kitchen alone. I'm sure that Foucault's watchtower Panopticon—with its omniscient empty room to supervise society's *mores* like an all-seeing prison guard—would have approved of our separation of the races in southern North Carolina.[6]

So race relationships were entangled in our peaceful suppers. I yearned for us to be Good at Heart, nevertheless. How could both be true? As a

---

[6] *Tim Tyson, in* Blood Done Sign My Name, *gives an excellent account of the dangerous social climate on racial issues in these days, especially in eastern North Carolina.*

chronically worried child and teenager, I wondered how to undo what we were doing to Josephine by exiling her to the kitchen stool. I came up empty.

Ansie would frequently proclaim to us her conviction about Josephine: "In another era, *I* would be working for *her.*"

People of all classes can be hyper-aware of race and class stereotypes. They will try their best to avoid stereotypes that would tarnish their view of themselves as Good at Heart—stereotypes such as a Wicked Stepmother or a Simon Legree, the evil slave-beater from Harriet Beecher Stowe's novel, *Uncle Tom's Cabin.* The Legree figure still appears in films about slavery even today, under various other names.

The family of my grandmother, Laura Fraser, tried diligently to be kind to their slaves. Her grandparents, Ladson Lawrence Fraser Sr. and Hannah Atkinson Boone, supervised a plantation near Sumter that they called Booneland, which became known as a good and fair place, even though—and perhaps because—it was a place for slaves to live.[7]

Whites in the South discussed this aspiration towards kindness to slaves among themselves, wanting to make *even slavery* into a situation where people could be Good at Heart. Here is an exchange of letters between two Frasers in my ancestors' family. It illustrates for me how seriously insulted a person can feel if his honorability as a slave owner is questioned:

On September 21, 1861, Thomas Fraser writes this letter from Germantown to his brother Ladson Lawrence in Sumter:

> Give my love to Father & Mother & all at home also to Sister Ada and the children. I have forgotten to say to you to tell Father it is my habit, when cotton opens . . . early in the season to require over 100 as the task—but I always allow the Negroes pay for all over 100. It is easier to get 150 lb. in September than 100 in October.

Thomas is sending information to Father, Ladson Lawrence Sr., about how he himself deals with "the Negroes" during the cotton season. Thomas may be boasting a little about his generous incentive system, or he may be giving

---

[7] These Frasers, my great-grandparents, preserved in a private journal (saved by my Aunt, Ansie Kirven Williams) the names, birth dates, and mothers of more than 150 slaves over three generations. This journal, paired with U. S. Census records from 1870 and afterward, may be useful to African-American genealogists. See my article in the National Genealogical Society Quarterly, Vol. 106 No. 2, June 2018, pp. 123-139.

advice. In any case, Ladson Lawrence Sr. apparently felt insulted. In his next letter on October 29th, Thomas is vigorously apologizing to Father:

> All I can say in reference to Father's having his feelings hurt about anything I said is this—I am not conscious of having said anything to Bro William or to you in my letter which could have given offence and I am sure I never intended anything of the sort. I have fully appreciated his kindness in having an eye to my plantation affairs. All I could have done, for I do not more remember what I did say, was to state my mode of dealing and give a word of caution, so as to enable him to carry out his purpose of doing me a kindness. I have too much, of the hard side of human nature to deal with here to be unkind to those whom I have left behind and for whom I have risked my all here.

What was the perceived offense? Perhaps Ladson Lawrence was outraged that Thomas wanted him to push slaves to pick more than 100 pounds of cotton a day, period. Or maybe he thought Thomas was accusing him of harshness, by thinking Father needed instruction to pay slaves for more cotton.

Whites cherished their reputation as benevolent slave masters. Ladson Lawrence Sr. may have imagined his benevolence challenged. In turn, Thomas may have felt his own filial loyalty questioned. Father may have taken offense at being thought unkind, and reciprocally Thomas is pleading, "Don't think me unkind!" What self-respecting Southerner, needing to be validated as Good at Heart, would *not* stiffen at being called disloyal to family or cruel to slaves?

Kindness as a virtue is still the coin of the realm in the South. Intense graciousness reigns. Under such "abominable circumstances" as slavery and Jim Crow, a white person's goodness always had to be proven. Southerners I have known can be competitive for Best at Heart—most charitable, most polite, speediest at lunging for the restaurant check. I'm reminded of potlatch, a fierce contest of giving. My husband Richard call this "After you . . . No, no, after *you*" behavior *the South Carolina standoff.*

In the South, land of former slave masters, there are different opinions about the ethics of slavery.

My grandmother Laura Fraser's great-great-grandfather, John Baxter Fraser, kept a journal on the daily operations of his farm near Sumter, which he supervised with slaves in the early 1800s. In this journal, published by the

South Carolina Historical Society as *Cotton Culture*, the story is a mixed account of both harmony and conflict. The relationship between Fraser and his slaves is described as "unusually close."

The editors of this journal continue, "He began with one or two slaves, and the number grew to fifty-six before 1820 . . . The planter, therefore, rarely punished a slave, although he was a man of violent temper . . . arising, perhaps, from his chronic unhealthiness with stomach ulcers."

John Fraser had a difficult life in a small log cabin on a cotton farm. He often quarreled with his white neighbors over debts. Once he beat up a white schoolteacher, Nathan Hanks, who overcharged him for his children's tuition. After suing Fraser for assault and battery, Hanks was awarded $200 by the court. Fraser also drank, running up bills at the Cross Roads tavern, where the Darlington-Sumter road intersected with the Waxhaws-Charleston Road. "Like virtually all Southern males of the period, Fraser ingested alcohol in immoderate quantities."

Even with a violent temper, illness, drink, and a hard life, Fraser in his 600-page journal records punishing slaves only once, with five lashes, for not meeting their task. Fraser and his older sons would often pick cotton with the slaves, for he had neither an overseer or a black slave driver. Maybe interracial kindness with him was simply about getting in the crops and not starving. "Judging from the relative absence of complaints about his slaves. . . . Fraser enjoyed exceptional cooperation." For three generations his slaves descended from the same family, and "the relationship between whites and blacks on the Fraser plantation was unusually close." In his will, Fraser kept his slave families together. Several times when local custom might have punished a slave, Fraser did not. When the slave Ben "broke" (drank) a bottle of wine as he carried several bottles home, Fraser only lamented his bad luck. When Milly and several other slaves overstayed their passes to a neighboring farm, Fraser did not punish them. To Fraser, a slave who ran away had "eloped." When the slave Toney disappeared with a supply of sweet potatoes, to be found months later in a Chesterfield County jail, Fraser merely returned Toney to work. Toney stayed with him for life. In 1805 Fraser emancipated an older male slave, Carolina, for his services (Moore and Moore. 41-59).

It is true that kindess by white people—whether during slavery or later during Jim Crow—might not reliably *feel, when received,* like real kindness to the black people to whom it is directed. What blacks often felt and still may feel, as I understand it, is condescension. To Southern white people who might be seriously trying to be good—perhaps silently competing for person

Best-at-Heart to black people—this hint of condescension can be a slippery trap.

I'm washing dishes. Mama rinses and dries.

Through the kitchen window, we can see our tiny magnolia in the yard. Daddy's pet tree. We are in Winston-Salem in the 1950s, before dishwashers.

"Some men are true gentlemen. Like your father."

"Uh-huh," I respond.

"I've met only a few others with such rock-solid principles. One was my English teacher at Coker College. James McBride Dabbs."

"Uh-huh?" I cooperate. I'm impatient to finish these dishes.

"Now there was a man. Just as good, just as ethical as he could *be*. Smart! But he cared about people, you could tell. An unselfish man."

"Yes, ma'am." Are these virtues leading to a critique of my flaws?

Mama stops. She dreams out the window, holding a wet plate in the dishtowel. Her eye is fixed upon some pure place, far from here. I take a breath.

"James McBride Dabbs. He suffered so much, with his wife dying, poor man. But he picked himself up and got back to work. Fine man, fine writer."

"Yes, ma'am." I take the point. Pick myself up.

"He was kind to me. He thought I had talent." Mama is coming back to the present now, wiping the knives and forks in a hurry.

"Uh-huh?"

"You missed some egg on this plate. Try it again."

James McBride Dabbs was familiar with the timeworn Southern effort to be extra-special-good to blacks. In his 1958 book *The Southern Heritage,* he pinpoints white attitudes toward blacks under Jim Crow: "we love them to death (242)."

Dabbs makes a heartfelt case that the South should put aside their fears and embrace integration, social justice, and love. He critiques Southern "virtue" as paternalism. All those efforts to demonstrate white goodness to blacks have harmed blacks further, by condescending to them, belittling them, keeping them down. Dabbs believes that in white minds, "the Negro was to remain, in relation to the white, a perpetual child (240)." Children do not have liberty.

The evils of slavery and its aftermath surely exacerbated white people's need to be Good at Heart. Dabbs is attempting to remove a veil from the Southern white mind. "We know we have done wrong," he says, referring to whites' super-kind treatment of blacks that is sustained by seeing blacks as inferior children.

In what sense do we "know," however? When you're urgently trying to pull your own Good-at-Heart baby from the flames, it's easy to fool yourself about your own kindness. Look how men have treated women so *very* kindly and *very* courtly in the course of civilization, while often perceiving them as childlike inferiors. Not many people set out to be villains.

> None do offend, none—I say none!
> *King Lear IV.iv.2773*

Dabbs hands a tough epiphany to Southern whites and to anyone whose seeming kindness may keep others down and beholden. "We converted the African Negro into the image of our own desire, a slave" and a biddable child (192). Dabbs paints injustice with a kind white face. How can this be true, when all the time white people thought they were Being Good to Blacks? But it can.

William Blake wrote in the late 1700s and early 1800s, when my ancestors first owned slaves. Here is one of his indictments against helpers of the poor:

> Pity could be no more
> If we did not make somebody poor
> And Mercy no more could be
> If all were as happy as we.
> William Blake, *Songs of Experience*

This is Blake's disturbing poetic charge of cause and effect: Society routinely sets up structures that will oppress poor people *so that* oppressors can feel good about being kind to the oppressed. Dabbs labels this chilling phenomenon the "paradoxical goodness within slavery (145)."

During my trips to the South, I once met a relative who felt he was doing a kindness to black children by keeping them out of white private schools. He believed that "once the black children learned their work was so much worse than the white children's work, they would be crushed." He was sparing them that disappointment. He sounded sincere—and yet.

Recently, I was told by relatives that my grandmother Laura Fraser believed that blacks were not fully human because they did not possess souls. This information helps me better understand one of the stories that my mother, Maisie Kirven, wrote in college in the early 1930s. The story begins this way:

> Shadrach was a melancholy nigger. I do not mean merely that he was morose and sober, for he was neither. Superstitious and amoral, he typified his race; but there was something not Negro, but Man.

Gathered near the back steps of the farmhouse, the "hands" and the child narrator become spellbound as Shadrach dances to his song, "I'm gwine to heb'n flyin', Lawd." His ritual ends in a sinuous pose, with one arm curled upward and the other trailing by his side.

Shadrach wears an amulet around his neck, a "huge, bony, white-hawk's claw." He believes that it protects him from his longtime foe, old Wart-Eye the alligator, who lurks in Scapo Swamp. When he loses that amulet, Shadrach knows he is doomed to die. His prescience is attributed to that "slight Anglo-Saxon taint" in his blood, for Shadrach is a mulatto.

The child narrator searches frantically for the amulet, but in vain. Shadrach is not afraid, though. He is heroically resigned. He goes about his usual activities until one day he is assigned to go along on a fishing trip to Scapo Swamp.

Later, a farmhand relates that Shadrach has died in a flaming boat propelled forward by his nemesis, old Wart-Eye, the alligator. His body is recovered, fixed in death, with one arm curled upward and the other trailing by his side—the very pose that accompanied his Christian song. His death is both primitive superstition and Christian prophecy. Like the original Shadrach in the fiery furnace, he keeps his faith during mortal peril, although no angels appear to rescue him.

In a blend of kindness and racist belief, Maisie takes pains to give the main character a soul, and then she allows him to save that soul—through his courage, his religious belief, and his bit of Anglo-Saxon blood. Shadrach feels victorious as he is dying: "I'm gwine to heb'n flyin', Lawd."

This story blends the racist certainty of the author with her sincere effort to be kind, to make an exception in the name of humanity. For this purpose, the author uses the "slight Anglo-Saxon taint" in the main character's blood—a phenomenon that might be notable to white nationalists today. The tension of this story—the possible clashing against the impossible—helps me understand how agitated my mother was at any hint of racial conflict.

When I was three years old, we moved from Fairmont to Winston-Salem, North Carolina. Mama wanted an ideal black maid, like the one Ansie had. Mama found Bertha. I was afraid of Bertha. She had brownish-black skin and a square, stolid face. Her face was not sweet and her eyes were not twinkly. Her expression mixed sad and mad in a way I couldn't decipher. She never said much to me, and I never dared to say much to her. Was she a helpless innocent or a hidden danger? She never smiled, laughed, or hurried. She took snuff. Whenever she sat down to shell butterbeans, she would first spit out the chew into a snuff cup. I tried not to let Bertha see my aversion. Her face may have reflected the longstanding contempt for blacks that hung over the whole country, North and South, like pesticide. In fact, she may have internalized that contempt, showing the world the same locked face of all the black women I noticed when I rode the regular Winston-Salem bus to grammar school.

Years later, I learned that my six-years-younger sister Cathy had a good old time with Bertha. They enjoyed making chocolate chip cookies together. Frequently! I was glad to hear about that, and I will always believe that my fear of Bertha was my own fault in some way. Maybe if I had been able to "loosen up," Bertha could have loosened up, too, and we could have been friends.

Mama did her very best. In 1948 when I was almost seven, Mama took me on a Christmas Eve visit to Bertha's house. We drove in the Ford to Shantytown, the place where I was told all Negroes lived.

I sat beside Mama in the car, with no car seats or seat belts. The sun had set, and through the car window I saw a row of houses plumb to the road's border. Mama parked right before one front door. Where was the yard? Where was the front walk?

"I'll come around and let you out," Mama told me. You walk straight into the house. Don't look right or left, you understand me?"

I took Mama's hand and stepped into the mud, for it had been raining. She knocked and pushed at the door without waiting for an answer, and we stepped into a small, square room. Bertha sat before a Christmas tree to receive us. Would she smile at me now? The room was sparsely decorated. On the left was a small brick fireplace with a cloth reindeer on the mantlepiece.

A little girl smaller than me peered out from behind Bertha.

"Oh, this must be the granddaughter I've heard about," Mama enthused.

"Betty Mae, say hello to Mrs. Sanders," Bertha prompted.

"Hello, Betty Mae." Mama bent down.

"Hello." Betty Mae was shy. She was a lighter brown than Bertha. More than ignorant, I wondered whether Betty Mae would darken as she got older.

"Say hello, say hello," the two adults bade us, and we waved to each other. Betty Mae had her hair done in tiny pigtails and pretty bows.

Vibrating loud from the radio was the new song, "Rudolph, the Red-Nosed Reindeer." Betty Mae beckoned for me to take the cloth reindeer down and then showed me its red nose. She told me the story.

Meanwhile, Mama was scrolling out compliments the way she always did, competing with the Rudolph song for the high notes in the room. She praised Betty Mae's dress and Bertha's fine stitching. She praised the radio, the rug, the little couch. The red-nosed cloth reindeer, the paint on the walls, the Christmas tree. As the sentences spooled out of her mouth, I could tell Mama was getting worried. The room began to feel unhappy. I thought we would stay until everyone was happier, because that was how visits worked.

"We have some cookies," said Bertha. "Would you like . . ."

Good. I prepared myself to take a seat, eat my cookie, and praise it.

But Mama had begun to panic. "Oh no, we can't stay. We must get back."

We couldn't stay? No cookie? Mama's hands were trembling. Had she run out of compliments? She thanked Bertha profusely, told me to shake Betty Mae's hand, and we bolted for the door.

I wondered whether Bertha lived among hidden dangers.

Some rush of terror within Mama had stopped our visit cold. Mama had spread around kindness aplenty, with great speed, and then we ran. We never returned to visit Bertha and Betty Mae. I wondered later whether Daddy might have warned Mama that driving to Shantytown at night, as a white mother and daughter alone, was madness?

The twelve-foot trip from Bertha's parlor back into our little locked black Ford felt like a long, long stretch.

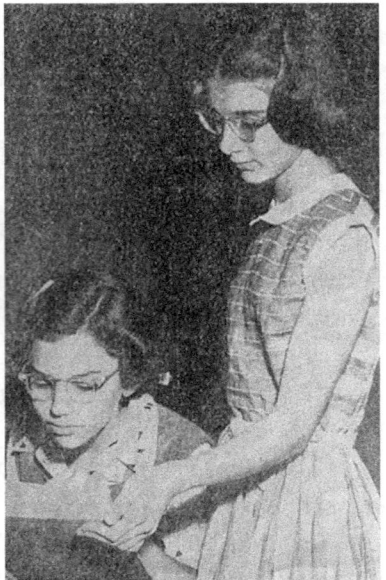

Freda Bluestone and Mariann Sanders at the Winston-Salem City Hall in 1955

Common knowledge says that children can make friends across races. Maybe that's what Mama was attempting with Betty Mae and me. My cousins in Eastover were playmates with Jook and Pansie Mae, the children of a black tenant farmer. Danny and Laura Ann and Pansie Mae had a rabies scare and went through the whole series of rabies shots together. My cousin Joe Chandler said that Jook was his best childhood friend.

Seven years after our Shantytown visit to Bertha, in 1955, I won the spelling bee for my school at the age of twelve, and I was sent to the Winston-Salem town hall for the brief finals.

Spelling felt good to me, as an unambiguous pastime in my ambiguous life. When I arrived at town hall for the finals, I met the competition, Freda Bluestone from Ardmore school, whom I liked at once. She seemed kind, she had a nifty name, and she looked different from my usual classmates—although in the photo, I see now, she and I resemble each other.

Freda won. She missed two words to my three. In this much earlier and much easier version of today's spelling bees, we missed words like "embarrass" and "bouillon."

After the contest, they shepherded Freda and me into another room. Two young black girls were there. It took me a minute to realize (how could I not have known?) that these must be the spelling-bee winners from the two black schools in our city. Winston-Salem had conducted two contests in two separate rooms—no doubt with the Good-at-Heart plan, as they probably thought, of saving the black girls from humiliation before the naturally superior-in-spelling white girls.

The photographer for the *Winston-Salem Journal and Sentinel* huddled the four finalists together for a news photo of the two black girls, Freda, and me.

Mama picked me up at City Hall. I explained the outcome and the newspaper picture. I thought she would be proud of me. She was horrified.

"They did *what?*" she shrilled. "Took a picture of *whom?*"

Mama spun around and drove back to the *Journal and Sentinel* office. She marched in and demanded that they divide the four-girl photo between the two black girls and the two whites. Furthermore, they should print each pair of girls on a separate page of the newspaper. I wondered if she was losing her grip.

I asked why.

Mama replied that I was too young to understand the machinations some people were capable of. "Outside forces" would be at work to take advantage of me, a white girl with a "perfectly shaped little oval face."

"What's going on with Mama?" I asked Daddy that night.

"It doesn't matter," he said. "It will be over soon. Don't worry her." Daddy was the type of person who just wanted to stay out of trouble. As did I.

Daddy knew a lot more than we did about the ghosts that haunted Mama, but he never broke her confidences.

As I reflect today, I suppose that Mama may have then believed that blacks were mainly docile, helpless pawns, foisted upon unsuspecting Southern whites by Yankees or Communists who were out to punish the South for The War or to ruin the country through miscegenation. These agitators would bring that long-feared black uprising. The Supreme Court ruling of *Brown v. Board* may have terrified Southerners with extravagant visions of such "Negro handlers."

Or perhaps Mama was afraid that Klan members would see the newspaper photo, find us, and burn our house down. It was true that Klan activity in North Carolina, always substantial, surged after *Brown v. Board* to fever pitch.

Or Mama may have imagined an even worse outcome—that her older brothers might ridicule her as naïve for walking into a political photo-op trap.

"Maisie, how *could* you be so idealistic?" the brothers in Mama's mind may have jeered. "Look at little Maisie, with her nose in a book and her head in the clouds." Mama's traumatic experiences with her brothers could not be healed by time. Being laughed at by her brothers once more would have seemed to her a fate worse than death—even though sometimes she praised them as the best brothers in all the world.

Five years later, Mama's worries about integration fed into my interview for admission to Duke University. By then I was wiser and more desperate.

The interview committee pitched me this one: "Do your parents have strong views about whether the black and white races should be separated?"

"My mother does," I replied, truthfully. "She believes in segregation."

"Do her opinions worry you?" they asked, eyeing me keenly.

I knew what they were fishing for. "Well," I answered. "I am a little worried. *About my mother.*"

They all laughed appreciatively, secure in their self-images as enlightened white people. This is how I was cynical and unfeeling enough to exploit my unknowing mother and join the "outside forces" of Duke University.

These days we have an enormous, many-sided and evolving relationship between blacks and whites in America. We've moved from slavery through emancipation, Reconstruction, sharecropping, Jim Crow, Martin Luther King, and Malcom X to the insistence that Black Lives Matter. We continue to ask one another whether different races are treated equally in their search for college admissions and jobs—and under persistent questions like these, this country's racial conflicts may in time yield to reason and calm.

To understand racial conflict more clearly, it helps to consider Carl Jung's theory of "projection" or "projective identification" as it applies to racism. The theory is simple enough—that we all *unconsciously* (without realizing it) project or "throw away" from ourselves certain feelings we are ashamed of having, feelings we do have but do not realize we have. That without knowing it or meaning to, we project—or throw—these feelings onto someone else.

To put it another way, Jung's theory of "projection" holds that we all have various "shadow selves"—aspects of ourselves that we do not like and probably do not even realize that we have.

All people fear their own "bad" qualities—whether these are qualities they actually have or simply fear that they might have—because they think their own society frowns upon these qualities. Jung calls this mass of denied or feared-as-bad qualities the *shadow self*.

> The shadow . . . cannot be accepted as a negative part of one's own psyche and is therefore projected—that is, is transferred to the outside world and experienced as an outside object. It is combated, punished, and exterminated . . . (Neumann, quoted in Becker, 95).

For example, let's suppose that a woman named Pam has a "shadow self" that includes the wish to ridicule other people. This "shadow self" is automatically and permanently in hiding, in her unconscious. Consciously, Pam herself cannot bear the thought that she would *ever* stoop to making fun of another person. If she ever does get close to laughing at someone, a mental "switch" automatically flips in her head and lets her feel very, very sorry for that person instead.

Then Pam meets a fellow named Squeak and notices that he often resorts to ridiculing others. Pam feels deeply moved to despise *Squeak's* behavior. She detests it. She is certain that the urge to ridicule belongs to Squeak, and *not* to herself. She is not aware that her own unconscious desire to make fun of others is now experienced as Squeak's desire. Therefore, she intensely hates *his* wish to ridicule others, without being in the least aware that she harbors the same tendency.

Pam's need to ridicule others, her unconscious meanness, has been *projected* onto Squeak, without any effort by her or any awareness of what her mind has done. This concept resembles suggesting that each person's mind has a special, automatic process of "laundering" or "disappearing" all the emotions that she most despises—while keeping her unaware that she indeed has these emotions herself.

Simply put, we each dread that we might be a Bad-at-Heart person. Our brain's solution is to deny—even to ourselves—that we have qualities we don't want to have. We don't perform this denial on purpose. It happens to us unconsciously, without our realizing it. We automatically cast out, onto other people, the qualities we see as "bad."

This casting-out of a "shadow self" can be silent and painless. Projection is nobody's fault. A person does not realize she is doing it.

The origins of many negative black stereotypes in this country may be caused by unconscious projections from the minds of white people.

One example is evident in the recently quoted Fraser letters, where a white father is worried that his son may have called him a harsh slavemaster. Here's how the mechanism of projection might circumvent that worry: An unconscious projection could cause the worried father's brain, or the son's brain, to project (throw) that supposition of harshness onto black people, rather than the father, in this scenario. This would be a typical act of the unconscious projection mechanism in each human brain. Although no one has planned to call black people harsh, nevertheless the thought does seem to appear. Familiar stereotypes of blacks might follow this pattern, without anyone being aware that an unconscious process has been at work.

The poet Langston Hughes has some elegant sentences that show how American whites may project their own bullying tendencies onto blacks, allowing whites to claim that black people are the dangerous ones—not white people. In his humorous 1942 "Simple" stories, Hughes has Semple, a character who represents the black resident from Harlem, say this:

> They drug me over here from Africa. They slaved me, they freed me, they lynched me, they starved me during the Depression, they

Jim Crowed me during the War. Then they come saying *they* are afraid of *me*. (*Voices and Visions*)

Exactly. This sack of accusations carries its own sack of answers. Semple is saying that it's absurd for whites to fear blacks, yet he's listing reason upon reason for whites to fear the anger of blacks—because whites are clearly projecting their own bullying tendencies onto blacks, claiming that it is the blacks who are the bullies. The unconscious mechanism of projection reveals that the savagery whites fear from blacks is the whites' own savagery, reflected back upon them.

When I was seven years old in the 1940s, I rode the city bus daily to Wiley School. I watched blacks climb on and steer wordlessly toward the back seats, where the black passengers sat. They rarely spoke, even to each other, and they avoided eye contact with me. They stared out of the bus window at something far away that made them sad.

The front seats were taken by fourteen-year-old white boys, tall and smart-talking, whose presence scared the daylights out of me. To escape them, I once chose a seat beside a black person. Everyone instantly came alive, even the driver. Everyone hustled me to a front seat, where I imitated the blacks by pressing my face to the window, trying to be invisible to the fearsome boys.

Whatever loathing was silently dished out to these back-of-the-bus black riders, they must have felt it a good deal. As a child I thought I could *feel* them feeling it. In that silence, they probably felt laden with all the unfavorable traits that whites, through the common mechanism of projection, denied within themselves. Only silence, and sometimes not even that, could keep them physically safe, as any reader of Richard Wright's *Black Boy* will learn. Their silence was ominous:

> What was he thinking, this docile Negro? . . . We have described segregation in pleasant terms, and for much of the time most of the Negroes have tacitly accepted the situation, and we have assumed they were telling the truth. They, however, were silent only because complaint was unhealthy. They could never believe in their hearts what under slavery they do seem to have believed—that he superior-inferior relations of segregation were true and right. (Dabbs 160, 171)

As I have grown older, I have learned more features of the wide-ranging blame that has been cast out unconsciously—meaning projected—by whites upon blacks. In one of Mama's stories often told in college, in a tale rumored to occur in the 1910s, her white family hears a hurried knock on the door one dark night. When Grandfather Tom opens it, he sees a terrified, helpless black man.

This black man tells the white family that the neighborhood menace, Benjamin Raven, has finally snapped and murdered someone. Raven is half-black and half-Indian, a racial combination of superhuman crazy-meanness. Raven went to the local store to ask for kerosene. When told they were out of stock, he leapt over the counter and slit the storekeeper's throat without a word. In this story, the quivering black man at the door begs Grandfather Tom for help. "Cap'n, you have to do something." In this story, black people themselves are terrified of this legendary, savage "black beast."

The slave culture seems to have created this Black Beast character, who stands for the fear-filled anger and hatred that whites may feel toward blacks, and as well for the fear-filled anger and hatred that blacks may feel toward whites. This mythic Black Beast seems at least halfway an unconscious Jungian projection by whites onto blacks. Indeed, this Beast looms large enough in the culture to represent black people's and white people's anger, both.

White people may well have been panicky to start with, because blacks outnumbered whites in so many areas of the slaveholding South. It would be understandable if whites had (unconsciously) projected all their own anger—as well as the anger they thought perhaps black people felt—onto a culturally projected Black Beast figure that looms up in the popular imagination to threaten everyone. He is a disaster waiting to happen—even if he is a fiction.

When my Uncle Tom told a small family audience the story of Grandfather Tom being ambushed and shot by a sharecropper, one woman listener in the family sighs and asks, "Now what about that man Roger Raven?" The imaginary Roger Raven is a terrifying brother of the imaginary Bejamin Raven. Those people listening to the story of one terror are eager to hear the story of another one, in ritual repetition. The stories of these mythic Black Beasts seem to comfort the listeners, in a repetition that becomes a ritual. It was Roger Raven. Or it was Benjamin Raven. This is a repeated story, told rhythmically, perhaps bringing to listeners the eventual comfort of the familiar.

Such stories of bloodshed and terror could expand to include the deeds that many men, black or white or Indian, have been known to do or have claimed to perform. In their mythic state, these villains become a constant presence in the culture and occupy the background.

These stories even make their way into politics. "Pitchfork" Ben Tillman, Governor and Senator from South Carolina between 1890 and 1918, told petrifying tales about a hypothetical "black fiend" to push his political agenda. He pictured for Congress this monster, worse than a beast, hypothetically raping pure white women:

> I have three daughters, but so help me God, I had rather find either one of them killed by a tiger or a bear and gather up her bones and bury them, conscious that she had died in the purity of her maidenhood, than to have her crawl to me and tell me the horrid story that she had been robbed of the jewel of her womanhood by a black fiend. [Ben Tillman's Fiery Tongue]

In his 1998 book *Shades of Freedom,* Judge A. Leon Higginbotham, Jr. documents "the role of the American legal process in substantiating, perpetuating, and legitimizing the precept of [black] inferiority (1998, xxv). He says the legal system in practice tends to suspect and convict black men of crimes, and to credit the false accusations of blacks by white people. The default perception is that "A Black Man Did It," Higginbotham argues.

Or as Langston Hughes put it so well about white people, "Then they come saying *they* are afraid of *me.*"

When Clarence Thomas wondered aloud whether the criticism he received in the process of his appointment to the Supreme Court was "a high-tech lynching," he may have been thinking of stories like those about Benjamin and Roger Raven. Maybe the criticism of him at the televised Senate hearing was just white people coming up with their scary stories about black people, once more.

Winthrop Jordan quotes a preamble to the South Carolina slave code: "Whereas, the plantations and estates of this province cannot be well and sufficiently managed and brought into use, without the labor and service of negroes and other slaves; and forasmuch as the said negroes and other slaves brought unto the people of the Province for that purpose, are of barbarous, wild, savage natures . . . for the good regulating and ordering of them, as may restrain the disorders, rapines and inhumanity, to which they are naturally prone and inclined . . . ." The descriptions in this introductory clause sufficiently make the following main clause, calling for protective action, almost unnecessary.

Harper Lee also knew the mind of the South when she created the plot of her novel *To Kill a Mockingbird*. The black male character, Tom Robinson, is wrongly accused of the crime of sleeping with a white woman. Tom is innocent, and he has even resisted the white woman's sexual advances. Yet he stands trial and is sent to jail by the all-white jury—even though the heroic lawyer Atticus Finch has represented him. When Tom tries to escape from jail, he is shot.

"Pitchfork" Ben Tillman, Governor and Senator from South Carolina from 1890 to 1918, would qualify to be a member of Harper Lee's fictional jury.

The Red Shirts, whose members included people in my family like my grandfather Thomas J. Kirven and his nephew Eckard Lee, rode to protest the black vote. In Tillman's state, he says, blacks of voting age outnumbered whites. Tillman denied the Southern slaveholders' reputation for brutality by intentionally projecting brutality onto the rich Northern entrepreneurs as the real slavedrivers. Before the Senate in 1896, he says:

> President Cleveland knows nothing about farmers, and more's the pity, he cares nothing about them. They are burning our candle at both ends, robbing us on the one hand with the tariff and robbing us on the other hand with the single gold standard. And they have asked us [the farmers] like beasts of burden, like dumb driven cattle, to bear these things and say nothing but to vote the party ticket.

Brutal domination, callous disregard, explosive anger—the qualities often attributed to whites are here cast out by Tillman onto blacks or rich Northerners.

Eckard Lee interpreted the Red Shirts as riding against the Northerners rather than against blacks.

Mariann: What's the Red Shirts?

Eckard Lee: In the South they put on the Red Shirts . . . Gainst the North was what it was . . .

Projection and scapegoating go hand in hand. They can happen routinely on either side of a painful debate. Our tall, imposing woman Latin teacher in our Winston-Salem high school was convinced that whenever the school band started to play "The Battle Hymn of the Republic," they were simply repeating an terrible anthem that blames—scapegoats—the South for The War. She would march out of the auditorium every time she heard that song.

It is 2002. I'm sitting in an auditorium at Fairfield University, where I work. The lecturer, Professor Jacqueline Goldsby, is screening some lynching postcards that were collected around a hundred years ago from the American South. These postcards have been recovered for research because they were donated by the relatives to whom they were sent.

The pictures are from postcards written by those who watched lynchings during the early 1900s. Amid each crowd at a lynching, dangling from a tall pole, is a burned corpse of a black man who has been designated guilty. Goldsby shows one postcard written to a friend or relative, then another. One of the witnesses to the lynching has written only one message on the postcard: "Say hello to Uncle Fred." Other postcard writers also seem untroubled and unmoved to have just seen a black man burnt and hanged.

The fictional generic "black beast" creature, so vividly imagined in the South of the 1900s, became a famous character as a well-known cultural projective identification. This character, known as Ben Raven or Roger Raven in my family's stories, was an old story. Lynching a black man would be an exercise in killing this same character yet one more time. Would this practice have become so routine that it was just an ordinary event to white audiences?

Chapter Seven:
Baby Paradoxes and Raising the Baby

The language of "Saving the Baby" is a metaphor, of course, which I've used to suggest the amazing potential for good lives that human beings do have, coupled with the understanding that human beings can be all too fragile. Our love of real babies is joined with our hope for the people they will become. Babies are the human race.

We try to care for these Babies with whatever strength and nurture we can summon. We wish for each of them a good reputation and the knowledge that they are Good at Heart. We know there will be struggles in life, always.

One famous human dilemma is stated by Ernest Becker: "The greatest cause of evil includes all human motives in one giant paradox . . . . The paradox is that *evil comes from man's urge to win heroic victories over evil" (135-36)*. Human civilization is subject to this paradox.

A dear cousin recently said this to me: "They thought if they didn't beat us, they wouldn't have good kids." Thank you, my dear cousin. You are correct, that is what they thought. Yet this very conviction—which is a version of Becker's "one giant paradox"—can itself lead to evil.

Hitler's father beat his son. Stalin's father beat his son, too. It's fair enough to say that Hitler and Stalin each had the *"urge to win heroic victories over evil."* Nietzsche, who was beaten as a child, broke down entirely when he saw a horse being whipped in the street. His pain reminds me of his statement, later in his life, that "morality is petrified violence."

In general, this seemed to be the reasoning: *To Save the Baby, you should Beat the Baby, because the Baby will ultimately thank you for forcing or teaching him/her to be a good person. It is your duty, and a virtuous thing to do.*

The custom of beating, with the idea that beating people would make them more virtuous, applies also to this nation's horrifying history of beating slaves. We have all seen films about slaves in the antebellum South being beaten, for many of the same reasons that children were beaten: disobedience, slackness, talking back, disloyalty, running away, recklessness, laziness, and all the rest. Not one of my own relatives has ever told me any story about beating slaves, although I still assume such beatings may well have occurred because I've seen the same movies that everyone else has. We all know the dramatic scene when the camera pauses to reveal huge, crosshatched scars on a slave's back. This "crime of the lash" is typically portrayed in our films as the evil of evils, the brutality of mankind exposed. After all, the specter of a slave rebellion—a catastrophic prospect—was thought to be "beaten back," so to speak, by beating slaves.

Even my grandmother, the famously kind Laura Fraser Kirven, would first admonish a wayward child and then send the child to her husband Tom, my grandfather, for "physical punishment," probably of the same kind that he himself endured as a child.

I've heard through my family of Kirvens that our great-grandfather Erasmus Kirven was "hard on those boys." Eckard Lee described to me what happened to Erasmus's son Thomas Kirven, my grandfather, as a boy: "They whipped him, but that didn't do any good." The adults then resorted to threatening young Thomas by invoking frightening mythic figures like "Raw Head" or "Bloody Bones." When my grandfather, Thomas himself, married and had children, he became the one in charge of physical punishment, and he in turn was reputed to be "hard on those boys" who were my five uncles Tom, Lawrence, Donnie, Coit, and Marion. I've learned from my cousins that several of my uncle's brothers believed that both boys and girls should be "disciplined" with beatings. My cousin Winkie told me that as a child her father, Marion, who took the belt to his own children, was always begging his mother Laura for a good report to his father Tom. There is one exception, for which I am thankful. My uncle Coit (the famous policeman) gave up his belief in beatings when his merciful wife, Harriet "Doll" Kirven, finally "put her foot down"—a phrase, perhaps Southern, meaning that she vetoed this kind of so-called "discipline."

Beating slaves and beating children—this is a pair of inhumanities. In an apparent contradiction or paradox, both have taken place in the South, that land of graciousness and hospitality. I've read that in these days, 90% of black people still whip their children.

The American South is not the only community in history that has believed in beating children. Laurence Stone describes how Europeans punished their children in his book, *Marriage and the Family in Europe: 1450-1700*. Over the centuries, European parents have convinced themselves that a beating would expel evil *from* the child and instill virtue *into* the child. This is why European parents tried their very best to be *diligent* or *resolute* about beating children. They might feel remiss if they did *not* hit their children *for their own good*.

In my research for this book, I happened to read *Flames After Midnight,* which details two atrocities that happened around the turn of the century in the town of Kirven in the Midwest (no relation to my Kirven family, to my knowledge). In this true account of a terrible event, the cries of young woman named Eula Ausley—a seventeen-year-old who was at that moment being beaten to death in the woods by the murderers—sounded to her neighbors, who lived a farm's distance away, like an ordinary child being "disciplined," which is a word often used for "whipped." (This one detail reveals much about humanity's history of what has been called "disciplining" children.) The neighbors did not intervene because they had regularly heard such cries before. Then a frantic investigation for the culprits mistakenly identified two black men, who were then burnt alive in the public square that night.

Maisie and Bill, my two parents, completely disagreed about how to raise children. One of Mama's undated letters of July 1942, soon after my father had traveled to the European Theatre for World War II, seems to be a continuing discussion about how to raise the baby. I'm two months away from being born, at this point. Mama here refers to the fetal movement inside her womb as the "fighting" of theoretical "twins" as she discusses how to "discipline" the yet unborn baby:

> The twins and I are fine—except that the twins have been fighting again, as usual. I'm anxious to get them where I can discipline them about that fighting, aren't you? Don't get worried about my using the word "discipline," Bub. I don't mean "spank," really. I *promise* not to spank them. I'll wait and let you do that. I'll bet you'll change your mind and agree with me, though, if they're as spoiled as they probably will be. But we'll find a better way than spanking to remedy that, won't we, Bub?

Maisie seems to hand over the issue to my father, Bill. Yet Bill is across the ocean, and his management is not available. His kind advice to Maisie, in a return letter, is simply to "spoil [the baby] as she wants to be spoiled" (February 9, 1943), but his advice was not heeded because he was away at World War II. As the months of separation stretched out to years, Maisie would return to the baseline convictions she had learned from within her own family, with her older brothers and her father as her predecessors. She did indeed mean "spank," and although that may sound like a cute word, it did mean a beating.

When my daughter was born, she grew big enough—at three years old—to feel like jumping on the bed, like those Eight Little Monkeys in the children's book. Then she decided she didn't want to stop. Oh, dear. I panicked and began to tremble. Was I supposed to . . . NO! There was no way I would do *that*. I caught my breath and came up with a distraction. I'd offer my little girl some ice cream. Ah, what a relief. Later, a kind psychiatrist, whom I consulted, explained to me the full range of alternatives to beating children—for instance, I could try bargaining with her. Yes, I could. And I did. The thought of treating her as I had been treated was sickening to me.

The psychologist Alice Miller argues in several books that the long-held conviction that children should be beaten is a damaging pathology that travels inevitably from generation to generation. It is nearly impossible to cure because it embraces a repression necessary for survival. She finds in history some spectacular examples of abused children driven by this pathology to become insanely cruel adults who slaughter millions—examples that include Hitler and Stalin. Most beaten children do not become monsters on such a great scale, yet their pathological convictions that it is good to beat their own children or control others with violence can be tenacious, mesmerizing, and damaging.

Miller's central argument is that beaten or abused children *must* believe that their own beatings *are just.* They must believe that their parents act from some superior wisdom, and they must find multiple ways to *support* their parents' actions. The alternative belief—that they are good children in a corrupt world with pathological parents—cannot be withstood by a small child. Instead, abused children take on the convictions of their punishers as a way of "putting to rest," or repressing, their own conflicted memories of being beaten. They do this in order to keep on living.

When they become adults, this repression is still in place. Beaten children become parents with a conviction that they must beat their own children. Unconsciously, they must affirm their vital certainty that their parents were good and right.

> Adolescents who have been beaten regard what they have experienced in their own upbringing as normal and a matter of

course. They think that what they have been taught—namely, that children need to be beaten—is right. And they don't question those views, because as children who have been physically intimidated, they are afraid to call their parents into question (Miller 1993, 55).

Plain good luck and fortunate circumstances—beginning with the discovery of my parents' World War II correspondence in our attic in Virginia—have enabled me to see how my parents were unhappily, even tragically misled by our prevailing culture and by their own different backgrounds.

Sometime in 1945, Maisie breaks. I am not yet three years old. In an August letter Maisie is asking Bill in effect to beat her own anger back into her. She is caught between her reluctance to beat her daughter and her conviction that there is nothing else she can do in this impossible situation. She cannot help it, any more than she can help breathing. She crosses over and reverts to the certainties of her original family. Identifying with the oppressive brothers of her childhood, she decides to beat her two-year-old daughter.

Despite searing memories of her brothers' taunts, Maisie gravitates toward the felt power that those brothers display. After all, those brothers were themselves beaten and now beat their own children, who seem to be respectful and obedient. That must be strength. Maisie needs strength. Her brothers' families do seem stable, and Maisie craves stability. Besides, her once-perfect Mariann has somehow become a disobedient and bawling child, as well as a turncoat who seeks out Ansie, Perry, and Diane instead of her own mother.

> Mariann has gotten in the habit recently of refusing to go to sleep until I come to bed with her, and hops in and out of bed from the time I put her to bed until I go to bed too . . . Maybe we can work out that little difficulty to the benefit of all concerned when you come home (August 16, 1945) . . . Mariann certainly is being insistent this evening about my going to bed . . . . I've already spanked her several times about bawling out lengthily . . . and don't want to have to do it again—tears me to pieces to have to do that . . . . Well, I guess it was one o'clock before Mariann and I got to sleep—maybe I shouldn't have spanked her. (August 20, 1945)

Maisie can't bear Mariann yelling at her, as if calling her a bad mother. Mariann seems to taunt her, and Maisie believes she has been cruelly taunted as a child, by her own brothers. She will fight fire with fire, challenging her brothers' type of force against her own child's apparent disrespect.

Maisie no longer invokes violence upon herself for mistreating an ideal baby, for she has now implanted a sliver of her past—the "physical discipline" that has seemed so necessary to the family where she originally belonged—into her model of an ideal future. She needs that piece of her past. She persuades herself that she can still have her serene and joyful home in her imagined future, where she can hold on tight to a perfect Maisie-and-Bill in which she is Good at Heart. Yet Bill must agree about physical discipline.

Bill never does agree about physical discipline. Yet he still goes along with Maisie beating her children, even while he is careful to distance himself from the scene. Bill and Maisie will have three daughters. The family will continue down this contradictory path.

On behalf of my parents, I am sad to know that this subject of disciplining children created a permanent disagreement between them. Yet on my own behalf, I am glad to have finally understood the nature of our parents' differences, which is made clear at last by their personal correspondence.

Mama beats my sister Cathy, six years younger than me, and my youngest sister Laura Beth, thirteen years younger. Daddy disagrees but stays away. It is a terrible sound to hear a child being beaten. Once when I am seven years old, at Mama's urging, Daddy takes out his belt and stands behind me, but he cannot compel himself to perform the act of beating me. He drops the belt in consternation. "I just can't do it, Maisie," he says. "I can't do it."

Maisie uses some strange words and phrases that I learn only gradually, by asking how they are spelled—words such as po'bucker, hottentot, buttheaded, pickaninny, ragamuffin, screaming meemee, Dracula's moll, bride of Frankenstein, whirling dervish, wreck of the Hesperus. We daughters are urged to behave ourselves in such a way that we could never, ever be described by these words. They are words of warning, taboos we should avoid. I wonder whether Maisie learned these words as a child.

Ansie once lamented that Maisie had a tongue like a knife. Diane remembers Ansie grabbing Maisie by the shoulders and telling her, "When you say things like that, in the heat of anger, you *wound* people in ways that can never fully heal."

In my early school years, I exist in a kind of fog. Many things refuse to focus in my head. One rare snowy day in Winston-Salem, when I am six years old and Cathy is an infant, I walk across the street to a strange neighbor's swimming pool. All is white. No one is there.

Is that ice thin, or is it solid enough to hold me up? I don't know how to swim. I step onto the snowy pool at random. By chance, I am at the shallow end. It is cold. I wander home. Blankets and yelling meet me.

Another time, when I am seven years old, I am visiting Ansie's house. At this moment I am by myself. Mama has warned me a hundred times not to go anywhere near the pair of roller-dryers fastened to the old-fashioned washtub in Ansie's basement. Those thick wooden spools are in constant motion whenever the washer is plugged in, rolling and rolling, ready to squeeze out the water from sheets and towels. They are clamped together hard. Mama has told me a hundred times that those rollers could squeeze away an arm or a leg from a little person, that they could even kill me.

I touch those rolling rollers, right at the line where they press together. They push my fingers away. Then I go around to the other side and touch them again. Instantly they suck in my arm, right up to the elbow. I scream. Diane leaps down the basement stairs and releases the rollers into my chin. My arm turns out to be fine. My chin has a small scratch.

When Mama has died in 1992 and Daddy is an old man, I summon the nerve to approach him. One question has always troubled me. In tears, I ask him, "Daddy, did you *then,* or do you *now* agree with Mama's views that children should be beaten?" He and I are sitting on a polished window seat, at my sister L. B.'s house in Massachusetts. I dread asking whether he was also *behind* the beatings, for I remember my parents vowing to take a *united* approach towards us children. Yet I must ask.

"Did she beat you? I didn't know," Daddy lies. He is a self-effacing person, volunteering little. "I must have been out of the house, at work."

I continue to cry. Daddy elaborates, sensing that I need a little more talk.

"No," he says. "I always believed in treating children with gentleness and respect." I am praying that *this* statement, at least, is true.

That evening, I approach my tall younger sister, L. B. She is rushing through the house, her mop of chestnut hair bouncing as she goes, cackling at every absurdity that comes her way. At her memorial service ten years from that day, a good friend will write on the *Memories of L. B.* page, "Her laugh was like a whooping crane."

I tell L. B. what I have asked Daddy. Her comeback is swift: "My God, Mariann. Better you than me."

I report Daddy's story of not being at home. "Yeah, *right.*" L. B. huffs and rolls her eyes. "That's a crock. He was there. He was always there." She laughs, and it is a soft whooping crane sound.

Not many years later, Daddy utters his dying confession to me that he has "fooled them all." I am gratified that Daddy will reveal himself to me in any way, however indecipherable that revelation may be.

"Good, Daddy," I say, as the casual adult child, determined to agree. "Who did you fool, exactly?"

"Everybody," he replies. "All of them."

I wonder if this "everybody" includes me, a willing fool.

When Mama was 77, in 1992, she died of cancer. L. B. traveled to our sister Cathy's house in Atlanta. By then Cathy was a family physician, and she was caring for Mama in the last stages of her life.

Mama lay on the bed in which she would die, and L. B. sat beside her. When Cathy left the room and they were alone, Mama pleaded with L. B.

"I can't understand it," Mama said. "Why have I never been able to be close to any of my three daughters? And you, L. B., you who were so smart, so funny, so lovely in every way, I would have thought that *we* could be good friends. What *should* I have done to strengthen the bond between us? What else *could* I have done?"

L. B. drew upon her last drop of courage and said, "Well, Mama, there were all those beatings. We could talk about the beatings, as a start to getting closer."

Mama turned her face away.

"What beatings?" she asked. "I never laid a hand on you. I never laid a hand on any of you three girls."

Father William, Bill, and Mariann in 1945. Bill is tying her shoe

Mama lived without any adult help from her culture, any "enlightened witness," in Miller's terms, who might have helped her understand the truth of her own childhood, whatever that may have been, and integrate it into her life (Miller 1990, 151). She was fighting a heroic inner battle all the time, against insurmountable psychological odds that she did not understand—that no one so isolated could ever understand. She could not speak her anguish to her daughters, who heard only sporadic and puzzling comments. Her dearest husband, Bill, could not cure her pain himself or induce her to seek professional help. She was too badly hurt to reach out. Mama held on so tightly to her dignity and privacy that she could not reveal her troubled feelings to anyone who might have helped her find relief.

If Daddy ever did try to persuade Mama that children should be treated with gentleness and respect—that *she* should be treated that way, and that she should treat her *children* that way—Mama was too damaged to hear him. In these circumstances, she did the best she possibly could in raising her children. She did better than her best. Sometimes healing never comes.

Back in the summer of 1942, when Mama was pregnant with me, she used to take early morning walks with my cousin Diane, then four years old. They strolled around the block in Fairmont and watched the morning glories open. They came to like each other then. They treated each other sweetly. Many years later, shortly before she died and had almost given up trying to be friends with any of her three daughters, Mama renewed her friendship with Diane.

Mama had lived in constant apprehension of being mocked by her relatives, or in constant hurt from having been humiliated by them—either or both. She feared other family members would belittle her, or worse, pity her if they discovered she was terminally ill with that shameful disease, cancer. She kept her cancer diagnosis concealed from everyone except Daddy and her three daughters.

However, as her illness progressed to its inevitable end, Mama did send a present to Diane without mentioning that she herself was sick. Diane did not understand that day why she was suddenly receiving a gift from Maisie. Diane unwrapped the box and discovered a perfect blue morning glory inside a translucent glass ball. This flower was safe. It was Spotless. It was Good at Heart. It was ideal. Each petal, clear as a blue pool, rich as fruit, was preserved clear of any shadows, forever.

That luminous blue flower was Mama's vision of her own Baby that might have been spared from the flames.

Scenes and Interludes

Towering Uncles

Cousins Julie and Larry remember when they were terrorized by Uncle Donnie on the subject of high-school math.

Donnie's face would turn purple as he tried to explain to his niece and nephew how to solve for x.

"God-*dog* it!" Donnie would raise his entire arm like he was about to split a stump, and then bring it down on the table, *slap-slam!*

Larry would stare at his book and keep his mouth shut, which was a sign of attention, for Larry was one steady talker.

Julie would lay her head on the table, on the verge of tears.

Donnie would pace around the large wood table in the living room, with each invisible piece of the great math puzzle in his uplifted hands. He would glue each piece into the air. *This* means *this* and so we have *that*. Then he'd do it once more. Got it now?

Clear as mud.

Donnie would roar, "You mean to tell me you *still* don't understand?" He would clutch his head to keep his mind from blowing up.

"No, sir, we don't," Julie would admit.

"Look here, Donnie, we're *trying*." Larry would add.

Those sines and cosines worked Donnie up. Why couldn't these children see? It was every bit as plain as he could make it. It was pure logic.

My own experience of Uncle Donnie was much milder.

Donnie never raised his voice to me. I quivered simply because he was an adult, and large, and I was half-poisoned by my own personal snakebed of internal fears.

Donnie and I would meet at Fairmont. I was a little girl visiting Ansie. Donnie would arrive at the door un-tucking his shirt soaked-with-sweat from his not-air-conditioned car, for he made long, hot drives over South Carolina for Investors Syndicate. He would drink a giant glass of ice water and stand by the fan, flapping his shirttails in its breeze.

Donnie's typical greeting to all the family, as my cousin Beau recalls, was "How's your corporosity sagaciating? Following Beau's suggestion years later, I discovered that Brer Rabbit asks the Tar Baby much the same question: "How duz yo' syn'tums seem ter segashuate? (Harris, 6)" This phrase, which I was then too young to catch, boils down to "How are you?" or maybe even, "How's your body thinking?" I do remember that Donnie liked comic fancy-talk. Want some more corn on the cob, Donnie? "Thank you, ma'am, but I've had a gracious sufficiency."

Donnie and I would sit down at Ansie's card table, near her business desk, and play rummy. Maybe Donnie figured I was too timid to handle his frustration. He would have been right. Never had anyone outside my immediate family struck me, but I took no chances. I learned those cards perfectly.

"Laws a mussy," Donnie would rumble. "Who dealt this mess?" I would jump, but Donnie would grin his merry, crooked-teeth grin.

"Looky there!" Donnie would act pleased. "You've got a Dream Hand, I do believe. You can draw once, put 'em down, and double the score. Can you add?"

I could add. It felt like a test, but one I had a good shot at passing.

My uncle Coit was more intimidating, even while he was being nice.

I can still feel myself sitting across the kitchen table from Uncle Coit in Sumter. We are playing rummy, and I am six years old. I'm trying not to admit to myself that Coit scares me. He ducks his chin and peers at me beneath angular black eyebrows. His eyes glitter with intelligence. He smiles. Why? Have I said something amusingly stupid?

There is a gun in Coit's holster, which hangs on his chair. He is a policeman, so he carries his gun *always*. Years later, I learn that he even sleeps beside it. That gun is fully visible as we play, drawing and discarding. Not wanting to be impolite, I don't mention the gun. I watch it, though.

Coit clears his throat. "Do you know what a Dream Hand is, young miss?"

I do. I explain a Dream Hand, then a Hand from Heaven.

"Bless goodness, she knows all that!" Coit exclaims, and then shifts in his chair.

Whew, I think. Yes, I am eager to be both innocent and good.

I imagine Coit catching a robber. *Hands up!*

On Christmas Day at The Farm, so they tell me, my uncles try to scare one another with Blood Rummy. They played through the afternoon, after the turkey dinner was put away. There would be much smacking-down of cards, and declaring of multiple wild cards, and piling of cards onto others' plays, and grabbing the entire discard pile.

Was there money? Maybe.

Ecstasy

Our family's hunting and fishing stories don't usually focus on chest-thumping. More often they're about slip-ups in confronting the great unknown of wild creatures, and humility at emerging intact. On a duck-hunting expedition, the usual hunters might be shielded by Great-Uncle Luke, so massive that he could stride through the briars and make a trail for them to follow. Or Larry would find himself in a freezing swamp, in his underpants, shooting ducks. Or Joe would wrestle and prevail over a big buck, and then it would take four men struggling for hours to carry the animal two miles back to the truck.

Kirvens have hunted deer, raccoons, ducks, quail, gators, and fish—no wild bears or lions, no "big game," no flirting with death. I have struggled, as a city-style animal-lover, to understand my family's motivations for hunting. Do they take some strange pleasure in killing defenseless animals? No, I've learned. The attraction of hunting is more mysterious.

I've asked my cousin Joe about the appeal of hunting. My question felt provocative, to me, because deer strike me with wonder, and I want to protect those seemingly fragile animals.

"Joe," I asked, "What is it you like so much about killing deer?"

Joe's eyes glazed over. When he answered, his tone was soft and musing. "It was so hard," Joe whispered. "They ran so fast."

I was jarred. Here was common ground. Joe, too, was struck with wonder at the sight of a deer. His words were reverent.

Maybe shooting a deer can feel like a kind of miracle. With a bit of lead and extra-careful eye focus, you can become a match for this impossibly swift and beautiful wild creature that inhabits another dimension. How is this possible? How do you have a line to this pure life?

My cousin Perry has used the word "ecstasy" to describe his long-ago afternoons hunting quail at The Farm. The word astonished me then, but I may be coming to understand.

Perry described to me the cool air, the special bright wakefulness of autumn, the hundreds of yards from one line of woods to the next, all touched by scattered brush. The older boys would set up a cry, and hordes of quail would rush out. It took his breath away. The magic of possible sustenance for hundreds of people, relief and plenitude, the hope of hunger vanquished all there in the sharp-edged fall sunshine.

Joe, Tom, and Larry Kirven with coon skins and coon dogs.

Larry Kirven with his "catch" in the 1940s

In the days before Myrtle Beach was gobbled up for real estate, Joe and his wife Sallie drove with friends to a spot where they could fish for a whole day. They set up camp among the sea oats in the dunes.

By late afternoon they had secured four glorious lines of flounder, swaying with the weight of the fish. They would be a mile or two from camp by then. Joe just walked the lines back up the shore, gliding them through the ocean water. When he met another fisherman, he just slid his flounder line beneath the other fellow's line. When Joe describes that fish dinner at camp as the best he ever had, it wasn't simply about the taste of fish. It was about life bubbling over.

All that said, hunting wasn't only about rituals and epiphanies. Uncle Tom had only one strict down-to-earth rule about hunting: "If you kill it, then you clean it, and you eat it."

Not much mystery or wonder there, but a good standard of practice.

Not Even My Dogs

Perry became the man of the family when his father died. Not that he was expected to stand on the front step with a shotgun to keep the peace. But as Perry grew older and stronger, he was able to tackle problems that neither his sister nor his mother could handle alone. Maybe because of his masculine upper-body strength, or maybe just because it was fated, he was nudged into canine control.

I would be visiting Fairmont, sitting in Ansie's office on the couch near the front window and writing out customer addresses for Ansie's business, The Town and Country Shop.

Infernal howls and visceral barks would explode all around the house. It was a siege of sound, like the werewolves were coming. Within a count of ten, I would hear Ansie's urgent voice.

"Perry! The dogs!"

This cry meant that my cousin Diane's collie, Laddie, had escaped from his pen and encountered Butch, a stocky mixed breed who ruled the neighborhood. Butch supposedly belonged to a boy who lived a few houses away, Sonny Huffines. But Butch was often left to roam free, for whatever reason.

So whenever Laddie freed himself while Butch also happened to be free, the battle would begin. Those dogs sounded to me like the animal ferocity of the entire planet had just exploded. I imagined them rushing into Ansie's front yard, ripping at each other with the snarling-est violence you ever heard.

Where was Sonny Huffines? Seldom at home, as I recall.

"Let me see! Let *me* see!" I would stick my nose through the venetian blinds, expecting to see blood and teeth and muscle.

"No, no!" I was told. "You don't want to see!"

Then Perry, in a fury himself, would charge out to separate the dogs. The screen door would bang helplessly.

"Get the hose! Turn the hose on them!"

Sometimes Ansie would be out there with Perry, because it would take them both to grab those possibly flesh-eating dogs by their collars and shove them back inside their two separate fences. The snarling would break into pieces, like a buzz-saw losing power. Then it would be quiet.

Perry would slam back into the house, grumbling and growling.

He knew it was monumentally unfair. Because of his XY chromosomes, he had been appointed semi-official dog-warden, with all the hazards of the job: the bared fangs, the springing hindquarters. Someone had to keep those dogs from killing each other, and Perry was tagged.

Sonny Huffines was perpetually absent. Every so often Ansie would step into the back yard to try a little one-on-one with Mrs. Huffines, Sonny's mother. Yet Ansie could not risk earning a reputation as an inveterate complainer, not in the small town of Fairmont, on whose residents Ansie depended for her family income.

Perry would plead, *Mama, why am I the one who has to do this?*

There was no answer.

When I visited Perry years later, we shared memories of those intractable dogs on the rampage, and I sympathized with Perry's assignment.

"Yeah," he told me. "Yeah. And they weren't even my dogs!"

Funny, they never are. Maybe we all end up quieting other people's dogs. Ha ha ha.

Courage in Plastic Bags

When I was in my twenties and too phobic to travel, Mama would pitch me the story of my legendary sister Cathy, who commuted 40 miles over the mountains to Virginia Tech in Blacksburg on a motorcycle in all weathers, daily, to finish her college degree. This story was meant to inspire me to buck up and face down my phobias with *will power,* the family solution to all hurdles. Cathy was fearless in the pursuit of higher education, said Mama.

One summer Cathy told me her own version of the story. Yes, she had traveled from Roanoke to classes in Blacksburg. She and her husband Mike owned one car and one motorcycle. Cathy carpooled with other Virginia Tech students, using the family car on every third day while Mike rode the motorcycle to work. They were on a budget. Times were hard.

Her commuting arrangement would last until final exams, when the student commuters had different schedules and were all forced to find their separate ways to Blacksburg.

Cathy rode the family motorcycle on exam days, all right, forty miles over the mountain to Blacksburg and forty miles back. In January, it was one frozen trek. The highway was treacherous with rain and low temperatures. Roaring on at sixty miles per hour, you were cut and numbed by the wind no matter how you dressed. Cathy had a heavy jacket and cap, but no boots, so she covered her shoes with plastic bags from home-delivered newspapers, fastened to her legs by rubber bands. By the time she reached Blacksburg, her feet were either well soaked or well iced.

Cathy has solidly adopted "No whining" as one of her life's mottos. Valor to the extreme. But even Cathy remembers those motorcycle trips as excruciating. And I became more curious about family traditions when I realized that Mama made this story bigger than life. My parents, who lived in Roanoke, owned two cars. Is there any reason that they couldn't have lent Cathy . . . just on exam days . . . oh, never mind.

Lost and Found

By the late 1930s, a big family was living on the farm at Eastover. Uncle Tom and his wife Eva had six children by then: Ophelia, Tom, Joe, Laura Ann, Danny, and Larry.

Everybody was busy all the time, caring-for or being cared-for, trying to get the cows milked, bring the crops in, put up with the weather, and keep the children safe. With six children underfoot, even when some were half grown, no one could keep an eye on every single child every single minute.

One cloud-covered Sunday morning, anxiety whirred through the family.

"Anybody seen Larry?"

Larry was four years old then, and he had been on the move since he had begun walking at nine months old. He would take off for anywhere, inside the house or out in the fields, fearless. That day, the person watching the younger children had been distracted for a minute, and that was all it took.

It had rained in torrents the night before. Everybody searching for Larry knew that rainwater would have filled all the plunging ditches nearby. One slip-in-the-mud step, and a four-year-old child could be in over his head.

Lah—reeeee! The whole family spread out through the house, the yard, and the barn, with their calls unanswered. Eva was frantic.

My cousin Laura Ann told me what happened:

The search widened to the nearby neighbors' yard, Laura Ann said. One neighbor said that she had seen a small child in a red raincoat walking up the highway. Tom Sr. rushed where the neighbor had pointed. There on the side of the road sat Larry, fascinated by the twirling and swirling water, which was rushing into a large pipe. It said to him, "Booga-lunka, booga-lunka!" He said it back.

Four-year-old Larry spoke to the gurgling water in its own language. The family rejoiced. Halleluiah! Booga-lunka!

No one had mentioned "grit" or any other word for "courage," during the entire search. But it was all right. Larry didn't drown, after all. He just learned to sing *Booga-lunka!*

Wanting to Go That Way: Funny No More

Spike was my uncle Tom's favorite hunting dog, half bulldog and half Walker hound. He could nose out coons nestled in trees, even the tall trees of the river swamp. Tom depended on Spike for night hunting expeditions through fields and rivers with male relatives and friends. Spike grew old in the service of his human masters until cataracts filmed over his once-keen eyes. But he could still catch a scent.

One night in the mid-1950s, old Spike set out with Tom and his hunting party. They were after raccoons. Tom's son Larry and Ansie's son Perry were in their early twenties then, along with Larry's older brother Joe. Each one of them has told me this story.

It was a cool autumn night, maybe too cool with too brisk a breeze, for the guys tromped through brush and curved around trees for hours without a raccoon to be seen or heard. Maybe Spike couldn't smell the coons in the wind. Maybe those coons were huddled down for the night. The guys kept on walking because coonskins brought a good price. Some "hard up" people even ate coons. Joe told me that once when he entered a friend's house, he saw a skinned, roasted coon on the table with an apple in its mouth.

After a long empty while, the hunting party arrived at a huge tree. They saw that one large branch was bent way down, so far that its whole spread of leaves was laid out along the ground in a dark cave of greenery under the half moon.

Spike came alert. On his old legs he walked down that great branch, slow and eager, and disappeared. No doubt Spike had smelled a coon, and he was closing in. They all waited in the dark. Nothing. Where had Spike got to?

It had been long enough—too long—when Tom finally heard twigs snap. Something was coming out. Tom switched his flashlight on and shone it down the length of that low branch, further and further, until the beam caught two red eyes.

Spike must have flushed a coon at last. Tom aimed his shotgun and fired. The eyes vanished. He whistled up Spike. No Spike appeared.

Tom walked the length of the branch and reached down into the leaves, and there was Spike. He had been killed on the instant by a shot in the head.

Oh, no. Oh, no. Oh, no.

Tom had taken Spike for a coon and shot him, with that same King Nitro single-barrel 32-inch full-choke shotgun that Joe had used to kill the mad dog, fifteen years earlier.

Wails and groans. Disbelief.

After they buried Spike, the men sat up around the kitchen table, wanting to talk and talk until it was all right. They knew it would never be all right. They lingered on the hows and the whats, mistaken this and that, plain old accidents, mean tricks played by fate.

Finally, someone said, "That was the way Spike would have wanted to go."

All right, then. That did it. They could sleep, eventually. They had shaped the end of the story.

Down-Home Recipes

In 2004, I told my sister Cathy that I planned to visit Joe and Sallie Kirven.

"Hey, I'll bet Joe will serve you his famous barbecued chicken," she predicted.

"Great," I answered. "I like barbecued chicken."

"Why don't you watch him and see how he cooks it?" Cathy continued. "I've always wanted to know. You could ask him, but he wouldn't tell you. There's *no way* he'd let you in on the genuine family recipe for barbecued chicken. It's been in the family for generations."

"Sure," I said. "I'll keep an eye out."

When we reached my cousin Joe's house that summer, the table was already spread. In the center was a thumping big platter of Joe's special barbecued chicken, leg-joined-to-breast pieces that each spanned a dinner plate.

Tender? The meat melted from the bone with one nudge of a fork. All the cousins cried mmm-*mmmmm!*

When we had finally devoured the last forkful of peach cobbler, I felt well fed and bold.

"Joe, that chicken is amazing," I said.

"Well, thank you, ma'm. We're right fond if it."

"I don't suppose you'd tell us the recipe?"

Joe answered, "Course I'll tell you the recipe. Get yourself a pencil and paper there! Write it down! Now, who does the barbecue-ing in your family?"

My husband Richard took down the ingredients and listened to the disquisition on how far down the pit should be dug, how big the drum chosen, how deep the coals, how far from the grill, how much sopping of the cloth and basting with the sauce, how frequent the turning, and how strong the intuition needed to tell when the chicken was done. Proper cooking took a *long* time, Joe insisted. It was not so much the sauce as the *process* that coaxed out the flavor.

After we had been schooled, my zeal spoke up again.

"Joe, how far back does this recipe go in the family? Who thought it up?"

"Well, now," Joe answered, "My daddy got this recipe from one of his good friends. Name of Harry Rhyttenberg. Now, Rhyttenberg, he was a Jewish man, but Rhyttenberg and my daddy, they were the best of friends their whole lives. Rhyttenberg was the one showed him the barbecue sauce and the *process*."

I have a picture of Joe's daddy, my uncle Tom, sitting on the porch at The Farm with Joe and Sallie, and Harry Rhyttenberg. Joe is courting Salllie at the time. They are eating chicken barbecued with the Genuine Jewish Southern Barbecue Sauce provided by Harry Rhyttenberg and perhaps his ancestors.

Later in our visit, Joe mused, "You know, there's another recipe for barbecue sauce in our family."

"Oh?" I was intrigued. "Where does this recipe come from?"

"Our Uncle Donnie," answered Joe.

"Really?" I knew Uncle Donnie as an insurance salesman, not as a gourmet.

Joe continued, "Back when the family lived in Eastover, we'd invite all the uncles over on Sunday for a barbecue. We had an old colored man who'd stand at the coals and baste the meat for us. Now Donnie, he would hide behind a tree and poke his head out to see how that colored man made the sauce."

"Was Donnie successful?"

"Oh, yeah. He figured it out."

"What was in the sauce?"

"I forget," said Joe. "You mix up ketchup and mustard with a dash of this and that and the other. Can't recall the proportions. I'll look around for it."

So that's another down-home recipe. Genuine Southern Jewish and African-American Barbecue Sauce as seen by Donnie at Eastover. Peace in the family.

When I lived in Connecticut, my friends *loved* my pecan pie. They told me, *You must have learned this from your family as a Southern girl.*

Every time, I tell them that it's the recipe from *Better Homes and Gardens* with a few extra pecan halves thrown in. Takes twenty minutes. Want the recipe?

They don't want the recipe. They want to *oooh* and *ahhh*. The next time I serve pecan pie, they say, *This must be an old Southern recipe from your family.*

So peaceful to imagine a down-home recipe for whatever you're eating. That way, you know the special, secret place where all the good food comes from. You eat in total contentment.

Afterwards, you sleep.

Peacemaker at the Wheel

Some people are thrust into the role of peacemaker. Their hard job is to prevent hurt feelings, and that job sticks with you until it's over. Everybody feels fine, but the peacemakers have the world's consternation on their shoulders.

This story comes from David Onsrud, the husband of my cousin Laura Ann, who entitles it "The Kirven Commanding Presence."

Lucia Kirven and her sister, Helen Adel Kirven, were riding in the back seat of a car driven by one of Lucia's daughters-in-law, Nancy, visiting from New York. This happened in Englewood, Florida in the 1960s, and to the embarrassment of all, it was revealed by Danny, who was there.

Nancy was driving, and the two Kirven sisters (daughters of Hugh Kirven) were sitting in the back seat. Danny, Nancy's young son and Lucia's grandson, was in the front seat beside his mother. Nancy was not familiar with the highways of Englewood and was taking directions from the two Kirvens in back.

The car approached a fork in the road. One of the Kirvens gave the direction to take the left fork, which was immediately countered by the second Kirven who favored the right fork.

"No! No! Don't go right! You will end up in a subdivision! Go left!"

"No! If you go left, you will go down the river! Go right!"

Next thing they knew, they were standing around the car, figuring how to get it out of the drainage ditch in the middle of the fork.

Years later, when the incident was recalled, Nancy revealed that she had not driven a car occupied by those two ladies *ever again.*

She said, "Individually, yes, but not together."

Nancy's noble goal had been to keep the peace. No one wants to hurt the back-seat drivers' *feelings!* You can't be *rude* to your relatives or elders.

Nancy's car hit the ditch, but no feelings were hurt.

Kiss the Shark

In the summer of 2001, chemotherapy was providing L. B. some relief. She could bask in the sun for a few minutes. She could walk, eat, and breathe with some comfort. She would toss me her standard jokes whenever I phoned during those anxiety-filled years of her dying, from 1998 to 2002.

"How are you feeling?"

This was the one permitted question, for L. B. despised sentimentality. She had been inoculated against sentimentality, she would say, by our mother.

"How am I feeling? I'm still walking and talking," L. B. would answer.

Or she would shoot back, "I'm here today. I'll be here tomorrow."

So in 2001, L. B. decided to have a good summer. On a surgeon's salary, she could afford some treats. She navigated a flashy red motorcycle along the streets of Winchester, while it gave off a satisfying hum. She purchased a green Audi sports convertible and took six-year-old Luke for drives while they listened to Talking Heads and Harry Potter. She steered Luke to museums and restaurants and movies and ice cream parlors.

She would die on May 6, 2002.

That 2001 summer, L. B. accepted every offer for an outing that she thought her body could stand. When Kathy and Steve Goldman, old friends from West Hartford, invited L. B. and Luke to a fishing trip off the Cape, L. B. drove there with Luke in her Audi convertible. She gave sports-car rides to all four of the Goldmans' squealing, spirited children. A photo at her memorial service showed her arriving and arriving and arriving once more in the green Audi, smiling, with a different kid every time.

The deep-sea fishing trip was a delight. Luke loved it. The Goldman children were enthralled. They caught and threw back some fascinating ocean creatures.

We have a picture of Luke, and each Goldman child in turn, holding a baby shark. Za zoom! Laughin' fit to kill!

We have a picture of L. B. kissing that baby shark.

Take that, mortal danger! Take that, approaching death!

Civil Conversations

Family disputes are no small threat. The Kirvens of the 1900s, racked by the choice of educational ideals *versus* farming ideals, may have felt deeply hurt. Then there were the Great Uncles of the 1800s, fussin' and fightin' over women and land, with lawsuits and guns. One brother would say of another, *Lock 'im up!*

Yet family customs have designed some peaceful rituals to hold these dangerous internecine feelings at bay.

David Onsrud told us a short-short story which he calls "Two Kirven Men Talking." This story needs an effort to approximate sound effects, which will be all but impossible.

The scene is a routine afternoon visit at someone's home. The women set out sweet tea and cookies. Two Kirven men place themselves comfortably across the parlor from each other, one on a well-stuffed couch and the other on a brocade chair.

The first Kirven man, on the couch, starts conversing in a deep rumble. He says, *"Frumlaroom bafrumla HUMla froomcrumpha phoom."* At least that's what it sounds like to Dave. It feels like a calm, meditative, inscrutable observation in a deep bass voice highly inflected with a South Carolina low-country accent. The Kirven man may as well be speaking Entish (as Tolkien would say) without the benefit of translation.

The second Kirven man, though, seems to understand his relative's statement perfectly well. From his decorated chair across the room, he responds amiably, *"Phroombla rumma HUMham rommacrum O!"* and then gulps his sweet tea. More deep bass. The men are tuning to each other in their lower registers.

Leaning on the doorjamb, Dave cannot make out a single word. Why can't these people open their mouths when they talk? Don't they need explanations? *Pardon me, could you repeat that?*

Yet the Kirven men recognize every companionable syllable, or they seem to. They reach an understanding that deepens with every throat-clearing rumble.

After a decent visiting while, the two Kirven men are absolutely satisfied.

They are full of sweet tea, cookies, and maybe each others' well-considered views. Dave remains unenlightened. He seems not to have had Kirven security clearance.

****

Is it different for Kirven women? Could be. My first talk ever with my cousin Winkie, whom I had never met, was in 2006. I was sixty-four years old, and she was older. Our chat was the polar opposite of David Onsrud's portrayal of Kirven men. We chatted at lightning speed. Cheery.

We found Winkie in the Still Hope assisted-living center in Columbia. My husband Richard and I threaded the labyrinth of halls to Winkie's apartment.

Cries of love and family feeling and instant friendship! Open-armed Winkie was an image of me. We looked as alike as our baby pictures had. We chattered on and interrupted each other, with no mention of the conflicts within either of our families. We were determined right away to "let sleeping dogs lie" wherever they happened to be. We talked up a storm, a *fast* storm.

Winkie took up her walker and led us to the cafeteria. She sprinted. She boosted herself along on that thing like it was a crutch with springs. My husband Richard and I hurried to open doors for her, but she beat us to them. We were wired up, straining to get beside her in case she fell. We were *quite a sight,* as the family saying goes.

Over lunch, Winkie and I hopped around some tough topics. She told me how she had become Strom Thurmond's first secretary in Washington. One day, he had called the University of South Carolina and asked for their brightest girl, and they had called Winkie to the phone! We chortled together over this wild chance.

Our laughter sailed straight over racial issues, and way past anecdotes about her father's temper. The cafeteria servers looked on, deeming us harmless.

"Did you agree with Strom's political views?" I asked.

"Oh, the newspapers *pestered* me to tell them what Strom thought. I learned to keep my mouth shut."

"Do you agree with those views now, today?"

"I've learned to keep my political opinions to myself." Winkie cackled when she said this. Fair enough. I wasn't going to pipe up with my political views, either. Not that there was time. We were in high gear.

"What about your father?" I served up this question to Winkie.

"He agreed with everything Strom said. My father told everybody, *"I like colored people. I love colored people. But I don't want anyone over there at the damned NAACP shoving colored people down my throat."*

I had heard that one before. Time to speed on. I echoed a familiar soft-serve opinion: "He wanted to relate to blacks one-on-one!" A useful notion for blurring controversy.

"That's right. And so do I." She put that one to rest.

Winkie had a family reputation of speaking her mind. I didn't poke. We drank in each other's babbling words while we downed our chicken salad and potato chips and imbibed our drinks. I poured an experience or two of mine into our talk-stream.

Over the key lime pie, Winkie held me with her glittering eye.

"I think we're both brainy," she concluded.

Yes, I felt that Winkie and I had glommed onto each other just like kin. We were supposedly brainy, speedy women, riding a cool river above inflammable topics, as we had both been "brought up" to do. Ha!

Whenever Winkie pulled us back into family stories, I jotted down a few notes for this memoir. Then we all rushed back to her apartment, jiggety jog, in the slipstream of her walker. We were a silent film.

"Stay the night," Winkie invited me, "and I'll take you down memory lane." She showed me her guest room, packed with memorabilia of her children and their children, next to a bed trimmed in eyelet cotton.

If I had stayed, Winkie and I just might have talked ourselves silly enough to slip into more perilous family topics, memories and feelings that people could whisper but would never repeat in ordinary conversation—what one cousin of mine calls "graveyard talk."

Yet I could not stay. Eighteen months later Winkie died, on Christmas Eve of 2007. Her sister Anne called me that night.

I've dreamed of chasing Winkie down the hall of old age.

"Winkie, wait for me! Let's really *talk* this time."

Danny and the Two Mules and the Hat

This story comes from my cousin, Diane Williams Yamamoto.

My cousin Danny was about eight years older than me. As I knew him, he was a good-tempered soul with a big laugh, wishful eyes, and an untamed black curl down his forehead. His face was often canted to one side, as if he saw the world from an angle invisible to others. He was a natural at making peace.

"Danny was a good and kind person," my cousin Diane said to me a few summers ago, in the living room of her North Carolina apartment. Like her mother Ansie, Diane has a flair for elegance. Her selective paintings, tapestries, and decorative lights create a soothing enclave of blues and purples in her home. She often chooses pieces from South America—especially Bolivia, the birthplace of her husband, Willy Yamamoto, who is every bit as good and kind as Danny was, and more.

Here is the story Diane tells from a time when she was nine and Danny was twelve. These are her words:

Every year at Christmas time, Mama and Perry and I left Fairmont just after breakfast on our Christmas journey, first to Mullins to "have the Christmas tree" (exchange gifts) with my Williams kin and eat an elegant Christmas dinner at my grandparents' table. Perry and I were anxious to continue the trip on to Sumter, The Farm, and the unusual freedom that we always experienced there: always many cousins, always adventure, always fun. I must have been nine or so. I was still a child with a gifted imagination who longed for freedom. I really wanted to be a cowboy. I had learned to ride the mules bareback but still fell or was bounced off from time to time.

Colt was a short-legged mule and my preferred mount, not as far from his back to the hard-packed earth as it was from the back of Ida, a mule whose long legs made her a foot taller than Colt. Danny agreed to ride with me through the pastures and fields and down through the edge of the swamp, where the shallow, almost-still stream had a thin skim of ice covering it. We were both bundled against the unusual South Carolina Christmas freeze. I was wearing a little hand-knitted tam[8] that my friend Margaret White had given me for Christmas. The mules were in a wicked mood, anxious to get back to the warm barn, and not happy to take two kids on a recreational ride. Danny and I both thought it would be fun to ride through the icy stream in true Old-West style. The mules did not think it would be fun, but with a few hard kicks

---

[8] *A "tam o'shanter" is a Scottish cap named after the character in a Robert Burns poem*

in the ribs, and a slap with a switch pulled from a bush, Colt and Ida plunged into the black water and hurried to the far bank.

Colt's charge through the water led me under a tree limb, which caught my tam and lifted it to dangle over the water. Danny on Ida crossed a little upstream away from the trees. I raised a loud protest that we had to retrieve my dear and valuable hat, that I would be punished within an inch of my life if we arrived back at the house without this irreplaceable, handmade hat. Danny agreed, after much convincing, to retrieve the tam. Ida did not agree. One trip through the icy stream was more than enough for her. Danny picked up a stout stick and began to whack the mule on the rump. After about ten stinging blows, long-legged Ida plunged into the water and ran to the opposite bank, passing directly beneath the limb that had stolen my hat. The limb caught Danny at chest level and scraped him off into the black, icy swamp water. Danny held the now-black tam in his hand. He was sputtering, cold, and mad as a wet hen.

Cathy and the Oyster

People can be cajoled into peace.

Once upon a time Maisie decided that her daughter Cathy should be made to expand her tastes.

Cathy ate meats and carbs and desserts as a child, but no vegetables. We both rejected weird or *squishy* foods—such as the eggplant casserole or cheese soufflé over which Mama once labored and before which we had to sit until we ate some, waiting until Mama, seeing only three of four bites gone, retracted her dictum. In fact, we never ate a morsel of those suspicious dishes. We slipped "bites" of them onto the wooden mini-shelves that came under the dining table as a handy resting place.

Mama was getting her focus onto Cathy's palate while I was at college. So I'm telling this story as Cathy told it to me.

Oysters were the delicacy Mama chose for training Cathy to be a gourmet and a lady, for one implied the other, and Mama longed for Cathy to be poised and serene in all social dining situations. Daddy was the implement Mama used, for he was naturally high-class and had a talent for inveighing.

The three of them sat at the dining table before a plate of gently cooked oysters, the kind you find in oyster stew.

Daddy stepped into his peacemaker costume, to please Mama.

"Cathy," said Daddy, "If you'll eat just one oyster, I'll buy you an ice cream cone." Ice cream was Daddy's favorite dessert.

"Nope," said Cathy. Or perhaps it was "No, sir," back then.

"Two ice cream cones?"

"Nope."

"Three?"

Cathy sat at the dining table with her arms folded. Daddy kept ratcheting up the number of ice cream cones. He could have been conducting an experiment on persuading children without force. Or maybe he was just amusing himself.

I can imagine Mama taking breaks for venting in the next room, stage-whispering her outbursts. *Bill! For heaven's sake!*

Daddy kept his calm attention on Cathy.

Finally he said, "How about fifty-three ice cream cones?"

"I'll do it!"

Cathy grabbed an oyster, reached it back into her throat, and let it slide down without touching her tongue. Then she rinsed her mouth with water. Home free.

Cathy collected all fifty-three ice cream cones, one occasion at a time.

Cathy loves this story. It demonstrates who she is.

A Squirt in the Hair

"Those Kirven boys!" wailed the high-school teachers in Sumter. "They ride to school on their cows!"

Was this true? Could you do that to a cow?

When I traced this tale down to *who* and *where*, I arrived at my five uncles: Tom, Lawrence, Donnie, Coit, and Marion. The time would have been way back in the 1910s to 1920s.

Yessiree, my relatives told me, those big boys would ride their cows to school in the morning after milking and back in the afternoon before milking. School was right up there beside Highway 76, just a hop and a skip away.

The teachers would flutter and sputter about what rules were getting messed with, as the story goes. And anyway, how *could* you expect to keep those Kirvens from causing a ruckus? And now that they were *at* the school and *with* the cows, you couldn't exactly send them on a slow cow ride all the way home, could you? That would be a waste of learning time. Well then, all right, the school could spare a little grass for those cows to graze on.

So anytime there was a recess, which was every so often, those Kirven boys would invite all the girls to come and meet those cows—especially the girls they might be sweet on. They would encourage the girls to lean on down, now, and take a look at how that milking was done. Then you could bet that *one* of those boys, and you never knew *which* one, would squirt some ooshy milk right up into some girl's hair. A different girl every time.

That girl would squeal in a way that was mighty satisfying to all the boys.

What could any teacher ever do about that? Just be ready with a little towel and say, "Well, *sweetie?* Just don't stand so close to the cow!"

Ridin' Around Town

Ida Dick was a nice lady who was related somehow to the Frasers.

Mama's full name at birth, she always claimed, was Mary Adelaide Muriel Delorme Kirven. "I was the last, so they gave me all the names they hadn't used up yet," Mama said to me. My trying-to-be-careful research told me, though, that Mama had all by herself substituted the name "Muriel" for the name "Dick" which she had actually been given as her third first name at birth. That was because Mama never, ever wanted to get within two miles of anything like a bawdy joke. She even had some serious objection to describing a happy person as "bright-eyed and bushy-tailed." She thought that was rude. Who knew?

Anyway, Ida Dick was a beloved and eccentric figure in the town. She rode her bicycle everywhere in all kinds of weather. On chilly days in Sumter, you could usually spot Ida Dick pedaling downtown on her bicycle, wearing a fur coat that actually draped over her wheels without catching any spokes.

On the day of her marriage, Ida Dick and her chosen beloved were apparently of the same mind about bicycles. They were scheduled to appear before the Justice of the Peace at the courthouse, but it was raining. So they just cycled to the courthouse in their raincoats while they held up their umbrellas one-handed. They looked as happy as they could be.

Buzz, Buzz

Cousin Beau's first year of higher education was noisy. During class, at dinner, in assembly, or any old time, the women of Coker College would hear the gathering roar of an engine, and they would need to rush to the windows. zzzzzzOWWWW!

This was in the 1940s, right after the War, and an airplane was buzzing the college! The women were thrilled in a scary way and scared in a thrilling way.

"Who is it? Who IS it?" They clamored.

The plane seemed to scorch the dormitory roof on its way past, so close did it skim by.

Who was it? That would be the daring and expert aviator Robert Johnson, Beau's beau.[9]

Who could resist such a mischievous and red-blooded courtship? Soon, Beau eloped with Bob. She would get married and see the world.

Beau's parents, Coit and Doll, were bewildered. How could her daughter interrupt her education, just like that? Was she in her right mind?

Yes, indeed.

Beau sums it up neatly. "They thought I wasn't independent," she says. "But I *knew* I *was*."

So Beau and Bob each hit the bull's eye in finding a life partner. Buzzing, soaring, traveling, shooting—and all the while they stood by each other. Photos of Beau and Bob usually show them leaning into each other.

Bo and Bob at their home in Columbia, c. 2009

Pink Ladies

Ansie Kirven Williams was a stylish and self-possessed aunt who could be either stern or gentle. She might have had a soft spot for me, thank goodness, because I didn't ever want to go up against her hard side.

---

[9] *Robert Johnson was a 2nd Lieutenant in the Army Air Corps, which became the United States Air Force. He went on to fly fighter jets for forty years. He soloed in a Steerman (open cockpit) and flew all the important fighter jets including the F-16. He earned the Order of the Palmetto, South Carolina's highest award. When he retired, he was a Brigadier General.*

She was strict with her children, Diane and Perry. Diane describes her mother's no-nonsense facial expression as *severe, severe, severe,* and *stern, stern, stern.* Ansie believed in following the rules, working before play, and behaving in a dignified manner. As the owner of *The Town and Country Shop* which sold ladies' outfits, she knew she had to be a mighty good example of decorum and self-containment.

Ansie had another persona, though. She could let loose and enjoy herself. At sixteen, she writes her mama from Hi-Y camp that she needs a dollar *immediately* because "a hundred dollars won't do me any good *now* if it gets here too late." Then she writes about "something more pleasant," meaning the pranks at camp:

> The camp is just like a big family. But the *family* was certainly in an uproar last night. They had a dumping spree upstairs, and some of us . . . from downstairs stayed up to see the fun. One girl especially, we wanted to dump so we stayed up until about 2 o'clock waiting our chance when we decided at last that she was asleep and crept into the room where she was. She sat up like she had springs in her legs and called out in a gruff voice, "*I* know what you came in here for. Get out!!!!" So as she was rather big (weighed about 200) we obeyed. You should have seen us creeping downstairs and sneaking back into our room.

This is the Ansie who would take her pre-teen grandchildren for a ride and then hit the accelerator when they urged, "Faster, Nana, Faster!"

This is also the fun-loving Ansie who brought me along to New York City for my first time on a wholesale-clothes-buying trip when I was fourteen years old and treated me to my first full lobster dinner. Strangely fearless, Ansie would even attend Broadway plays and visit restaurants. Sometimes her good friend Jessie Fisher, the mother of her son Perry's best friend Gerald, would come with her, and they would take in the sights together.

During some of these years, my cousin Laura Ann lived on Long Island, where Ansie and Jessie could visit her. Once the three of them dined together at an inviting restaurant on the way from New York City to Long Island.

And so it happened that Laura Ann was able to stun her younger cousin Perry, with her up-to-the-minute news about his mother, by mentioning that Ansie and Jessie had each ordered a "pink lady" at dinner when they were in that Long Island restaurant.

"I didn't even know then what a pink lady *was!*" Perry still exclaims.

Laura Ann had to explain slowly to Perry that a pink lady was, in plain fact, an alcoholic drink. How to comprehend this? *"My own mother!"* Perry could not imagine his mother ordering a *drink*. And in *public*.

Wikipedia tells us that a pink lady is made with Plymouth gin.

> A pink lady is a classic gin-based cocktail with a long history. The egg-whites and cream mix create a foam that floats on top of the drink, giving it a unique texture. The Pink Lady is traditionally a very feminine drink choice, colloquially known as a "girly drink" The pink lady may have appealed to women who did not have much experience with alcohol. Ironically, the Pink Lady is very dry by today's standards, with its gin base and slight grenadine flavoring lacking the extreme fruit flavor or sweetness that modern drinkers associate with girly drinks.

Ansie and Jessie, unlike Perry, had no trouble whatsoever imagining that they could order a pink lady.

Many years later, trying to figure out how his mother had ever become an imbiber of cocktails, Perry related to me a Christmas Day scene when he and Gerald were presented with their first bicycles. It was a big deal. Earning a Christmas bicycle took an eternity of mowing lawns, and now their labor had paid off.

When Perry and Gerald were about twelve, in the late 1940s, Jessie Fisher and her husband Willis came over to Ansie's house for Christmas Day. The three adults had secretly stored two bicycles near Ansie's garage in a separate building called the "cook house," which was a throwback to slavery days and their aftermath. No cooks had lived there for a long time.

Early Christmas morning, in a ceremonial display, Ansie and Jessie and Willis marched out to the cook house—stayed there for sort of a long while—and then returned down the driveway, steering two new bicycles by the handlebars.

Ah, Christmas Joy! Merry Christmas, Perry and Gerald!

Ansie, Jessie, and Willis seemed even happier than the two boys. They were giggling.

Somehow, it took several more trips to the cook house for the grownups to complete the delivery of those bicycles, and each trip took all three of the grownups. They got bicycle parts. Printed directions for gears. Bells. A tire pump. Spare parts. More spare parts.

Each trip was funnier to the three adults. They giggled more.

What was so attractive about that cook house to those three adults?

After Perry was told about the Pink Ladies, he finally had a clue.

It's Your Father Speaking

Marion and Mabel's three daughters supplied Marion with a woman-filled house. According to their cousin Beau, however, Marion had wanted a son.

In response to unspoken wishes, daughters can step up and act like sons. Beau knew about that, being a crack shot and riding in an F-104 Star Fighter.

Even so, women will talk like women—interrupting each other continually and multi-listening. Simultaneous conversations in one room.

Uncle Marion may have cracked beneath woman-talk. He pushed back one day when Mabel and his three daughters were spending the afternoon at home. They were discussing this and that, all of them talking at once, so that Marion would probably have needed to cover his ears.

Suddenly the phone would ring.

One of the four women would answer.

The caller would be Marion. Unnoticed, he would have slipped out of the house, marched to the pay phone on the corner, and dialed his own number.

Anne, for example, might pick up the phone. "Hello, Kirven residence."

"Let me speak to my *wife!*" It would be Marion's voice, mock-indignant.

"Daddy? Is that you, Daddy?"

"*Yes. It's your father speaking. Put your mother on the phone.*"

"Where did you go, Daddy? We thought you were here with *us*," Anne would wonder.

"Well, when I was there, I couldn't get a blankety-blank word in edgewise, now could I?"

Marion would snort out of the corner of his mouth, in his Groucho Marx voice. "*Put the damn phone in your mother's hand!*"

Mabel would pretend calm. "Where are you, dear? What's the matter?"

"I'll *tell* you what the matter is! If I want to be heard . . . "

It wasn't always easy to tell whether Marion was furious or just kidding.

Your father is an alien menace, or he's one of the family. Guess which, ho ho.

Sometimes, Marion would just stomp downtown to Western Union and send the women a telegram.

Sorry! Sorry!

Larry was good at killing snakes. When he was seventeen years old, he and H. P. Stokes were in Rocky Bluff Swamp one morning when they spotted a yellow-brown snake, semi-coiled, climbing over a log toward them. Larry grabbed his .22 rifle and shot the snake through the head. They brought the carcass into town and measured it. Sixty-one and a half inches long, thicker than a man's arm, about eight pounds, and fifteen rattles. Larry celebrated his good aim and narrow escape.

In his daily rounds, Larry would be on the lookout for dangerous snakes to dispatch. When he drove by a venomous snake on the road, he'd often get out of the truck and whack its head off with a hoe blade. Or he'd grab the snake by the tail and fling its head two or three times against a nearby post, and then throw the snake carcass into the trunk.

One night in his high-school years, Larry had a date. Worried about being late, he planned to pick up his lovely girlfriend first, then make a little stop for refreshments on the way to the drive-in movie. Larry was a courteous guy. He told the girl to relax in the car while he went into the store for sodas and candy.

Meanwhile, there was a snake corpse in the trunk waking up from its afternoon blow on the head. Decidedly not dead, it squeezed through the crack in the back seat and slithered over to the driver's door and up the side. The steering wheel was the perfect plaything for it to wind itself around.

Yes, the snake appeared beside the steering wheel. Girl and snake met face to face.

Screams. Howls of rage. Door slammed. More screams, with furious words.

Larry had the sodas in his hand but a furious girlfriend in his face.

She wasn't hurt, but it was a long time before she spoke to Larry again.

Special Letter for Tom

Dread of social disgrace—now there's danger for you! Chills the blood.

When Grandfather Tom was sixteen, he got a scholarship for a business course at the Commercial College of Kentucky University. There he studied law, business customs, mercantile correspondence, bookkeeping, and mathematics—and he earned the right to talk to their faculty in the future. He might have been preparing to manage a farm—if he could just find a way to purchase the land. He would have finished his business course in the late 1880s, and his first letter to Laura was in 1892. That means there were four or five years in between when he could socialize as a single man.

Eckard Lee told me this story.

At one time during his bachelor years, Tom lived in a cabin with his brothers, who would become the Great Uncles Jim and Bob. They may have found work southeast from their father's farm in Dovesville, maybe earning enough to buy their own farms one of these days. Tom and Jim and Bob were all working, but they had their nights to themselves.

Tom's social life began to annoy Jim and Bob. He was coming and going every hour of the night—into the cabin, out of the cabin, always "visitin' people," so that Jim and Bob could get no peace.

Tom had excess energy, it seemed. Jim and Bob thought they'd play a prank to slow him down.

So Jim and Bob forged a letter to Tom. It was a joint and painstaking process, written in what those two imagined was a *feminine* handwriting, round and flowery, using a fancy *feminine* prose style. They wanted it to appear that it was written by a certain young lady that Tom had been seeing while he was socializing with many ladies and "runnin' around at night," all of which annoyed the devil out of Jim and Bob.

One particular woman swooned over Tom, as Jim and Bob had been told, but the two had never exchanged letters. Now here was a chance for Jim and Bob to employ their fertile wits. After they had finished their creation, they folded the letter, sealed the envelope, addressed it to Tom, and added the lady's return address in the corner. They were especially proud of their official-looking stamp.

Jim and Bob were pretending to nap in their bunks when they heard Tom unfold the letter.

In the silence, they imagined Tom reading this supposed lady's sugary compliments (written by Jim and Bob), praising him for his blue eyes and manly deportment, and bestowing upon him her admiration and deep regard. Jim and Bob had taken care to make this lady seem just a bit more eager than ladies usually were in those days.

Tom was emitting little yelps. Jim and Bob kept their eyes closed and tried to silence their chuckles. They knew Tom was reading about the lady's overwhelming pleasure and honor that she and Tom were of the same mind, and that Tom was noticing her suggestion that together she and Tom could easily formalize their engagement during next week's visit, in the company of her Papá.

Tom cried out, "Oh, my good Lord!"

Ah! Tom must now be reading about how *gratified* the lady was that Tom's words had left no doubt of his intentions. How greatly it was her privilege to comply with his wishes. And how extremely pleased she would be to spend her entire life endeavoring to make him happy.

"No, no, no! Jim! Bob! Wake up! I got trouble!"

Jim and Bob rubbed their sleepy eyes. They saw that Tom's face was buried inside his large and sweaty palms.

What's that, brother? Oh yeah, give that letter here. Uh hmm, uh *hmmm!* With all the socializing you do, brother Tom, maybe you find it hard to recall what you tell *this* lady, what you tell *that* lady? Women sure can jump to conclusions. Too bad. And what is this card here?

It was the lady's list of instructions on *How to talk to Papá*. Oh my gracious, said Jim and Bob while they each kept a straight face, we got to put our heads together and get you out of this mess.

Well, Tom surely did look like he was too scared to go visitin' on *that* night. This lady's Papa would probably denounce him to every other Papa in the country. There was no way out.

Tom stewed for hours, searching for words that might soften that lady's rage when he explained . . . . But Jim and Bob just shook their heads. Yes, by heaven, the whole business was a doggone shame. Let's think on it some more during tomorrow's workday.

That night, when Tom was finally asleep and snoring, Jim and Bob lay awake congratulating each other on their lady-handwriting, their lady-sweetness, and their list of Papá-instructions. In the middle of their glee, Tom sprung up from his bed. He had heard every word.

So how did Tom feel about this trick his brothers had played on him? My cousin Larry, who looks a lot like Grandfather Tom, is especially fond of the saying, *If I spit on the grass, it would catch fire!*

So did this side-busting prank scare Tom away from all of his visitin' people and runnin' around at night? The story just doesn't tell us.

Up a Tree

In the 1950s in Winston-Salem, North Carolina, a ten-year-old could still walk on suburban streets, alone, without adults panicking that she might be abducted by some dangerous reprobate.

So I walked in our suburb regularly. My friends and I lived on parallel streets named for trees in the pastoral world. My usual walking trek reached across lawns, from Sylvan Road to Roslyn Road to Arbor Road to Oaklawn Avenue. Or I might stroll down Spring Garden, the road that crossed all others like the tops of two Greek *pi's* side to side.

Marjorie Randolph lived on Oaklawn Avenue, the last parallel road. In our church choir, I stood next to Marjorie and admired her strong voice and lively opinions. Her father was a psychiatrist who didn't want children to feel too much blame. Once when I threw up during a sleepover at Marjorie's house and began my frantic apologies, Angus Randolph was nice enough to shush me.

"You don't need to be sorry," he said in his merciful voice.

One Saturday afternoon I set out toward Marjorie's on a lark, without phoning first. She'd probably be at home, and if not, it was a good day for a walk.

I sauntered up Sylvan Road to Spring Garden, then crossed each street in turn: Roslyn, Arbor, Oaklawn. I turned right on Oaklawn, where Marjorie lived in the tenth house down. When I'd walked past a couple of houses, I spotted three bulldogs jumping about in the next yard. Too late to turn back now.

A bulldog's face was my definition of a fighting face. Squeezed-up, pugnacious, and about-to-bite. The three of them trotted up to me, growling.

No one was visible in the bulldog yard. I scanned the street. It was a peaceful, idyllic, abandoned street. Those bulldogs could outrun me to Marjorie's house, and besides, the Randolphs might not be at home.

I did what I had read about in so many storybooks. I climbed up a small pear tree in the yard. That tree was neither thick nor tall, and my legs dangled a few feet above three sets of bulldog teeth. The dogs sat beneath me and thumped their tails. I discovered that if I shifted my weight, even a little, the tree would flex toward the ground in a comely pastoral arc. I stayed very still.

So I was treed. I was a little abashed, but stubborn. I'd wait as long as the dogs could.

I knew how this story ended. The animal in the tree always won.

The occasional car passed and ignored our vignette. It must have looked like a silly game to adults going somewhere, and if I waved at them too vigorously, the tree would bend. The bulldogs and I studied each other. An hour or so passed by.

At last a car pulled into the driveway. Rescue! It was the owner of the house, back from the store. He apologized all over the place. He shooed the dogs away, invited me into his living room for a chocolate cream, and then sent me along home with a whole box of those sweets.

Was I ever proud of my shrewd escape, my patience, and my reward!

Mama hollered at me, "Why did you go into the house of a strange man and eat whatever candy he gave you? What have I told you?"

Despite my common-sense explanations, I was now up another kind of tree. My victory faded to defeat. Eventually, Mama had a little phone conversation with Mr. Bulldog Owner, and afterwards it was *Hmmph. Even so.*

Chocolate creams have been my favorite candy ever since.

Fumes of the Patriarchy

This is a story by David Onsrud.

Aunt Grace was a likeable, pleasant, and generous person. She kept herself busy and enjoyed conversing with everyone.

Her husband, Uncle Julian, the son of Eugene E. ("Hugh") Kirven, was a quiet person who took in everything happening around him without saying much. Whenever he listened to people while they talked, I would get the feeling that he was analyzing the talker, weighing within himself the credibility of what was being said. Without question, he had the Kirven temperament, often referred to as a "short fuse." He was the undisputed ruler of the home, very seldom questioned. I don't recall ever seeing him smile. He had the seriousness of the engineer who was carrying a lot of responsibility. His conversations were short, his statements to the point. He was an alumnus of Clemson, a civil engineer, who supervised many Darlington Highway projects. He would keep workday events separate from his home life.

Once at supper, Uncle Julian stated in his pointed style that some *woman* had run into the rear of the macadam truck while it was spreading the blacktop, driving her car well into the hot asphalt. That was it, no further comment. He did not answer his wife Grace's questions about the incident. Nor did Aunt Grace ever speak up and explain to Uncle Julian that the crack-crack-crack of his ice cubes, when he stirred his iced tea, irritated the heck out of her. She kept it all in.

One evening in the 1940s, Aunt Grace planned to drive to the store.

The car, a 1938 green Chevy, was parked at the curb. Grace left the house but at once returned to tell Uncle Julian that the car wouldn't start, probably a dead battery.

At the curb, Julian cranked the Chevy without success. Then he instructed Aunt Grace to get in the car and let him push-start it with the pickup truck. He positioned the pickup behind the Chevy, reached into the car window where Aunt Grace was sitting, set the choke and throttle, put the shift lever in second gear, and turned the ignition switch to "on." He told Aunt Grace to depress the clutch pedal while he pushed her with the truck, then let the clutch out when he blew the horn. The car should start. Aunt Grace understood and was ready.

For many years Aunt Grace would talk about the event that followed, nervously but humorously reliving the experience each time.

Uncle Julian climbed into the pickup, eased up to the rear bumper of the car, and began to push. Aunt Grace steered from the curb into the street, and Uncle Julian pushed up to a good speed. Then he blew the horn.

Aunt Grace let out the clutch, and the engine started. The car jerked. Aunt Grace gripped the wheel tightly as she drove to the end of the block, made a high-speed left turn onto the short side street, continued without slowing to the next corner, made another high-speed left, then executed speedy left turns No. 3 and 4. This maneuver put her back on Sanders Street, where she had started.

She was amazed to see Uncle Julian standing in front of their house, next to his truck. She stopped, held on to the wheel, and stared straight ahead.

Through all four high-speed turns she had imagined—she was sure she had felt—Uncle Julian still behind her, still pushing. She had feared he was in one of his temperamental moods, but she asked no questions.

Hmmm. Why? She could now see that her husband Julian had indeed not been behind her and pushing her, after all.

So was she now waiting for her husband's official permission? Perhaps waiting for him to say, *Go right ahead and drive to the store now, Wife dear?*

Why, Indeed?

The first Kirven prank that I put up with? It turned sour to me in an instant.

It was summer. I was visiting Fairmont. One afternoon—unannounced—a grown man and a boy walked through the front door and stood expectantly on the hall rug. They seemed to be in high spirits. The man was large and loose-limbed, with a grin suggesting that everything in the whole world was a hilarious joke.

I called Ansie. Unperturbed, she walked over to greet them and introduced me.

"Mariann, this is your Uncle Lawrence."

I had not yet met the boy, who may have been Larry, because I had not yet become acquainted with The Farm. Anyway, I felt that the adult guy—Lawrence—was taking up all the oxygen in the room.

They were paying Ansie a spontaneous visit from Sumter, and the man's goofy smile told me that he was quite pleased to be surprising us.

Standing there in my childhood, I thought, *Time to be polite.* I stuck out my hand to this man, Lawrence, and began, "Pleased to . . ."

The guy snatched my hand by my thin wrist and flapped my hand back and forth close to my nose, so that my fingers hit my face, rat-a-tat-a-tat.

He had a question for me: "Why ya hittin' yourself, huh, huh, why ya hittin' yourself?"

I jerked away and stared at him. Who was this person, anyway?

It was great fun, you see. I *seemed* to be hitting myself, but in fact *he* was rat-tat-tatting on *my* face. Ho, ho, ho!

Ansie had him apologize. *It was just a joke, honey, you didn't mind, did you?*

This encounter proved to be a sort of initiation for me. In later years, I would sometimes be tricked by some relative or other into "hittin' myself." Or some family member would sneak up behind me and cover my eyes and stay mum, which was the signal for "Guess who?"

Or we'd all play "The Bears are Coming Tonight," where a bunch of us sang as we skipped around the house in the nightmare darkness, until the secretly designated "bear" would emerge, snarling, from behind some bush or tree, and everyone would be scared out of their freaking minds.

Jokes like these never took hold with me. I didn't much like scaring people.

He Had a Beard

Our family's local homegrown horror story, "The Mongoli," may also have come from Sumter. Diane shared this story with me long before I would be a Girl Scout who would gather around the campfire to hear about The Claw.

Diane said that this story began on a road near The Farm. That made it sound far away and exotic to me. For years, I did not know exactly how a person reached The Farm, or how distant it was.

It was one evening on some road near The Farm, Diane said, that some of our cousins were walking home when they heard a noise up yonder, right next to the side of the road. Was it an animal, maybe, trapped or wounded? They kept following the sound.

When they came nearer, they heard groans coming from a drainage ditch. They craned their heads and peered *way, way* down the ditch, maybe six feet down.

It was no animal. It was . . . *a man!*

And oh, my Lord in Heaven! That man's stomach had been *eaten out!*

His whole stomach! *Eaten!* That man was barely alive!

And that poor man was trying to speak to them! Our cousins leaned way over, twisting themselves into that ditch, actually brushing against that man's tooth-marked stomach itself, until they could hear his weak and scratchy voice, and he could say only one thing:

He had . . . a . . . beard! He . . . had . . . a . . . beard!!

Diane would lean over me with stretched eyes and hands like talons.

He had a beard!

"Aiieeeeee!" I would shriek, rolling over onto the bed to protect my own stomach. I would go stiff.

Diane would continue, *They found out that creature who ate out the man's stomach was called . . . a Mongoli!"*

My wails would bring in the adults. "What in the world? Children?"

Then we got to some questions without answers. What did a Mongoli look like, exactly? Did Mongolis live near Fairmont, too, maybe in the woods?

"Tell it to me again," I would beg Diane, and sometimes Perry as well. "Again."

I wanted to test myself to see whether I could be brave the next time. Yet the next time, that story was just as excruciating. It was terrifying. It was addictive. The whole stomach!

One time, Diane and Perry hunted down a picture of a mandrill, which is a rather frightening relative of the baboon, except with red and blue marks on its face and a red butt beneath its tail.

That picture wasn't nearly as spine-chilling as the story.

What He Offered

Here's a story that might be about whites' supposed fear of blacks, or it might be about Southern whites' excess of politeness. Both or either. Or neither.

Sometime after her children had grown to school age in the 1970s, Diane began selling Avon beauty products door-to-door in the Raleigh-Durham area. As the Avon Lady, Diane rang doorbells in suburban and urban neighborhoods. Those answering the bell were not always friendly, sober, or even sane.

"I don't think I was exactly naïve back then," Diane says in retrospect. "But I do admit to being optimistic."

One day, Diane the Avon Lady was admitted to an apartment in downtown Durham by a short, thick, middle-aged black man with an irritable expression and a volume of dark hair. He motioned her to a chair near the door and placed himself across the room on a couch.

Diane is a petite woman with large, sympathetic eyes. Her voice is mellifluous. As she sat in the designated chair and delivered her optimistic speech for Avon products, the man's frown grew deeper. He stared at the floor.

Finally he erupted. "You're like my wife!" It was not a compliment but an accusation.

Diane shifted in her chair and continued her Avon speech more softly.

Before long, the man hissed, "Bitch!" as if to himself.

Diane rose from her chair, hesitating. She clutched her Avon bag.

"Bitch!" snarled the hulking prospective customer. And then, louder, "I'm going to kill you!" His raised eyes were glassy, perhaps seeing mainly his own rage.

When he lunged off the couch toward Diane, she darted through the apartment door and slammed out the main door to the street and then tore down the sidewalk as fast as her feet would take her.

"Did he run after you?" I asked her.

"I didn't turn my head," Diane replied. Then she mentioned, "He had offered to kill me."

After that incident, Diane tuned up her strategies. When she came to a new address, she rang the bell and took a good two steps away from the door. Then she chatted with the resident for a while before entering the proffered room. And she always scoped out the exit route.

Later, at a dinner party in Raleigh, Diane told this story in a matter-of-fact way, without any screaming or waving of hands.

Some Northerners were among the guests, because by this time North Carolina had become a popular place for retirement. Good prices, great food, *gracious* people.

When Diane reached the part about the short-thick-angry-black guy offering to kill her, the guests from the North fairly shouted with delight.

"Oh, you Southerners!" they chortled. "Such good manners! What a delicate way to say it, that he *offered to kill you*. You people are a riot. We'd be swearing up a storm."

That is how Diane's story of near-death for Avon's sake has become a story of Northerners chuckling about "soft" Southerners.

"The man was ready to kill me," Diane says. "What's so *soft* about that?"

Uncle John and the Refrigerator

Great-Uncle John King Kirven was the fourth of nine brothers, all sons of Erasmus Goodson Kirven. He was born in 1864, after Josh and Hugh and Jim, and before Bob and Tom and Luke and Joseph and Edward. I have no photograph of John. I have a photo of six other brothers posed together. And the huge 1911 photo does not include the brothers John, or Edward, or young Joseph, who died as a child.

Why no pictures? Family lore has it that John was not especially genial and did not seek out his brothers' company. Perhaps John thought that his brothers had treated him unfairly, so he decided to return the favor. A letter from Great-Uncle Hugh to his daughter seems to accuse John of outright stealing: "He took Edward's registered cow."

One relative told me that Great-Uncle John was inflexibly anti-Kirven. I can only guess what that may mean. John married Anna Blackwell, and they had only one child, a daughter named Emie. She became an attorney, and her career brought her wealth. She is said to have donated $100,000 to the University of South Carolina, yet not one cent to help any Kirvens.

Even so, John King Kirven was regarded by the Kirvens as family. And as family, he had an unspoken claim, resembling the code of hospitality to strangers in *The Odyssey*. John was also diabetic, which made him more needy. Later in life he had to wear a wooden leg. Diabetes had claimed half of the leg he was born with.

So it happened that John came to live with Tom and Eva's family at Eastover, for a while. John may have been cantankerous and mean, but he felt that he could cash in on his Family entitlement to room and board. Perhaps his daughter Emie was too busy as an attorney to take him in. No one remembers how long John stayed, but the family did not return from Eastover until 1944, the year that John died at the age of 80.

Emie would pull up in her car and let out Great-Uncle John, who would stump toward the Eastover house, muttering and cursing to himself all the way, as irascible as any pirate on the high seas. He would have been in his 70s by then—diabetic, pained by his leg, and not real happy to see more Kirvens.

During his stay, John was forever suspicious that these Kirvens were after his money. Once he accused Eva of taking some of his money to spend on a new dress. My cousin Laura Ann remembers that after that particular encounter, her father Tom simply asked John to leave. Did he? No one remembers. All in all, Laura Ann says, the family treated John well. There were no fights. It was more of a freeze-out between the Kirvens and the self-proclaimed anti-Kirven.

John would keep to his own room, generally, because he didn't want much to do with the family. He had one dietary requirement—a big dish of cold oatmeal every day. Eva would cook that oatmeal in the morning and put it in the refrigerator for John, all covered with waxed paper. Sometime during the day, John would hobble out from his room, remove the oatmeal from the refrigerator, and hobble back where he could eat his oatmeal in solitude and peace.

One afternoon the family heard John make his way to the refrigerator, open it, and then close it, and then thud back to his room and shut the door. Family members may have stayed right where they were, thinking, "I sure don't want to run into John at the refrigerator and have to try to talk to him."

In John's room, though, all hell broke loose. The family came running. John was spitting on the floor and yelling, with total disgust on his face. Little pale globules were scattered all around him.

So what was the trouble with John this time? Lord have mercy!

Well, John had gotten a bowl of fish roe from the refrigerator, by mistake. After all, fish roe does look somewhat like oatmeal—with a porridge consistency, a bit rough and a bit smooth.

John had carried that bowl to his room and dug in eagerly with his spoon.

I can imagine John bellowing, *Ugh! Ugh! What's wrong with these blankety-blank people and their blankety-blank food?*

He may have suspected that somebody was trying to poison him or pull off some prank. After all, he knew that he was living among Kirvens without being genuinely liked. Who *put* that fish roe into that refrigerator? Doggone it!

Flannery O'Connor might have said that John Kirven "learned his lesson" in this encounter, mild though that learning was.

Popping for Peace

Here is a win-win story about young black lives and young white lives. Both of which do matter, as we know.

Even Jung could probably not find any shadows in this story.

Racial conflict is one of the many issues involving schools these days—fights on buses, threats in the halls, regular screening for weapons. Some people worry about race-related violence.

Sumter's schools were integrated along with the others. My cousin Joe Chandler Kirven, a schoolteacher and later a school principal, dealt with racial issues during his entire career. In the Southern idiom, he declares that some of the finest teachers he has ever known were black.

In one elementary school where Joe was the principal, unrest among students would swell during the day, so that at the final bell, both black and white children would be fractious. Joe took note of this distress.

So he borrowed a big popcorn machine from one of the movie houses downtown and brought it to the school secretary's desk, right there next to the official Entrance and Exit doors. He taught a custodian how to run the machine. And right beside that popper, every school morning, Joe placed a hefty bag of un-popped kernels, and then he asked the custodian to please start that corn poppin' at about two o'clock in the afternoon.

Those smells of puffed-up corn and melted butter would waft through the school air, into halls and into classrooms, odors that got more delicious as 3:00 pm got closer.

When he tells this story, Joe brushes some imaginary popcorn-y fingers under his nose: *mmm—MMM!*

If you did not fight or yell or tease when you were leaving the school, you got a bag of popcorn. Otherwise, you didn't.

At the bell, Joe himself would be standing outside the school, next to the schoolbuses, waiting to give a popcorn bag to each of the many, many peaceful students.

He reports that by and large, those students just as quiet and peaceful as they could be.

Excerpts from Interviews with Relatives

Here I asked my relatives if they would like to be interviewed for this book. I didn't ask them specific questions. I simply encouraged them to talk about what was important to them.

Beau Kirven Johnson

When Beau tells me the story of Uncle Donnie, she expresses her conviction that love and pain are intertwined.

Donnie was the financial savior of the family who gave up a medical career for a job at Investors Syndicate to supervise investments for his siblings and their children. Many of my cousins' college costs were paid by Donnie, through his love for his family. Yet at the same time, for twenty-two years, Donnie was also in love with "the sweetest girlfriend," as Beau calls her, who was a teacher in Sumter. She was willing to marry him, but at last Donnie had to make a heartbreaking choice. Beau says that these were Donnie's thoughts: "I can't contribute anything to a marriage because I contribute to this family. I'm committed to this family for the rest of my life."

Mariann: It sounds like it was very important to you to be faithful to the people that needed taking care of.

Beau: "Always someone."

Beau's husband Bob is a retired Brigadier General with a distinguished military career. He was called overseas for some periods, and to Washington, D. C. for eight years. Bo traveled with him. Yet they chose as their home Columbia, South Carolina, which was close to Beau's parents in Sumter.

Beau: "We would not have left Mama and Daddy, because I was an only child, and that would have gone too far. It would have broken their hearts. Because when we did have to travel overseas, they were terribly lonesome for us and worried for us. But when we came back, Bob's job was at McIntire Air Force Base, closer to Columbia than it was to Sumter. And not only that, he had made friends with all the fellow pilots, and so all of his friends and our social activities were here, and yet we were still close enough if Mama and Daddy needed us, to go right back to them. And we went to see them very frequently, and every Christmas and Thanksgiving they either came to our house, or we went to their house. More often, they came to our house. And they were very comfortable with us living this close."

Over the years, Beau made several adventurous trips to New Mexico and Arizona with her daughter and best friend, Betsy. Her last trip was in 1976 with Bob, but there were also compelling reasons to be back in Columbia. By then Betsy was busy in Charlotte with her job, and Bobby—Beau's son—was close by and having difficulty with his marriage, and so Beau and Bob felt tied to Columbia.

Beau: "And then Daddy died when he was sixty-six years old, and my mother spent two years in Sumter, and after that, she was so lonesome she couldn't stand it any longer. So we tried to find her a house close to us, over here. And we found one right down the street. And she stayed in that for several years by herself and was quite happy there. And then when Bob had an opportunity to go to work in Washington on the Hill, and did some real good for the Guard, we moved to Washington. And Betsy—being Betsy—was so special, she took care of Mama. Moved in with her and married in Columbia."

So for a while, all the loved ones were being taken care of. Especially dear to Beau was her mother, Elizabeth Howard "Doll" Kirven, who was the model for Beau herself as a mother. "She never lifted a hand to me," says Beau.

Beau: "Then when we came home from Washington, D. C. [after eight years], Mama came to us and said, 'I can't stay with Betsy indefinitely, because Betsy has to have her own life, but I have decided that I don't want to stay by myself at my house. So I want to come down and stay with y'all.' Of course, we said yes, we'd love to have you. And from then on we've been here, until she died four years ago at Christmastime."

Beau wrote a substantial tribute to her mother, published in *The Sumter Item* on December 28, 2002. She writes, "Doll devoted her life to her family . . . She was 93 years old, and lived an active, healthy, almost charmed life . . . Doll lived to see all of her grandchildren and great-grandchildren. She was truly blessed, and they are truly blessed to have known her."

Not long after Beau's mother passed away, her daughter Betsy at fifty years old became fatally ill and succumbed in a few months. Once again, the fruit of love was agonizing pain. The process of dying collided with the closeness of love.

Beau: "We [Beau and Bob] didn't find out until less than three months before Betsy died that she was going to die. And that was a strange, weird feeling, and she felt different. She came home to stay. And I was so shocked that I was not really myself, and she was not really herself for those last three months. And so I felt—my feelings now are, I didn't get close enough to her before she left. There are things I should have told her before she left. And they still haunt me. She was right here in the house. She was different because she was dying. And I was different because I knew she was. But she was in such a precarious position that I was afraid the slightest little thing . . . she was holding herself together just as tight as she could, and I was afraid to say anything, because if I did, I might shatter that little bit of hold that she had over herself. And she felt the same way about me."

Mariann: You both didn't want to hurt each other, and you were both in shock.

Beau: "Yeah, and she was so afraid to say anything to me because I might fall apart. And now when I look back on it, we both should have talked to each other. If I could tell anybody in the whole world anything, it would be, 'Go ahead, make the effort and try to communicate to each other, because there's so much that needs to be said, because if you don't say it then, you'll never have another chance to say it. And you'll regret it for the rest of your life.'"

Beau knows that everyone who embraces love is at risk of feeling left behind, at some unfathomable distance, when a loved one passes away.

Beau: "There's not a day that goes by that I don't have some recollection about Betsy that is so painful, because she was not only my daughter, she was my best friend. There's not a day goes by that I don't think of something I want to ask Mama. Mama was really bright till the very end. And I keep thinking, why didn't I ask her this? Why didn't I ask her that? I need to know. And she could have told me, but I didn't think to ask her."

Beau continues: "You know what's so sad, is almost every month or two, somebody else that was a close friend dies. Because we have reached the ages of 86 and 81, and what's important are friends. I try to support Bob every time he loses another friend. It's beginning to be very painful for him that his friends are passing away, right and left. We go to a funeral about every two months. We went to one two weeks ago, and the very best friend that I ever had in my whole life died about six or eight months ago. We used to be the kind of friends where you'd just get on the phone and visit endlessly. But as long as Bob and I are together, we'll be all right. I do know that if anything happens to me first, he's going to need a lot of attention and love, and I'm hoping that the Kirvens in Sumter and that you and Richard will reach out to him."

Mariann: I'm sure we will. He's probably thinking the same for you.

Beau and Bob have traveled the world together during their lives, whenever the conditions of Bob's job in the military have required travel.

Beau: "Bob never showed any anger toward me in our whole lives. We did have to travel overseas, and then when Bob had an opportunity to go to work in Washington on the Hill, and did some real good for the Guard, we moved to Washington for eight years. But he has been the most wonderful husband anybody could have ever had. I'm not saying he was perfect, but he certainly took care of me."

Mariann: Every picture we have of you and Bob, Bob is leaning toward you with his arm around you. That's how he feels toward you.

Beau's travels westward with her friend-and-daughter Betsy carried a similar feeling of companionship and exhilaration. For a while with Betsy, as with Bob, Beau could know love as pure joy, without the pull of multiple obligations or the weight of grief.

Beau: "But when I made those ten or twelve trips with Betsy to New Mexico, and on to Arizona, on the Indian reservations, when Bob was deployed elsewhere for two or three months, where I couldn't go . . . I've always loved anything Western or Indian. The first time was just so great that I kept going back, and then after—our last trip was in 76, Bob went with me. If I could have lived anywhere I wanted to in the whole world, it would have been New Mexico. If I could have followed my dream, I would have painted and lived in New Mexico."

Beau astride her father's motorcycle

Cathy Sanders Andrews

Cathy: "I just keep plugging away. Doing the best I can. Putting one foot in front of another."

Mariann: When you and Mike had children, how did you decide to raise them?

Cathy: "Didn't make any decisions, really. It's the way it developed. I took it as it came."

Mariann: Can you give an example of taking as it comes?

Cathy: "Not really. At each stage of the children's lives, I reacted to what they were doing and didn't try to model myself one way or another. I was just trying to get through day to day."

Mariann: Did you and Mike have talks about how you were going to raise your kids, or did you automatically agree?

Cathy: "Of course we didn't agree on everything. But there was no master plan. It just happened."

Cathy's answers remind me of the sentence Voltaire writes in the final chapter of *Candide:* "Let's work without speculating . . . it's the only way of rendering life bearable." Unlike Candide's small group, though, Cathy and her husband Mike did have a goal:

Cathy: "Our family plan . . . was for me to get through medical school and have a practice. It was a plan for us as a family, not an individual plan. So then what happened in January 5, 1975 was that Mike had his motorcycle accident, which threatened to derail the family plan. That was in Roanoke. Some woman tried to make a left turn through him. Broke his hip, knee, and ankle. He was in the hospital for a month. Two days later I had to go back to school. And it was my last semester. So I had to make a choice: Sit there and pat his hand, or go back to school. I went back to school."

Mariann: Who took care of Mike?

Cathy: "The hospital, while I went back to school. And I'd come by and sit with him and study an hour or so in the evening, and that was it."

When Cathy graduated from medical school, their choice of a place to live was based on concrete specifications, rather than on concepts or feelings.

Cathy: "When I went to medical school, Mike had to stay in Roanoke without taking promotions elsewhere. IBM used to be called 'I've Been Moved,' and in order for him to move up in the company, he would have to move here, and there, and there. I had seven years of school to go to, which means he had to stay in Roanoke, which is not a large center, which means he sacrificed part of his career for me to continue in med school. At which point, when I graduated, we had to find a place that allowed him to at least advance to some degree in the company, and a place where I could set up a practice and not have to move. The three choices were White Plains, San Francisco, and Atlanta, and we liked the thought of Atlanta better."

Mariann: I want to ask about choosing where to go.

Cathy: "San Francisco was expensive. White Plains was cold."

Mariann: When you chose Atlanta, you were in driving distance of both your families. Did that have any influence on either you or Mike?

Cathy: "I think I was thinking that I could go back to The Farm for a little while, it was close to the family, but I think San Francisco is too expensive, and White Plains is too cold."

Mariann: If there had been a job you really wanted in Roanoke or Richmond, or someplace close to the parents, and a job for Mike, would you have chosen to live closer to them if all things were equal, or were you glad you ended up far enough away from them, in Atlanta?

Cathy: "That had no bearing whatsoever on my decision. It made no difference where the parents were."

Cathy emphasizes that **ideas** have not steered her life, while she has put one foot in front of the other.

Mariann: Did you feel you wanted to create a family that was like the one you grew up in, or that was different?

Cathy: "Never thought about it. It was not a concept I entertained at the time."

Mariann: So you would help out family if they were really sick. Did you and Mike automatically have the same set of priorities?

Cathy: "I have no idea. We didn't talk about priorities. We talked about practical. We did what we needed to do. We didn't abstract about it. We were more concrete about what we did."

Mariann: It sounds like you have a good system set up [in Cathy's medical practice], where you know how to manage patient responses.

Cathy: "Family medicine is 50% psychiatry, and I've been doing it for 27 years."

Mariann: What are your guiding ideas in psychiatry? What do you find yourself doing?

Cathy: "I don't have any specific guiding ideas. I do understand human behavior. It simply comes from experience in dealing with people. I individualize it, because I've known most of them for twenty-plus years."

Cathy has also renounced **comparisons** as a guide, while she has put one foot in front of the other.

Mariann: Did you feel you wanted to create a family that was like the home you grew up in, or that was different?

Cathy: "I did my own home. I did not compare it to the other."

Mariann: [Cathy has just described two kinds of men.] Do you think you knew [which kind Mike was] when you picked him?

Cathy: "I had no concept of that. I was 18. Didn't consider any comparison, at all. Don't even think now I'd make any comparison. I do my own individual thing, and I really don't compare with others."

Mariann: Looking back, do you feel like you treated your kids the way you were treated?

Cathy: "No, I feel like I treated them the best I knew how to then. Did the best job I could. And I didn't make any comparisons."

Mariann: Cathy has a solid belief in accepting the world as it is, with all its limitations. As she was growing up, the saying "Don't bang your head against a brick wall" was meant to express this version of resigned acceptance. For example, Cathy defines two categories of men and has adapted herself to this situation:

"There are really two kinds of men in this world. There are the ones that will stick by you no matter what, and there are the ones that are going to look elsewhere. Mike is one that will stick by me whatever else I do. I think our father was that way. I think Richard is that way. But there are other men that will wander. Mike is not one of those. It's in their personality."

She has accepted as matter-of-fact that our parents were financially limited, and that she and Mike also, early in their marriage, could not afford a lot.

Cathy: "I remember that our parents had to borrow sixty dollars in 1955 for us to go to Camp Kanuga. And they had to mortgage the house for it. And they had to pay it back over a long time so that we could all go to Camp Kanuga. We all four stayed in a cabin, and it was a church camp. You were having your period and couldn't go swimming, and I couldn't understand why you couldn't go swimming. And somehow I wasn't allowed to do what I wanted to do. I remember that. I was six and you were twelve."

Mariann: And they borrowed $60 so that we could go there.

Cathy: "It was 1954. Might even have been sixty-five dollars. But that was a big deal."

Mariann: I remember it would be summer, and it was hot, and I would say, "I want to go to Crystal Lake." And Mama would say, "We have a perfectly fine vinyl pool here—remember that little thing?—and I'll put the hose in it, and you and Cathy can sit in it."

Cathy: "Oh, I remember making a circle out of the hose, and filling it with water on the back concrete terrace. And we called it 'Crystal Lake' because that was a wonderful thing we occasionally got to do, but it was very rare. So we pretended."

Mariann: Was Mike working for IBM?

Cathy: Um-hm.

Mariann: So you had the one income.

Cathy: "That's the only way we got to go to the lake. We'd go camping, and our friends had a boat, and we got to go skiing. So we got to go camping with them. But I never bought disposable diapers, although they were available. I couldn't afford them. I couldn't afford a lot of things that I wanted for my kids. Once I finished school and had a job, and paid off loans, I suppose it got easier then. I had a big loan to pay off."

Mariann: Did Mama and Daddy help you at all?

Cathy: "They did let us borrow enough money to buy our first house. And we paid them back with interest. They considered it an investment. When we sold the house, we paid them back. Because at that time the cost of housing was continuing to go up, and the house was a good investment."

(Cathy accepts another fact of life that I have never been able to accept—that her time for visiting, and other people's time for visiting, is just plain limited.)

Mariann: Did you make many trips when you lived in Atlanta to see family?

Cathy: "I had all I could do. Pretty much we didn't visit anybody. I had too much to do. I was going to school, had a family, you know. We went out one time with the kids to visit Mike's mother when she was living in Albuquerque, and I think we made one or two trips to The Farm when the kids were little. Once I started back to school, that was it. I didn't have the luxury of making trips."

Mariann: Do you wish the people from Sumter had visited you more?

Cathy: "Never thought about it. I've invited them. They did come to Amy's wedding. They all did."

Mariann: That's terrific. That's wonderful.

Cathy: "I thought so. They did come to her wedding, but I hadn't seen them in years. I'd say, 'Y'all come,' but I didn't make a specific invite. They'd say 'Y'all come,' and occasionally I do show up. I don't feel bad, and my feelings aren't hurt. That's just the way it is."

Mariann: So it sounds like as you went through life, you had enough to do what was set in front of you, taking care of your family and your kids and your job, and the whole visiting family concern . . .

Cathy: "Well, I would visit family when I can, but I can only do so much, and you have a set of priorities, and you go 1-2-3, and if you can get to 4, you do 4, and if you have time for 5, you do 5, but you start with 1."

Mariann: Richard and I have had talks about how much visiting we are going to do. And the kids are our first priority, and after that, we negotiate.

Excerpts from Interviews with Relatives

Cathy: "Well, you have to negotiate. You're not the same person. You negotiate everything, whether it be who you visit—you negotiate what you eat for dinner. Well, life is negotiation with your spouse. We've been married 42 years. It's all a negotiation. What time you go to bed is a negotiation."

In negotiation with a spouse, as in all life's negotiations, you can influence others but you can by no means control them. This fact is another parameter of life Cathy has fully accepted.

Cathy: "I can control my behavior, but I can't control anybody else's. If they ask me, I can give them advice, but that's all I can do."

Mariann: Do you feel you can control your earning situation?

Cathy: "To some degree. Not entirely. I can't control the global economy. Nor can I control the current state of medicine. But I can take care of what's in my own backyard."

Mariann: Do you feel like you have control, to some degree, over your relationships with your family and your friends?

Cathy: "As far as my behavior is concerned. But I can't control how they manage it. I don't doubt but what I influence my patients quite a bit. Of course I do. To make them healthier? Absolutely. I wouldn't be practicing if I didn't think I had some positive influence. I have only my cognitive abilities when I treat people. I can write a prescription. I physically don't do that much: I'm not a surgeon. I'm a cognitive physician."

Mariann: So with family, you don't have control over their behavior.

Cathy: "I have limited control as far as my relationship, and how I obviously manage that relationship. I'm sure my influence has some effect, but there's a difference between being able to effectively deal with somebody and control them. There's a difference between control and having an effect. All families have folks whose behavior is somewhat less than ideal, and you can only influence it to the degree that you respond to them. You can't control them, but you can control your response to them."

Finally, Cathy believes, none of us have control over the arc of our lives. Cathy tries to influence her patients to realize that limitation. By lowering their expectations, as Cathy has lowered her own, she teaches her patients to adapt to reality.

Cathy says that "life gets more difficult as you go along. If you notice as we age, when we're young, our children get better. But our parents get worse. They deteriorate with time. And our children get better. When you're young, you're watching your children improve, and when you're old, you're watching your parents deteriorate, and at that time also your friends are deteriorating, and life gets a little more difficult. And I have this discussion a lot with patients who are suffering with dealing with children and with aging parents, and I say: Look. Your parents are going to get worse; you realize this. And you just have to accept that, and it's gonna happen. Your kids are going to get better. I notice that people in their 50s and early 60s have a little more angst about that situation. By the time people get to their 70s, they are a lot more accepting of it."

Once or twice Cathy has repeated this saying to me: "Life's a bitch and then you die." This stance seems only in part a joke, to Cathy.

Prompted by Cathy's view of life, I looked up the philosophy of Stoicism cultivated in ancient Greece and Rome. I found these sentences, among many others: "The Stoic ethic espouses a deterministic perspective . . . a Stoic of virtue . . . would amend his will to suit the world and remain, in the words of Epictetus, 'sick and yet happy, in peril and yet happy, dying and yet happy, in exile and happy, in disgrace and happy, thus positing a completely autonomous individual will, and at the same time a universe that is "a rigidly deterministic single whole (Stoicism)."

Mariann: What was the hardest kind of thing that you went through?

Cathy: "The hardest thing I did was take the two kids when they were little to Lakeside Amusement Park. Michael was 18 months, and Amy was two and a half years older than that. I had no means and couldn't afford to have a carrier or carriage or anything else to put them in. It rained and it was very dirty. I did it by myself, and it was a very difficult thing to do. But I was getting to treat them anyway. And they enjoyed it a lot. So it was probably difficult dealing with any lack of means of getting the kids what I wanted to get them. Couldn't do it. Had to make their clothes. Couldn't buy them. Couldn't afford them. Kids these days have all kinds of equipment to take care of babies. I had nothing like that. I had to wash the diapers. I had six weeks of diaper service. After that, I had cloth diapers. I couldn't find disposable ones. We went camping with two kids and cloth diapers. And a tent."

Mariann: Good heavens.

Cathy: "Yeah, it was tough."

Mariann: Mama said that you commuted to medical school over the mountains on a motorcycle.

Cathy: "Not quite. What happened was, we had only one car. Mike got a wild hair and decided he wanted to get a motorcycle. So I said, Aha! That's my ticket to school. So in order to go back to college, I had to have transportation. So I rode the motorcycle to the car pool, parked it in the parking lot, and then rode up to Blacksburg. Except when I had to be the driver in the car pool, and Mike would have to ride the motorcycle to work. And then that worked out well except when we had exams and the car pool ended, because everybody's schedule was different. So I had to ride about 45 miles for a week, when exams were. It only happened about nine times, maybe, that I had to ride the motorcycle for a week, back and forth.

"I could afford a rain suit, but the motorcycle didn't have any glass seal, as they do now, nor did it have a glass or plastic seal for the hands, and the equipment I had was somewhat inadequate, and cold weather was somewhat of a problem, so what I did was wrap up as best I could, put the helmet on—I did have a visor on my helmet—but when it's twenty degrees, I don't think there's a damn thing that will warm you up enough. And when it rained, it was a real problem, because I didn't have adequate shoes. So I put bread bags on my feet, with rubber bands. Didn't work real well. And when it began to rain—have you ever ridden 45 miles an hour, in the rain, for an hour and a half, with it coming at you at 60 miles an hour?"

Mariann: I can't imagine how you did it even once.

Cathy: Cold.

Mariann: That sounds like a kind of heroism.

Cathy acknowledges pleasure as she does pain. She takes it as it comes. She relishes playing golf with Mike and with the other members of a medical insurance group to which she belongs. She is a talented cook who does justice to good food. She even remembers long ago when our family of four shared a T-bone steak: "And I liked the bone. It had the sweetest meat, so I liked to chew on the bone of the steak. I still do."

Mariann: Do you think that your life changed by going to The Farm?

Cathy: "It influenced me significantly. I don't know how much it changed, if at all, but I certainly enjoyed it. The family did come to Amy's wedding. They all did."

Mariann: It seemed to me that Cathy had a grand time when she and Mike traveled to The Farm and saw all the cousins again. A few years before that, Cathy happily attended the Kirven Reunion in Darlington, South Carolina.

Cathy has been careful to be a good example for her colleagues and patients, which has been an act of love.

Cathy: "I do the right thing for my patients, and I do what I think is right, and I can be an example. And I've pretty much done that, in my office, I've been an example for doctors of how you treat patients, how you run a practice, how you do the right thing. And the patients are friends, who come in and we talk. Sometimes I can convince them to do what they should be doing, and sometimes I can't, and sometimes I think I have to set an example. That's why I exercise. I have to stay physically in shape to set an example. If I'm fat and I'm smoking, I can't set an example."

Cathy's primary care office, by her design, has no glass walls between patients and secretaries or nurses. In her office, patients know and feel that they will receive loving care.

Cathy cares for both patients and grandchildren with love: "I feel pretty good about the grandchildren. They are learning how to be responsible people, and they're learning what the World is like. And they certainly know that they are loved."

Julie Kirven Griffin

Julie's adolescence was spent in the close company of her older sister Ophelia, whom a blood transfusion had afflicted with fatal hepatitis. Beneath the watchful love of her family, Ophelia was dying, and she knew it. For long years before her death, Ophelia's bedfellow was her sister Julie, fifteen years younger.

Julie: "And I guess I went through depression, not knowing what it was. I remember sleeping with Ophelia downstairs at night, so that Mother could rest, and not have to get up. Mother had to take care of her all day. I remember Ophelia telling me, 'I know I'm dying,' and I said 'no you're not, no you're not.'"

Julie's life stopped to make room for Ophelia's death. During the years that might have been the bloom of Julie's youth, she was lost, smothered, depressed, and unsure how to live. The responsibility to comfort the dying fell upon Julie, and so did the damage. It was no one's fault. Being there for your family, a labor of love, can still be perilous. Only when Ophelia's need ended could Julie begin to see past her crushing burden.

Julie: "When Ophelia had to go to Duke and stay there for so long, the medical expenses were so big, because she didn't have any insurance, and so Daddy couldn't pay again, and I know that he was scared, he was very angry and agitated and feeling like here-we-go-again type of feeling. That was never said, but we all felt it."

Mariann: No wonder you felt smothered. You had somebody's impending death right up against you.

Julie: "And I didn't know how to deal with it. And Ophelia's thought was, when I die, take care of Tom and Daddy because they are the ones it's going to hit hardest. So even when she was sick . . ."

Mariann: She was taking care of them, and you were taking care of her.

For a time, Julie had opted out of life. She could not feel.

Julie: "Situational depression, you know."

Mariann: Phee was sick for a number of years.

Julie: "Oh, yeah. Yeah. And things that I would have done as a teenager with parental support—it wasn't there. And so I went to college with a feeling of being smothered, like I don't know what I'm supposed to be doing, what am I supposed to be doing at this point in my life? Then Lynwood came along, you know, I guess he was my salvation."

Mariann: When in your life did he come along?

Julie: "In Lewisburg, second year in Lewisburg, and then we both went to East Carolina together. And then after the funeral, we got married."

Mariann: When you left Phee's funeral . . .

Julie: "We left the funeral, he came and picked me up, and we were supposed to go back to school, and I said I just can't go back to school. You know, bless Lynwood's heart, I took all this with me into marriage, and right away a baby, and it was just like [laughs] it took me a while, bless his heart, it took me a while to . . . I never talked with anybody about it, you know."

With marriage to Lynwood and the birth of her three daughters, Julie joined the course of her life. She had known emotional paralysis, though, and she carried that knowledge with her. Her trial would yield to a blessing, as years passed. Decades later, she compares the sequence of her life to that of Moses—first tried by God, then blessed by God.

Julie: "God has prepared me through things that happen to you in your life, like Moses. When God was preparing Moses to lead those Israelites out to Egypt. Years before, he had been raised in the palace, so he had the education. He killed the Egyptian, he went into exile in Midian for forty years, and then God said, Okay, Moses, I've got a job for you to do, and he said N-o-o, God. I'm not ready, you know, pick somebody else. I'm not ready."

In the story of Julie's life, too, she found herself suddenly blessed. Whether it was fate, Providence, or an epiphany, Julie was summoned to help people who carried emotional burdens, as she had for so long. The summons was persistent, she believes, and would not let her refuse.

Julie: "One day I was in church at a ladies' meeting, and this one lady came in and was talking about mental health and volunteering, and so I went to volunteer there, and that led me into a job. When I got out of school, mental health school, there wasn't a job in mental health for me, so I went into special education and taught special education for thirteen years.

"And then she called me, and she said, 'I'm getting ready to retire, and I want you to take my job.'

"So I went for the interview, they offered me the job, and I went back to my principal and told him. So when they called to say they wanted me, he said, 'Leave her alone, let her stay here, she doesn't need to be anywhere but here [laughs].'

"They said, 'No, we want her here.' So."

Because Julie had herself been tried with emotional pain, she could help people in those straits. Her trial had turned into a blessing. Helping people deal with their lives felt wonderful.

Julie: "I feel like, that job, I never went to work a day that I went to work. I never felt like I was at work."

Mariann: I think that is a blessed feeling.

Julie: "Oh yeah. You know, the ability to be there, and to help, and to know you are helping a lot of single moms. We raised money to be able to support the workers there, and I learned a lot from the psychiatrists, and the psychologists, and the social workers while I was there. And being able to help the children in the group homes, who came in with no clothes, and to be able to provide for them. And the love that was nurtured from my mom and my dad with the taking in of the children was expressed in my job.

"I could relate to the women coming in there who had been through such a traumatic experience in their life, spiraling down—maybe they had a flat tire, or maybe they couldn't pay the light bill. They had children that were depending on them. And to be able to say, we can help, with the money that we've raised. To be able to give them a check to buy that tire, or to feed those children, or to help the children that would come in from parents who beat them or abused them, to be able to get right their life a little bit better …

"But whenever you go through something, you can always help somebody else go through it, when you've been there. And you can let them know, hey, there's an incident. You let them stay in it. That's life, there's an incident.

"If you were to have a heart attack, or if you were to cut your finger, cut your foot, or have diabetes, you go to a doctor, they can have a course of treatment for you. Mental illness strikes one in every five people. And they don't know where to go to get help, they don't know who to see. That's part of the problem, too, is having to realize 'We don't know what to do.'"

Helping mental patients became an active pleasure to Julie. It brought her joy to help family members in need, too. From the beginning, her family's rallying cry had been, "Family first!" Now as an adult, she could be there for family members without the disabling strain she had felt in having to be there for Ophelia.

"I never saw, when my dad leaves the house, that he didn't kiss my mother or kiss her when he came back. That was such a bond there, and she was always there for him and with him, even nursing him through his illness. And it gave me great pleasure to take her home with me after Daddy died, and keep her for a while, and then she got sick with leukemia. Her breast cancer came back, and she also had leukemia. And to nurse her through that, I felt, oh, that I could not be down there [at The Farm], you know, I had my family here, they were in school, I couldn't always go down there. I'd go down on the weekends and stay all weekend. I'd stay up Friday night, and all day Saturday, and Saturday night, and sleep on the way home Sunday.

"I think that if you have emotional support, you can weather just about anything. If I can have my family, I feel blessed, and I feel rich. It doesn't matter what I have in my house, my home. I want a comfortable chair, a comfortable bed, and everything else doesn't matter [laughs]."

Mutual support within the family circle has become both an imperative and a joy.

Mariann: It sounds like you and Lynwood also mutually support each other.

Julie: "I don't know what I would have done without him, when I had the Guillain-Barré. He was a blessing there. And my sister Lou [Laura Ann], she came, and she stayed with me during the day, and Lynwood stayed with me at night."

Mariann: And you've been helping Lou in her illnesses.

Julie: "Oh, I couldn't do any less, for her, from what she did for me. And even if she hadn't, I still would."

Back in the days when Julie slept beside Ophelia, she craved a bit of freedom and a sense of her own boundaries. Even back then, she realized that the good project of helping and being helped could not itself make up an entire life. One person cannot completely merge into another.

Julie: "And I remember getting up in the morning after I slept with her at night, which I didn't sleep that much, you know, because she was awake a lot, and I would talk with her, and we would talk, and get up, get on the horse and ride in the morning, and just a few minutes of freedom, before we would start."

Years later, after her ordeal with Guillain-Barré in the prison of her own body, Julie resists being too closed off, too protected. She needs some measure of freedom, her latitude, her saving distance from other people. She needs to feel that she has borders, that she is intact.

Julie: "I think the mutual respect is what comes in there. If you're able to give that mutual respect. A lot of people think they can give it, but they can't."

Mariann: That's a very good way to put it. They're all for it, they just can't do it.

Julie: "They like to think they can do it on their terms. You need to respect that person on their own terms. The way they need to be respected."

Mariann: It's not respect to say, "You shouldn't feel that way. Feel this way."

Julie: "Well, we went through that, too, you know. I've had a tough time since I've been sick, making an emotional adjustment to my limitations. And that's been real, real hard, when you're used to being up, and going, and doing, and then being imprisoned with the fatigue that comes, and you have to rest, but [Lynwood] has been very sweet with all that."

Mariann: That's how you can tell if somebody really respects and supports you, when you get in a real hard time and they don't lose their temper and they're real sweet. You've supported him through his heart problems.

Julie: "Oh, yeah. I could do no less there either, you know."

Mariann: You find out what they need, on their own terms.

Julie: "It's love. It's like there is not a step-by-step guide. No rule book. Lynwood didn't think I could take out the garbage, and he didn't think I could take it to the dump, and he didn't think I could do this, and he didn't think I could do that, and before [my illness] I did all that just great. But sometimes I feel smothered, like he does not want me to do certain things when I feel like I can do it. I feel like he limits me."

Mariann: You mean after you were sick?

Julie: "Yeah. After I was sick. Like the canoe out there? I wanted something that I could run. Something that I could do. And then he didn't want me to do it by myself. I said I've been instructed in water safety, I know how to swim, I wear a life jacket, so what's the rub? So one day I went to see Brandi. And it was pouring down rain, cats and dogs, going and coming. It was an hour and a half trip. And when I got home I told Leigh, I said, you know, the funny thing, Lynwood says nothing about me leaving in the rain, or coming back home in the rain, pouring down, so dangerous, but let me get out in that canoe, he says [slaps her hands], I was just trying to take care of you. So I think he finally realized that I need a little space in making decisions about myself."

Julie continues, "If I could choose where I wanted to be, I'd be back on the Farm. I like the Farm life. That's where I would choose to be, if it was workable between the both of us. I'd be right next door to The Farm. It's maybe for the best that I don't. But that's where I would be. Family has always been very, very important to me, and I feel like that being there when my brothers are going through what they're going through right now, that I could be supportive of them, and cook a meal once in a while, go to the grocery store, whatever, or look after Joe and let Sallie do something, but I think, with my health being what it is, if I were there, it would probably be detrimental."

Mariann: That you would go past your limitations?

Julie: "Yes. I had a good friend—we cultivated this relationship when I was working in mental health—it took him three years to walk over my doorstep into the health center, into the office. He'd get to the door and he couldn't come in. I knew he wanted to volunteer, but he could not make it into my office, and he had to do that to be able to volunteer. He wrote the most gorgeous poetry you ever read in all your life, it was so deep. He wrote one called, 'Put Ketchup on It and Keep on Chewing.'"

Mariann: I like the title!

Julie: "He wrote that when things get bad in life, put ketchup on it and keep on chewing. And he wrote the most restricted feeling of being in a locked ward, and the angel looking down on him and spreading light. And he trusted me and could talk with me, and he said his first psychotic break was when he found himself dancing naked on top of the Beth Israel Synagogue, and when his psychosis passed, he was standing naked on the top of the temple. And he said, 'I was so embarrassed, and I didn't know how I got there.' And I said, well, what did you do, Tim? And he said, 'I looked for my clothes. I got them and put them on. I went home and got into my bed and closed the door.'"

In Julie's house, she doesn't tell visitors or family what to do, and they don't tell her. But the house operates under her rules, so that she has her emotional space.

Julie: "When Matt and Jackie were living together in Simpsonville, they would come here for the weekend and I would say, 'I'm sorry, when you're under my roof you will not sleep together. This is my house, and you will abide by that.' And I think that Matt and Jackie were convinced that they were not going to marry, that they would just live together for the rest of their lives. And then one day they came to church with me on Sunday, and the preacher said something about family, and how that affects family when you live together and have children, and I'll have you know the next week, they called Leigh and Lynn in the middle of the night. They went down to the Magistrate's office, they got married, and then they went to Krispy Kreme for their reception [laughs]."

Mariann: So they had a sudden change of heart?

Julie: "Had an epiphany, I guess."

Julie lives a negotiated paradox between freedom on the one hand and rescuing or being rescued on the other. She knows that being thoroughly protected can suffocate a person. Sometimes you have to wait until someone crosses your threshold before you can reach out.

Diane Williams Yamamoto

Diane remembers very well her father, George Williams, even though he passed away when she was five years old. For the time she knew him, he was a gentle and fun-loving presence.

Diane: "The side slats of the youth bed looked like a ladder, and I said: 'Can I make a ladder out of that?' My mother would have died; she wouldn't have let me do it."

"And [her father] said, 'OK.' And he said, 'Where are we going to put the ladder?'"

"And I said, 'Let's put it in on the wall, and climb up and touch the ceiling,' because the ceiling seemed a long way up to me."

"He said, 'OK.' And he held the side of the bed up, and I climbed up, and I touched the ceiling. I felt like I was a hundred feet tall. But I had touched the ceiling, and that was loads of fun."

Mariann: he sounds very kind.

Diane: "This was before his health was bad, so I had to have been very young. My mother—it was after Pearl Harbor, and everybody was doing what they did, and my mother was going to Red Cross classes at night, and he was left with the chore of putting us to bed. And it was early. And I was certain that he was not wanting to just sit home and do that, so he said, 'Let's go to the movie.'"

"And I said, 'I have my pajamas on.'"

"And he said, 'Well, let's put your clothes back on, and let's go to the movie. Or if you just want to put your coat on over your pajamas, we'll just go to the movie.' So I thought that was wonderful. And so we went late to the movie, and I think my mother beat us home. He must have left her a note [laughs]. But anyway, she looked concerned [laughs]."

Mariann: Her father also demonstrated to her, as it happens, that utter safety can feel confining.

Diane: "I can remember my father, even, because he played, he was fun. You remember the expression 'snug as a bug in a rug'? And I said to him one day, 'I want to feel snug as a bug in a rug. I want to see what that feels like.'

"He said 'OK.' And he rolled me up in the living room rug. He left my head out. I didn't really like it very much, and I said 'a little too snug [laughs].'"

Diane didn't want to be quite that snug, and she found the small town of Fairmont, North Carolina somewhat boring and intrusive, too snug, as small towns often are.

"Well, I wanted to be as far away from Fairmont as I could get. I didn't like it there. I needed to be away from everybody knowing exactly what you were doing and deciding whether it was good or bad. I wanted to be in a bigger place. And I wanted to get out and see the world."

Diane says that from her earliest years she has wished for an adventurous life with a sense of fun and freedom. Maybe she caught that spirit from her father.

Diane: "We [Diane and her husband Willy] set out—he was in graduate school here [near Raleigh, North Carolina], and I stopped working when Wilito was born. And we weren't making very much money at all. And so when he finished graduate school, he needed a job, and he needed the adventure of trying something new. He was offered a job in Thibodeau,

Louisiana. That sounded like a wonderful adventure to me, and it was an adventure for sure [laughs]."

Diane: "We went to Louisiana, and we found a place to live, and it was in a hundred-year-old house, and we had an apartment. And our living room was what had been the foyer of the old house. And then there were two big rooms—I think one had been the dining room, and one had been maybe the living room, and then there was a small kitchen that only had a sink in it. No counter. No cabinets. It had a sink. And that was the kitchen."

Mariann: For the sake of freedom and laughter and adventure, Diane has learned to expect the unexpected in other people. Adventures can verge upon unpredictability and chaos. But Diane can tolerate that. She has a laid-back, amused appreciation of the human comedy.

Diane: "I was asking questions about the schools in Louisiana, and I didn't really want my children to go to Catholic school. And I wasn't impressed with the kids that had been to public school. And so I said to an acquaintance, 'I'm a little concerned about the schools, and I would like to ask some questions.' And they said, 'Well, if you're concerned about the schools, just go to the dime store and get a certificate and fill it out, and you teach.'"

Mariann: Hoo! That's a surprising answer! Go ahead and be the school [Both laugh].

Diane: "Yeah. And I thought, Ooo-oooo. I'm not a schoolteacher. I don't know about elementary school or anything like that, and I thought ooo-oooo. I bet a lot of the teachers just do that. So."

Mariann: The political climate in Louisiana was just as risky as the educational climate.

Diane: "I don't think we ever would have been really a part [of that Louisiana society]. Some people were very helpful and very good to us. There was a great deal of unrest because they were trying to unionize the plant. Or maybe the unions had already gotten there, and that's where I saw the big fight outside the plant. And there were two other families that moved down there. One was from Ohio, the McKees, who finally moved to New York, from there. And we all left about the same time, but the Bourgeois got sugar in the gas tank, and so did the McKees, got sugar in their gas tank."

Mariann: I don't know what that does. Does that ruin your gas tank?

Diane: "That will ruin your motor, I think. But we never got sugar in our gas tank. I don't know whether we were too strange? The people that I talked to, they said, 'Well, you sound like you're from Mississippi.' They knew I was not from there, but Mississippi was as far away as most of them could think."

Mariann: If you find yourself in incompatible waters, it may be time to take your search for adventure somewhere else—especially if you are in a society where you are being scrutinized, like Fairmont.

Diane: "It was a very closed society. We had a little girl that baby-sat some; her name was Madeleine Kelman. She had looked after Wilito and Pepe some when Brian was born. I think it was before my mother came. And she looked at me one day and she says, 'You're a Yankee.' And I said, 'Madeleine, I'm not a Yankee.'"

"'You're a Yankee.'"

Diane: "And I said, 'I was born in South Carolina, and I grew up in North Carolina, and they're both south of the Mason-Dixon line, and as far as I know, all of my family are from the South.'"

"'You're a Yankee.'"

Diane: "And I said, 'Madeleine, where do Yankees come from?' And she said, 'Any place north of Baton Rouge [laughs].'"

Mariann: Diane and Willy's adventures seemed to take them, by chance, from one closed society to another.

Diane: "When we moved back to North Carolina, we moved to High Point. I went to the strangest Christmas party I've ever been to, and I was thinking, 'OK. We're going to go and have a good time.' But we were at a Christmas party with the people who worked in the plant, and all the women sat on one side and looked very dour, like they were there because they had to be there.

The men were lined up on the other side of the room, and one man got up, and he played his guitar and sang religious songs, and we had a little punch, and a few cookies, and I said, 'Willy, let's get out of here [laughs].'"

Mariann: Diane doesn't express anger or even frustration at such scenes. She simply laughs as if she has seen another peculiar phenomenon and will now keep moving through life. One way to have an adventurous life is to look upon life itself—whatever happens—as an adventure, and Diane seems to have that cast of mind. She has a ready laugh. Her connecting phrases are matter-of-fact, as if to document the next strange thing that happened: *But anyway. Yeah. So.*

Diane: "I had two babies. But anyway. And we stayed in Louisiana until I said to Willy, 'We don't have any heat in this house.' I had checked the temperature. And I said, 'It gets cold enough here, sometimes, in the winter, that we're going to have to have heat.'"

Mariann: In early childhood, Diane met varied personalities among her father's relatives. She learned to relate to her grandfather—a "hard man" extremely different from her father–with a kind of fascination, and she tried to understand him.

Diane: "I mean, if you wanted an audience with my grandfather, you went to him. He was not a bad man. But he was hard. He had grown up hard. And he had a very Old Testament view of the hierarchy of the family."

Diane: "My Grandfather was orphaned when he was eight. His mother died as a result of childbirth, when his younger brother was born. He said that his formal education stopped when he was eight years old. And he said he looked at the back end of a mule from then on, holding the plow. But he learned the value of a penny then. And he used to give me a nickel, from time to time, which I really wanted to spend on a package of chewing gum or an ice cream cone. And he would say, 'Now, you save half of that.' And I used to look at the nickel and think, 'Well, this is one piece of money, and I really don't know how to cut it in half. If I cut it in half, would it be worth anything? And it would be too little to buy an ice cream cone.' But I was afraid to ask how I could save half of that. He did it on purpose. He liked to confound me. I guess my face was funny."

Mariann: Diane and Willy finally settled not in Louisiana or in High Point but in Raleigh, for Willy had "adopted" Raleigh, and they both felt at home there. The adventures continued, for each of her four children is an adventure to Diane. By appreciating distinct personalities, she makes her way through unpredictability and confusion with her first child, Wilito.

Diane: "It would have been better if Wilito had been a little bit more disciplined student, because I would have all these teacher conferences, and they would show me his desk, and it looked like a giant pregnant rabbit had made a big mess in his desk [laughs]. It was utter chaos. And he didn't care, and he didn't want to do his homework, and he didn't want to do what he didn't want to do. And when he was in the first grade—and he was very sick when he was little, and he had asthma, and he couldn't breathe, and it was very, very scary to me a lot of the time—his first-grade teacher would just let him lie on the floor when he felt like it, and he was a smart enough kid that, because he didn't want to do whatever it was that they were doing, he just lay on the floor.

"I was concerned. I was thinking, what in the world is going to become of him? He's going to flunk out of the first grade, or the second grade. And he seemed to be a constant concern for his teachers, as he went along.

"Wilito and Helen were extremely young and extremely immature when they married. But they seemed to be very happy and very well-matched, and they are both very bright, and both very vocal. And they disagree loudly sometimes [laughs], and that's OK, because they both have a lot of volume [laughs]."

Mariann: Sounds like an even match. It sounds to me, from what I've seen, that they are both very involved in their children's lives.

Diane: "They're very involved in their children, and they are both very helter-skelter. I don't know how anybody gets two shoes on that match."

Her second child, Pepe, was another adventure.

Diane: "I had a conference about Pepe in the fourth grade. The teacher said, 'I can't find a way to motivate him. How do you motivate him?' And I said, 'He's very interested in sports, and if he had something to read that was about sports, he might be . . .' And the teacher said, 'Well, there has to be a broader field of interest than that.' And I thought, 'Oh, well, you're the teacher. You're the one that studies all this. I don't know anything about it.'

"But anyway. It was not a very good conference. I've had good conferences and bad conferences, and kids are so different. You'd think they would be more alike, if they were kin to each other, but that's just not the case."

Mariann: Indeed, Brian was different from Pepe.

Diane: "Brian has his music, and all his ties here. He's settled. He was always that way, when he was a child, he'd just make the best of the situation. Like Dr. Spock said, 'Leave them alone, and they'll entertain themselves in bed in the morning and you can just sleep a while longer.' He did it. Everybody else just climbed out of the bed or screamed for attention, and Brian did that.

"In the moving picture we have of him when he was a baby, he fell down in the snow, and he really wanted to get up, and Wilito tried to pick him up, but he was just too heavy, and so Wilito finally just plopped him back down and let him loose, and he landed on his butt again. He didn't have any gloves, and there was snow on the ground, and he put his hands down and that was very uncomfortable because he couldn't get up that way, and so he didn't become frustrated and cry. He took his hands off and he put his feet out and just started kicking his feet. He'd have a good time right there on the ground. But I thought that was so revealing of exactly who he is, and his personality. And all the others, too. Wilito tried, he was doing his own thing, well OK, too hard to pick you up."

Mariann: Diane wanted her children to have a taste of freedom in their play, to have adventures and learn how to manage them.

Diane: "Willy wanted to come back here, and it was fine with me, and so we brought the house on Arrington Road, where we lived for so many years. And it was good. It was a neighborhood. All the children knew each other. There was a great amount of freedom for the kids there. And I wanted that for my children, because the farmland was over on the other side, and they could go out and wander there forever in those pastures. In going to The Farm, you know, I had that when I was down there, and I thought that was just pretty wonderful. It was good for my kids. They had that sort of freedom, and it was good.

"And the kids now have to make play dates, and the mama or daddy takes them. It's almost like the formal English visits that they used to have, and to me that seems unnatural. It's so nice to walk out of your house and say, 'Let's go kick the can' or 'Let's go let the dogs chase the cows.'

"When Julie was about ten years old, she had a very short haircut. And she was the only girl, playing with her three older brothers. But one summer it was so hot, and she was swimming, and it was just such a deal, all that long hair, and all that chlorine, and so we said, 'Would you like to get your hair cut off short?' And she said OK. And somehow she was out in the field with Brian and Vance—the little boy across the road and maybe a couple of other little boys—and they were chasing the cows with the dogs, which was great fun, fun for the dogs and fun for the kids. The cows roamed. They were in this huge pasture, and they were never brought into the barn. They weren't milk cows. They were experimental cows, I think, for the university. And they would charge the dogs and charge the kids. They were semi-wild creatures, and they were protecting themselves and doing what cows in the wild do.

"And the man came over the hill, and he was after the kids for chasing the cows. Well, the boys and the dogs disappeared, because they had done that before. And they left Julie to hold the bag. And the man thought she was another little boy, because she had a short haircut, and she had on jeans just like they did. But she felt like that was the most unfair, terrible thing, to be left holding the bag for all of them, and they were on the other side of the hill, hiding with the dogs and keeping the dogs quiet [laughs].

"She was really bent out of shape about that. And I said, 'Well, next time don't go.' Yeah. Well, I knew the boys were going to go. They weren't hurting the cows. I mean, how could those little dogs hurt the cows? And it's not bad training for them to learn to scamper out of the way of a cow. And know exactly how the cows behave, probably a good thing to know."

Mariann: You felt like they weren't really in danger.

Diane: "No, they weren't in danger. They were more in danger from the wrath of the man [laughs] than they were from the cows. But it didn't bother me at all that they were out chasing the cows. I knew they shouldn't be doing it, but I didn't feel one bit guilty."

Mariann: Nobody was getting hurt.

Diane: "No! It was just a little innocent mischief, as far as I was concerned. And there were a lot worse things to worry about. Things where discipline should be enforced, things they could and couldn't do. They were not bad kids. I was just letting them find out for themselves, you know. If they got a little bit too close and got scared enough, they wouldn't do it again.

"Wilito and Pepe are very close in age, and they're very close. And Brian was two years younger and a totally different personality. And he and Julie, who are three years apart, played together just really well, and they shared a lot of the same friends, and they really had a good time, other than Brian taking over and leaving her to hold the bag in the field with the cows, but that wasn't so bad. I think she learned from that experience."

Mariann: Diane believes it's good to let the children find out how to deal with the world themselves, as she herself had done:

Diane: "When Wilito hit the second grade, he had a different teacher. And she was a good teacher. She was—not a cruel teacher, but she required more of him. And they would complain about various teachers, and I'd tell them what my mother would tell me when I would say something. It gives you a chance to get to know somebody different, and to learn how to get along with them. It's good training. It really is."

Mariann: In the quest for freedom and fun, it seems, a person weaves in and out of impediments and dangers, even threats. Each person—and Diane thinks of children as smaller versions of people—has a distinct way of negotiating life's roadblocks, and that distinction should be respected. Here Diane is discussing her daughter-in-law's mother:

Diane: "I was really happy to have a chance to go with Yvonne. She rode with us to the mountains when the grandchildren were really little. And she thought I was utterly crazy because I had a water-pistol fight with the grandkids. It was too undignified for her. And she's very precise, she's very bright, but you'd think she was a total dingbat to listen to her sometimes. And she's one of the most honest people I have ever known in my life. She never covers anything.

"But Yvonne—and bless her—she's bipolar. And I don't think it was known that she was that way until she announced to her husband, 'I'm going to kill these children.' She was out of her mind. And he knew, because he knew that it wasn't hyperbole; she meant it. And so she is still on medication, and periodically she gets tired of taking it, and she will crash, and do some things, and so. But I think she must have been a pretty terrific mother. All of the kids have done well."

Mariann: To me, the feeling of Diane's description is not fear, not worry, but appreciation and delight. Diane does not bear down and try to control everything and everyone. She laughs. She comes by this attitude naturally, but she is also deliberate and self-aware.

Diane: "I've tried to make some things better than my childhood, like being so serious about some things. I've tried not to be so serious."

Mariann: So you raised your kids with a looser or freer spirit.

Diane: "I hope so. I hope so.

"[The Raleigh area] is a great place to live and work. Helen's family are here, because they came from Canada, because of the economics. It's a more metropolitan area. I mean, there are lots and lots of different kinds of people. You don't feel the brunt of prejudice here that you do in a smaller, more provincial atmosphere. And so it's a good place to live."

Mariann: The free spirit that Diane seeks for her children is made possible by stability and safety in the family. Hints of chaos are tolerable with secure surroundings, and Diane has always sought the security her home lacked after her father died.

Diane: "I think I was intent upon producing what I didn't have. It was important to me to have a home with a father and a mother and some happy children. I always sort of envied people who came from a home with both a father and a mother. It sounded good to me. Sounded secure and safe."

Mariann: For the father of her family, Diane chose a gentle and kind man who was himself valued and protected—very safe—as a child.

Diane: "And you know, your father seemed to me to be a very nice man. And he was always very kind to me, as was your mother."

Mariann: Do you think that Willy is like him in some way?

Diane: "In a lot of ways he is. He's a very safe person. He was very protected, growing up. He was the boy. And he had three sisters. And their job was to take care of him. And he's the one who had the education. He was the golden egg in that family. And the thing was, to make sure that he was educated, and safe, and that's why he's here—they sent him here so that he would be safe, and not be involved in politics in South America, which was not safe. They used to worry about him all the time, and they'd say, 'No, no, you can't climb the wall, you'll get in trouble.' And he'd climb the wall anyway, and not get in too much trouble, I don't think.

"He adored school. I think his school years in Bolivia were the happiest years of his life. He still loves school, and he was a very good student. He was at the top of his class. I think he was very obedient. He was not rebellious."

Mariann: From this auspicious upbringing, Willy came to love social situations and parties, and he was able to feel at home with nearly everyone.

Diane: "He likes social situations, and he likes food with everything. He doesn't feel awed by somebody's high rank. That doesn't bother him at all. And he recognizes—and is interested in—not necessarily to compete with or feel lower than—some of these people."

Mariann: By chance or instinct or design, Diane chose a father who would be safe as a husband, safe as an advising parent, and safe as a role model.

Diane: "Well, it was a strange thing, because I had never seen a husband-wife relationship. So I guess I was—I guess that made me hard to live with. And maybe I chose Willy because he's very easy to live with. Willy was a kind parent. He used to do a lot of talking, and he would reason with the children. I couldn't get very far. I don't think he got much farther than I did."

Mariann: Beyond safety with parents, Diane cultivated a secure community for her children. She wanted them to have stable, longstanding relationships with each other.

Mariann: You were saying that you wanted a more complete family with a father, and I wondered if four kids came because you wanted them to have one another for company?

Diane: "I wanted them to have family. I wanted them to have family when they were adults, and to be able to depend on each other. They know each other better than anybody else. They grew up together. I wanted them to know each other. And if Brian had been a girl, he would have been the last one. And when we had Julie, she was the last one no matter what. But anyway, they grew up very close. They knew each other when they were in high school."

Mariann: Growing up close is good for friends as well as family, Diane believes. Communities of friends take time to form.

Diane: "I said to Willy when we moved back here to the Raleigh area, 'This is a good place. I hope everything is good for you here. Because I think it's important for us to put down roots, and for the kids to know people and grow up with people, to be in one place. It's a matter of friends and relationships. It takes a long time to really get to know somebody. And I think growing up with somebody is the best way in the world to get to know them. I thought it was important for them to have friends that they knew, and not just pop from place to place and have to get used to a new school and try to make new friends and be accepted or not accepted."

Mariann: Willy had another job opportunity in Tennessee, but he and Diane turned it down. Here the call of adventure clashed with the values of safety and roots for the children. Safety prevailed.

Diane: "It was a good thing that we stayed put, because it would have been really hard to go. The money would have been a whole lot better there. And it would have been an adventure to go. It would have been fun, but we would have had to uproot the kids. And they really wanted to stay where they were."

Diane has always wanted her children to feel both rooted and free. Here is how she expresses that combination when her children were younger:

Diane: "It was a neighborhood. There were neighborhood schools, and all the children knew each other. There was a great amount of freedom for the kids there. And the kids enjoyed each other. They grew up to play in the street. And they keep in touch. They know the people they grew up with."

Mariann: To know extended family is to draw another circle of stability. Ansie's father-in-law was a difficult man, who even blamed her for her husband George's death. Diane recounts this tough fact with considerable understanding:

Diane: "I think it was very difficult for her, after my father died. Because I think my grandfather Williams in a way blamed her for my father's death. He was hurt that his son died, and it had to be somebody's fault. So it must be hers."

Mariann: Nevertheless, Ansie wanted her children to know George's side of the family. So she made a dignified peace with her father-in-law's blame and silently accepted his dictum that she would get no financial help. Ansie regularly took Perry and Diane to visit the Williams family in Mullins, South Carolina.

Diane: "My father-in-law drove all the way to Fairmont to tell my mother not to expect any help from him. This was shortly after my father died. He told her that he had given all the help that her family would have to my father when he opened his car dealership."

Mariann: "Your mother must have been strong indeed to take that."

Diane: "Well, she did. But she didn't choose to sever ties. She decided that we needed to know grandparents."

Mariann: The need for children to know their grandparents influenced Diane, as it had her mother. It gave Diane and Willy one further reason to settle in the Raleigh area—for her four children to know Ansie and for her to know them.

Mariann: Did you choose to go back to Raleigh because it was where Willy had a job? Why not a small town in Ohio, or in the North or the West?

Diane: "I guess because of family. I guess because of my mother. I was really concerned that my children would not know a grandparent. We moved to be close, really, to my mother. And she needed—she was alone. She had friends, but I felt like probably she needed to know her grandchildren, too."

Mariann: Cultivating this kind of safety demands constant work—the work of vigilance, care, guidance, time spent, priorities balanced, decisions made. Even with all these efforts, safety and security can be elusive.

Diane: "I wanted a life of adventure. But when you have little kids, you don't have a life of adventure, you have a life of hard work, looking after little kids. Life is hard work. And having a house full of kids is not an easy job. And as children grow up, they don't always do what you tell them to do. They don't always do what you think is safe, or what you would have them do."

Mariann: Once Diane conquered an alligator to keep her children safe. She told me this story at the beginning or her interview. I think she likes the story, and so do I.

Diane: "We were staying in Fairmont with my mother. And it was during that time that I killed the alligator, because it was approaching my children. And I didn't even know what it was. I chopped its head off with an edging tool. Like that. He was approaching my babies, who were playing under the pecan tree."

Mariann: Good God.

Diane: "And I just snatched up the tool and went running. He was somebody's alligator that had gotten too big to be a pet. And they had to let him loose—I guess he was supposed to go to the swamp, but he didn't head to the swamp. He headed toward my family."

Mariann: I never heard that story.

Diane: "Oh, yeah. And I thought, 'I'm going to Louisiana. Maybe I'll have a chance at another alligator.'"

Mariann: Was your chopping tool as big as his neck?

Diane: "Well, yeah. It was a half-moon-shaped edge. It was like a hoe, except that the edge was curved rather than being straight across. There was something that you could actually press very firmly on and bounce on with your feet, in the ground. Just an edge. And so I—I attacked the alligator, and I killed him. I chopped his head off."

Mariann: He didn't attack you?

Diane: "I don't remember. I remember seeing him going toward my babies with his mouth, doing that [moves her hands like jaws], and I thought, Oh, no."

Mariann: Most work to keep children safe is not so dramatic, in Diane's experience, but it is much more wearing. She was the disciplinarian of the family, because Willy was usually at work. Her mother was also the disciplinarian. Her views on handling young children are subject to competing theories and circumstances.

Diane: "Well, I think you discipline your kids mostly to keep them safe, not to bend them to your will. Mostly I was concerned that they could get killed. Or they would be in the position where a predator would take advantage of them or steal them away."

Mariann: Was your approach like your mother's?

Diane: "No, because I have a lot less control over my disposition and my temper than she did. Yeah, I'd get mad with them. And I don't think it's realistic not to get mad with people. I don't like to bully people, I don't want to intimidate them, but I would like them to listen to reason."

Mariann: How did you discipline the kids?

Diane: "I would spank them, when they were young. And I decided that really wasn't very good, along about the time that they were beginning to be school age. I didn't like hitting them. I didn't like it at all. It felt awful, to do that."

Mariann: Was that a departure from your mother?

Diane: "She used to spank, and I think she must have come to something like that conclusion, too, because mostly we were talked to. I spent a lot of time in solitary, in my room. With my own children, if things were really out of line, if they were unfair to each other or to some of the other kids, I would talk to them about that and send them upstairs, and I would tell them just exactly what my mother told me—go and find an acceptable way to say that [laughs]."

Mariann: One night Diane found herself in an impressive "all-knowing mother" role, and she didn't need to say a thing:

Diane: "Pepe was the one that gave me a run for my money, really. He would do things. He would take off on the tricycle and start screaming. When they were maybe ten, or eleven, he had a friend names John Mason. And they were going to spend the night in a tent, so he pitched the tent right outside the back door. It was possibly this high at its peak, with enough room for the two little boys maybe not to suffocate in it. And then somebody called Pepe—some girl, I think. And so I went out there to tell him he had a phone call. And nobody was there. And the bicycles were gone. And so I thought, well, they will be back before long, because they certainly don't want anybody to discover that they're gone. And I was getting a little madder, and a little madder, and I thought, well, I'll crawl into the tent and wait for them [laughs]. They came back very quietly, and they opened the tent to get in, and if I had been Godzilla . . . John Mason was scared to death. He remembers it even now. He thought I was magic to even know [laughs]. I don't think it bothered Pepe at all. But I made them come inside. I said, you can't sleep out here tonight. They had ridden their bicycles into Cary, in the dark of night, with no lights. And they didn't even know how it was that I realized that they weren't there. And I don't think I ever told them."

Mariann: As the children grew up, Diane made it a point to be there after school, to talk to them when they most needed a mother's guidance.

Diane: "I think homes are determined by, well, both the father and the mother, but more the mother. I think that the culture is passed through the women, and not the men."

Mariann: What do you mean by culture?

Diane: "Values, and tradition, and the way things are done."

Mariann: Like for example?

Diane: "When I finally went back to work, Wilito was in the seventh grade and college was looming, and we didn't have very much money at all. Wilito was in the seventh grade, Pepe was in the sixth grade, Brian was in the fifth grade, and Julie was in the second grade. And I said, I really need to work myself back into the job market. And that's when I thought, well, I really need to be at home when the kids are home. Because some people think that when kids are old enough to know better than to burn their fingers on the stove, then you can just leave them at home. But I was thinking, that's the beginning of when you need to be at home with the kids."

Mariann: That has to do with values? Talking about what went on at school?

Diane: "You don't want to control relationships, but you want to be able to monitor what's going on, and who their associations are, and if you see something developing that's not very good, you would like to be able to— maybe nudge them in a different direction, and reason with them about things. And they would say no, no, no, no, no, and then they would think about it. And I think they need limits, you know. They don't need to be just free. They need their own limits reinforced. They need to have an excuse not to do some of the things that they are invited to do sometimes. Mom won't like it, she's there, and she'll see us. I felt like I wanted to be at home when they were at home.

"Plus, you know, I just liked to get to know them, and I liked my kids. But anyway, I thought, well, what can I do part time? And the first summer I sold Avon, I thought I was going to have to quit. Because they were young, and I would come home and there would be a fight. But I managed, and then school started, and they got older. I think kids listen. I think after they digest it and have taken it in, you see it coming back."

Mariann: Diane realizes that no amount of supervising or listening or even "playing Godzilla" can keep children entirely safe, because the world is full of dangers. When her daughter Julie came out as gay, Diane's first response was to be afraid for her.

Diane: "Julie was very honest about it. And it was a huge thing for me, and for everybody, because you think of all the—well, the danger, really—and all the hurtful things that people say. And I worry because she's a small person. She's always been very open. And everybody—I mean all her neighbors, they all know. And she seems to get along well with them."

Mariann: I believe I can sense the fear rising and falling in Diane's voice whenever she talks about dangers to her children. As someone who can welcome adventure and freedom, Diane also has a keen sense of peril. She does not want to be a worrier, but she is no stranger to terror.

Mariann: Perhaps the most frightening time in Diane's life was when her mother developed Alzheimer's. In those early days Alzheimer's had not even been identified, and there was little help from the medical community. The disease was gradual and confusing. Was something wrong with Ansie, or not? Sometimes Ansie would speak on the phone as if from an "altered universe" of suspicion and strange perceptions, while at other times she would be cheerful and lucid.

Diane shudders to recall that time before Ansie's disease was certain, when she let her mother drive Brian and Julie the two hours to Fairmont. The children wanted to visit their grandmother, and Ansie wanted to take them, and Fairmont had always been a safe place. And yet . . .

Diane: "I don't know how old they were, maybe nine and twelve. And she took Julie and Brian, and I let them go with her in the car, and I knew that she was not right, and when they left, I thought, I've let my children go with her in the car, and I was very afraid. But they looked after her when they were down there. And she had had two wrecks, before that. And I didn't want to make her feel less. And so I thought, I'll never do that again. I just can't do that. It was wrong, and I shouldn't have done it, but nothing happened. But Brian and Julie couldn't keep a car on the road, and they couldn't keep a wreck from happening. I wasn't concerned about them being in Fairmont with her, because they would be able to manage, and to call somebody, to call home. That was the last time they went to visit."

Mariann: Before long, Ansie came to live with Diane and Willy, and she stayed through her worsening Alzheimer's disease until the end. Yet a person with Alzheimer's cannot feel safe and comforted, even among dear family members. These times meant work for Diane—the hardest and most exhausting kind of work—with meager results of security, safety, or comfort. "It was a pretty dreadful time," Diane says.

Mariann: Still, Diane remembers earlier and better times. Before Alzheimer's arrived like the serpent in the garden to prey upon Ansie's mind, she and her grandchildren rejoiced in one another's company. They went on adventures. They had fun.

Diane: "She would take them, one at a time, and they would all go. She was smart. And they would have a very good time. They would go to the zoo, or they would go down to Columbia, where they watched the moon walk, the first walk on the moon. I think they were at Marion's house. They were young, and that was fun. They got to stay up till the middle of the night and watch the man walk on the moon. It was memorable, memorable. And she would take off and go places and do things. They got to go with her. And she was a free spirit, she loved to go, there was nothing better than getting in the car and choooo! And I blame her for Wilito's love of speed in the car. Go fast, Nana, go fast! Put it in passing gear! And she would do it. Tear off down the road. And your teeth would go to the back of your mouth. She had that car then, eight-cylinder engine. She enjoyed herself. She could laugh heartily. There was nothing better than to get out and [slaps her hands] go, and the faster you could go, the better it was."

Mariann: Diane remembers Ansie as a solemn and stern mother. Yet there was another Ansie, the other half of the "split personality" Diane jokes about, who knew how to have fun. This other Ansie sounds to me remarkably like Diane's father George—the one who would take her to the movies at night in her pajamas, the one who would make her a ladder that could reach the ceiling.

Excerpts from Interviews with Relatives

Larry Kirven

Once when Larry was a young father in his thirties, he looked down and saw death. He was out on the property doing a routine job at the time.

Lary Kirven in the 1940s

Larry: "I was working on a deer stand. And I guess it was not too long after little Tommy had died, and Lauren was at the swamp with me. And I had nailed a cotton-picking spindle into the tree, and I wasn't standing but about five feet off the ground, and I was fixing to nail a nail into a board above my head, and at the moment when I swung the hammer, the spindle popped out from under my left foot, and I went over, head first, with the momentum of my swing and the hammer. Well, I don't guess it took me but two seconds to hit the ground. But as I was coming over, I knew I was going to break my neck. My whole life, from the time I could remember as a child in Eastover, it went through my mind [slaps his hands], and when I hit the ground, I knew I was dead. I just knew that my neck was going to be broken, because I came down on my head. Well, the hammer hit me right here, in the middle of the head. The board came down, and I took eleven stitches in the top of my head. And I was so stunned, and I didn't know anything. And then I heard Lauren say, "Daddy?" And I realized it was him, and as I got back and got my senses together I realized I wasn't dead and I was covered with blood—of course, it probably scared him to death—and Lauren was about nine years old. And he drove the car back to the house, with me in it, and I called Sarah over there to drive me to the hospital."

Mariann: Larry has told me this story several times, and it seems fixed in his brain. His son Lauren was nine years old in 1977, after Larry's father had died in 1975 and close to his mother's death in 1977. His son "little Tommy," who carried the family name of Thomas Jackson Kirven III, had died not long before. So the deaths of family members were all around him, converging upon his own near-fatal fall. He looked death in the face at that moment, and it looked back. Larry vigorously warned and advised his other children, to protect them from harm. Still, his children were too young to have seen what

Larry had seen in that fall. His teenage daughter Karoline a few years later took a big risk, with frightening results.

Larry: "It's just like I told you. We were talking about Lauren and those spending the night at the swamp and Karoline wanting to be down there with them. She gets up, and I ran and told her to get in the bed several times. I guess she was testing me to see if I was going to go to sleep or going to let her go. She finally somehow or other slipped out of the house and went down to the swamp on the mo-ped. Then Lauren and one of his friends in the meantime had gone on to town. The headlight on the mo-ped was out, but it was a bright moonlit night that night. When Lauren and his friend returned from town, he cut the lights off on the truck to ride through the farm to the swamp, and that's when they collided with the mo-ped about, I reckon, 1:30 or 2:00 in the morning. Karoline and one of the boys were riding double on the mo-ped coming back toward the house. When they came to tell me about the accident, all I could envision was Karoline being killed when they told me they had an accident and she was hurt. And of course, you know, I had already lost little Tommy."

Mariann: And almost lost yourself.

Larry: "Yep. And it was a very—I don't know how to explain it, but it was an awful, awful, awful feeling to know that something else has happened pretty terrible, and she [Karoline] of course broke her leg."

Mariann: Glimpses and forecasts of death are more than awful when you feel yourself helpless, unable to prevent the worst. Another loss that must have felt like death took place when Larry and his brothers sat down with their fatally ill father, Tom, to discuss the future of The Farm.

Larry: "Daddy was real sick, and you know he had . . ."

Mariann: Laryngeal cancer?

Larry: "Yeah, in the throat. And I guess Daddy kind of figured things weren't going to get any better. And he had a meeting with Joe, Tom, and Rusty, and myself. He wanted us to come together with The Farm. And I hated to tell him. But I told Daddy, as much as it hurt me to tell him, and I guess I had tears in my eyes when I told him, that there wasn't any way that three families could be supported by The Farm, when two people already could hardly be supported by The Farm."

Mariann: So you and Joe told your dad at that time that you couldn't be part of running The Farm. You couldn't keep your own jobs and at the same time run The Farm, and yet watching somebody else run The Farm, it was frustrating that you couldn't control what they were doing.

Larry: "That's right. That's right."

Mariann: The remaining two brothers, Tom and Rusty, worked hard to save The Farm, but as the 70s turned into the 80s, the economics of small dairy farms were stacked against them. In 1989, hurricane Hugo dealt the last blow of running The Farm as a business. The land had supported the Kirven family since 1912, but the era of agribusiness had now arrived to quash the small farmer.

So death and loss surprised Larry in the middle of his life. Yet his earlier good fortune came as an equal surprise. At the same time he sought to make a living, it seemed that a living was seeking him. In his senior year of college, his first job walked right up to him.

Mariann: Did you ever consider living anywhere else other than The Farm?

Larry: "I entertained that idea when I was in college. As a matter of fact, I had applied for a teaching job in biology in Eatonton, Georgia [four hours away]. My biology professor had had some contacts, and I guess somebody else in those areas had contacted the school and said that they had openings in these fields for these teachers.

"But in the meantime I came home for Christmas—this was my senior year—and a boy that had graduated from Presbyterian College told me he was leaving Furman High School, which was a District Two school in the county, and that he was a biology teacher. Well, that was my major. And so, during the Christmas holidays, I got an application and filled it out for Furman High School, and I never thought any more about it. I was still entertaining the idea of going down to Eatonton, Georgia to get a job.

"I guess it was somewhere around the middle of the spring when we were on the campus. And I saw a gentleman who was the superintendent of the schools, District 2 schools, walking across the campus.

"So I went over there and talked to him, and I asked him, just quizzically, 'What are you doing up here?' And he said, 'I'm looking for you.' Well, that kind of caught me, threw me back, you know, and I said, 'Looking for me? For what?'

"And he said, 'Didn't you apply for a job as a science teacher for the district?'

"And I had to think for a while, because I hadn't even thought about it. I said, 'Yessir, I did.'

"And he said, 'Well, the job is yours if you want it.' Just like that.

"So that was kind of like, overwhelming. He seeks me! But he had gone to the administration office and found that I had pretty good grades."

Mariann: Larry took this offer as it came. He welcomed this teaching job, only ten miles away from The Farm. During his four years there, he discovered that the work was bigger than the pay.

Larry: "I figured it up one day after the hours I spent out there, and the coaching, and the sports that I was teaching, and the hours that I was spending at scouting games and going to football games on Friday nights and the time I was spending out there with other things—I was making 48 cents an hour."

Mariann: Just as Larry was beginning to think he needed a better job, two better jobs walked into his life.

Larry: "After the four years I was teaching—and I don't know whether it was fate, whether it was luck—but anyway, they were going to build a new school bus shop in Sumter, I was teaching down at the school, and here comes the County Superintendent of Education with this man from the state, which I didn't know at that time, and he said, 'Somebody up here wants to speak to you.' And this was about November of '65. Anyway, I was offered the job, after a slight interview. If they liked you, and they saw qualities in you that they thought could fill the job, then basically the job was yours.

Excerpts from Interviews with Relatives

"So he called me back and told me he wanted me. And in the meantime, the Superintendent had called me, and unbeknownst to me, he wanted me to go back to school and get my Master's Degree and stay in the school system. And he kind of caught me. But anyway, I was married and I had a child on the way, and I was making $4,800 a year and I got a $3,000 raise to take the state job. That was a big, big jump for me. And so, naturally, I made the decision, and I took the job, and I stayed in the job for 37 years."

Larry needed only to appreciate his good luck and choose one job over the other.

Although the middle of Larry's life was heavy with deaths and portents, a steady stream of welcoming events has buoyed him up since childhood and sustained him through the hardest times. Once these two jobs walked into his life, and once he was settled with a wife and child near his parents' home, on the lot that his father deeded him—after all these pieces were in place, there was no more thought of going to Eatonton, Georgia. For Larry loves the place he was born. He can imagine no place better.

Larry: "Of course, working on the farm as I grew up, I got to love the land. I felt part of it. I enjoyed seeing things grow. And I guess it was always a part of something I wanted to do. I didn't really want to go that far away. I enjoyed the things that I grew up with, and I guess I just didn't have any desire to go somewhere else. I don't mind going off on a vacation and seeing other things. I think that's wonderful. But it ain't no place like home."

Mariann: Carol told me that you all went off for a month, but after a while, you wanted to come back and work on the land, because you didn't think anything could be better than that.

Larry: "Well, it was. That's right. That's right. But it's just something that kind of grows on you. It kind of gets in your blood. But I enjoyed working the land, and I enjoyed seeing things grow, and give you a yield, and help you make a living. And you just can't make it on The Farm. We rent it out now, but I enjoy the little gardens that I do and the things that I do."

Mariann: Larry does enormous work, much more than planting little gardens. He is the one who tends The Farm now, with tractor and four-wheeler and backhoe. He drove us around the fields and beside the swamps. He explained his plans for trimming some trees and planting others, banking the earth for swamp paths, refurbishing the deer stands, altering the water flow in the fish pond, clearing brush that chokes new growth, and working the soil for vegetables. From the window as we rode, I imagined that I was seeing the landscape of Larry's heart.

Larry: "I guess Daddy always wanted things to look nice and wanted them—I won't say manicured—but he wanted things done the right way and things not to look ramschackle, so to speak. He used to have us out there when we were growing up, to where we'd have a windstorm, back in the spring of the year, and we'd have to get out there and literally dig the sand off the fences. But over the years, when Daddy got older, this practice went out the door. And things just kind of never did get maintained like it needed to be done, and I guess I've taken it upon myself, but nobody else seems to do it but me. I don't know whether it's because I think Daddy might be looking at me or . . . but he's always wanted to leave The Farm to the children, and he said, 'Son, I'll tell you one thing.' He said, 'Land is something they don't make any more of. And if you've got it, you better take care of it and hold on to it as long as you can.'"

Mariann: For Larry, the land holds memories of gatherings with plenty of family members, back when childhood and mischief seemed to hold no real dangers.

Larry: "Well, now, having a big family—family was always very important to me. And I've always looked at our family and the closeness that we had and everybody kind of gravitated toward Mama and Daddy, especially during the holidays, all Marion and Coit and Lawrence and all those, and all the cousins, and of course Ansie would come down. Every Christmas the uncles always brought the fireworks for us [laughs], but they ended up shooting them off. I remember Perry was about maybe thirteen, and of course Ansie didn't want him to have a BB gun or nothing like that, but Coit insisted he was big enough to have a BB gun, so Coit went down to Stubbs Brothers Sporting Goods in Sumter and bought Perry a BB gun."

Mariann: Would Ansie let him shoot it?

Larry: "Well, I'm getting to that. But anyway, he's around there shooting it in the yard, and Ansie wanted to make sure that he had it unloaded. And Perry shook it, it was one of these 500 shot things, but he had BBs rattling in it [laughs], and we were all standing up on the front porch, and he said, 'See, Mama, it's unloaded,' and he cocked it like that, and I was standing over there, and he said, pow, and of course there was one BB left that whapped me right in the back. I don't know whether he ever got that BB gun back or not. But we always had a big gathering, like I said, at holidays—Fourth of July, Thanksgiving, and Christmas. I remember Jo, Marion's daughter, telling about her daddy when he said, 'We goin' to The Farm,' and his daughters said, 'Oh, Daddy, we don't want to go,' and Marion said, 'Get in the car. We goin' to The Farm. Shut up. I don't want to hear no more about it.'"

Mariann: It was as if The Farm drew together the whole spirit of the family. Relatives made their way to The Farm no matter what, and they would return again and again.

Larry: "Cathy came down. We didn't make company out of anybody, everybody fitted in, everybody worked, everybody pitched in, everybody did what needed to be done, whether it was feed the hogs, feed the cows, feed the chickens, whatever. It was all part of what we did, and Perry and Diane would come down quite often, and Perry would help with the combine-ing, in the summertime. As a matter of fact, Perry—I can't remember whether it was his sophomore year [in college]—got some kind of blood poisoning, and he had to drop out of school, the civil engineering that he was majoring in at N. C. State. He came down, and he got a job with the highway department the rest of that year, and that summer, and stayed down here with us the whole time."

Mariann: Lou [Laura Ann] was telling me that he helped build one of these exits.

Larry: "The bypass. I guess you probably came in on it, you turn off on 76. Well, that was part of the bypass that Perry worked on when he was down here."

Mariann: So Perry literally paved the way to The Farm, and the others paved it metaphorically. Larry still feels his life is arranged around the family gatherings for those who remain.

Larry: "I guess our families have gotten smaller. So we don't have the big gatherings, but we still enjoy getting together. I kind of look forward to it. Family means a lot, and even though I don't have but two children [Lauren and Karoline], Carol [Larry's second wife] has two, and we have one grandson, Lake, and then granddaughters, Logan Lee and DuBose, and we all try to get together, birthdays and things like that, we try to do it."

Mariann: The spirit of The Farm is large. To Larry, this spirit includes the values of his parents, which he feels are diminishing in younger generations. To keep your word, to be careful in the face of danger, to persevere in school—Larry inherited these moral codes directly from his parents, as he describes their effect on him:

Larry: "Daddy was telling us that his generation, coming along, their word was their bond. Basically they didn't sign any piece of paper. If they told you they were going to do something or going to help you, that was it! Or if they were going to give you something, that was it. And that's one of the things . . . whenever I tell somebody that I'm going to do something or say I'm going to do something, I try to honor that commitment. I don't think saying these things means as much to the younger generation as it was instilled in us as we were growing up.

"Daddy said. 'God gave you parents to help guide you growing up, to keep you from falling into the same pitfalls and holes that they fell in when they were growing up.' I told Lauren and Karoline, 'We can see things that you all don't see. You all think nothing's going to happen to you, but we've already been down that road, and we know what to expect.' And I said, 'You might think we don't understand, because your generation is different.' I said, 'But it wasn't so much different when we were growing up. You're just exposed to a lot more. You have more transportation than we did.'

"Both of my children, they don't do things I would prefer them to do. I give them advice. Sometimes they take some of it. But like a lot of children, sometimes they respond by saying things that they think you want to hear. It's just like when they were going to school they couldn't quite figure out how I knew why they weren't in school if they cut school. What they didn't know was that I had the attendance teacher. I said, if they are not in school, I want you to call me immediately when the roll is checked. I never did tell them exactly how or why I knew it, but I had feelers out. They were at an age where they needed to listen to me, and I wanted to make goddamn sure that they understood, and I was doing it for their own good."

Mariann: Larry is doing for his two children what he believes his parents did for him, with his mother's encouragement and his father's discipline.

Larry: "I guess if it hadn't been for Mama's encouragement, and the letters she wrote while I was in college, I might not have stayed in college. Absolutely. Mama had a big impact on me. I think she was a big influence in looking at things the way I did. But Daddy also was a big influence. Now, he disciplined us, don't get me wrong. But it taught me that he wanted us to know and understand that you don't do certain things, or that when you are told to do certain things, you need to go ahead and get them done. And he didn't do it out of malice, or out of anger, or anything like that, he did it out of I guess sometimes frustration because he couldn't seem to get our attention any other way. But family, it was instilled in me, is very important."

Mariann: Larry takes in his parents' behavior toward him as kindness. They were doing him a favor, in the same way that his parents were generous to their neighbors in need.

Larry: "My daddy was a hard taskmaster. In other words, he was a hard worker. He never said the words, 'I love you,' but by his actions he showed that he cared very much for his children, very much for Mama, and he was always trying to make other people feel good by doing things for them. I don't think Daddy ever knew a stranger. Mama and Daddy took in two or three kids that couldn't get along with their parents, and they came out and stayed all the way through high school, like E. M. [Joe Chandler's football companion at Presbyterian College]."

Mariann: Larry's whole life may have been sustained by the sense of a dwelling-place that his parents bequeathed to their children. Now in retirement he still feels the strength of that support. It is the gift of a way to live, just like the job offers of his youth that walked right up to him.

Mariann: is it true to say that when you're doing for the land what you think should be done, and doing it right, that you are kind of "in spirit" with your daddy?

Larry: "I get a pleasure out of it. An enjoyment out of it. It's like a therapy, almost."

Mariann: Do you feel like it connects you with your dad?

Larry: "I think so. I've had several people to tell me that I look more like Daddy. I act more like Daddy, than like anybody else in the family."

Mariann: I think you look more like Grandfather.

Larry: "Well, that's what Karoline said when she saw Grandaddy's picture, she said I looked more like Grandaddy than anybody else in the family."

Mariann: What do you think you mother would think? About you doing the work you're doing these days?

Larry: "I think she would approve, and she would be pleased. I think Mama kind of wanted us to stay close."

Mariann: To each other?

Larry: "Yeah, to the family. I felt that I'd like to have something—I don't guess you'd call it a legacy. I don't have any legacy or anything like that, but I hope that what I've tried to instill in my children would take, and they'd see some value in what I've tried to show them and tell them, and hopefully I'll have a little bit of something to leave them that they'd appreciate. And I know I appreciate what Daddy tried to do for us."

Mariann: Those sound to me like they are legacies. I mean—you feel like you have a legacy from you father.

Larry: "Yeah."

Mariann: To Larry, the land endures, outlasting death. While Larry is tending the land, doing as his father would have done, it feels almost as if Daddy and Grandaddy are alive. The land bridges those tragedies and terrors that have visited Larry in his lifetime, and Larry has been taught how to appreciate that bridge and walk across it.

Anne Kirven

Mariann: Anne chose to write the results of her own interview, below:

When I reflect on my own life growing up in Columbia, South Carolina, it brings to mind many memories of our family life.

My Daddy [Marion Kirven] was a successful insurance salesman, and Momma was a stay-at-home mom with us girls: Winkie, myself, and Jo. Winkie was four and a half years older than me, the "middle child," and Jo was the baby of the family. Growing up, I was tight with my dad. I would help him fence in the yard, pack the car for trips, and cut the grass. I guess I was kind of a tomboy. We never had to worry about not being taken care of. We always knew we were safe and had a home and food, the result of my dad's success. Momma was always there for all of us, but Daddy set the rules. At times, I felt she never spoke up or gave Daddy any flak. As I got older, I thought she needed to stand up to him at times, but it was not her nature. So I, being the "middle child," would speak up to daddy and voice my opinion during trying times, and on occasion he would listen to me.

I left Columbia after graduating from high school and went to Charleston for nurse's training. I met Allen, and we were married when I was nineteen years old. We lived in Charleston until 1964 and then moved to Columbia. We had our three girls: Cheryl, Barre, and Leslie. Allen and I had our times of disagreements and financial difficulties. My daddy felt Allen should be the main breadwinner, but I carried the majority of the load.

He would say we needed to agree to disagree. Allen and I had three children under three years old, and I was working full-time. We didn't have any extra. Daddy would tell Momma, "Mable, you need to take the girls down to Stride-Rite every three months and get their shoes." We had to polish them every Saturday night, and if I came over he'd say, "When was the last time you polished those shoes?" My daddy had two pairs of shoes. One of them went to the man to get them polished, and he wore the other. When I was in school, he would tell me, "You need two pairs of shoes. You wear one one day, and then you take them off, and wear them out and you wear the other."

Before moving back to Columbia, I spent many weekends at my parents' house when the girls were little. I wanted to be around family. When I grew up, you see, my mother's mother and father lived right down the street from us. They were always in our life. And it was a good thing, I mean, we'd go down there and spend the night with them and you know, we'd eat breakfast and she'd fix us all little cups of coffee, like you used to drink when you were little, and it was good.

On Sundays and on holidays, we would eat dinner at my parents' house. All of us would come, us, Winkie and Bobby and their children, Matt, Gray, and Amy. Jo and Bill lived in Boone, North Carolina. We would have more food than you could eat, and every dessert you could think of.

When I finally moved back to Columbia, I lived off Leesburg Road. I would get up before anybody would get up, any of my children, and I would cut through the back way and go up and have coffee with Daddy. Then I would go back home.

Allen and I did not always see eye to eye. He was somewhat domineering—similarities to my dad. We divorced in 1968. I remember reading a lot of books when I got divorced, like Co-Dependent No More and all these inspirational books. You feel like when you're young and your daddy's the head honcho, that's how it should be. And then you get older, and marry, and then you're like, I don't want it to be like that in my marriage. I never made any opinions when I was married. I never made any choices about anything. You know, Allen and I built a house, and I'd like so-and-so, and he'd say, put it in a folder, but when it came to it, I had that folder and there was nothing in that house like me. He didn't have room for it, or it cost too much. It was strictly his house.

Now that I am on my own, I can pay my bills and I have money for the things in life I need and deserve. It's like, "How'd that happen?"

Laura Ann Kirven Onsrud

Laura Ann wrote her own summary, because during her interview the recorder malfunctioned.

When we lived in Eastover, our nearest neighbors were about a mile away. There were not many other children to play with. The brothers and sisters played with each other or with the cook's children. Danny and I played with Pansy Mae at times. One afternoon when we were playing in the back yard, a rabid cat bit Pansy Mae on her hand. Danny and I rushed her over to the spigot to wash the blood away, and we ran to get help. We had to get rabies shots. There were many animals that were rabid that summer.

David and Laura Ann Onsrud

When we moved back to the Old Home Place in Sumter, there were neighbors that were nearby, and there were family members, aunts and uncles, living in town.

In the summer there was usually a relative or two visiting. When we gathered for meals, the table was always full. After eating, everyone helped with the dishes. There were times when Ma Ma and Daddy cared for a child that was in an unhappy home situation. They lived with us just like family, and everyone had work to do. It wasn't until many years later that I learned that my parents had gone to court to get custody of a child due to his home situation. And everyone had work to do on the farm. My parents always had room for one more. Our door was always open, especially when a child needed a place to stay. They could take them in and treat them like family.

Daddy had a fish pond dug, and it was stocked with fish. Daddy and the boys made a swimming pool. They poured concrete to form the sides. An Artesian well supplied the water for the pool, and a pipe was fixed so that water would drain into the big pond.

In late August before time for the family to separate for various reasons such as college, jobs, or service, the whole family—Ma Ma, Daddy, and all of us children—would come down to the pond for a leisurely afternoon.

After David and I married, I moved to Long Island where he worked. I got a teaching job in Smithtown. Life was different. We rented a small house, and then the following spring we bought a house in St. James. Dave's family was nearby in Smithtown. Dave always helped his family with the yard work or with what they needed to be done. And when our neighbor was unable to cut the grass any more, Dave cut his grass.

After Dave's father died, his mother moved to Florida. During holiday times, we made the effort to visit my family in Sumter and his mother in Florida. Sumter was halfway, so we stopped in Sumter going down and coming back.

When Dave's job on the Island was over, he went to Connecticut to work. I stayed on Long Island, as I was teaching. He came home weekends. Dave worked in Connecticut until a job opened up for him on Long Island at Brookhaven National Laboratory. He worked there until he retired. Then we moved South. We chose Simpsonville, South Carolina, because his sister was in Greenwood and his nephew was in Mauldin, and my family was in Sumter.

I especially remember that trips were made South during my father's illness. I would come down to give some help to the family. Daddy was sick with laryngeal cancer and died. Afterwards, Mama got sick and was failing. I took a week off and came to Sumter to visit and help out. Shortly after that visit, Mom died.

After getting settled in Simpsonville, we could visit family. We were always taught to help out when there was a family illness. My sister Julie was ill with Guillain-Barre, and she had to be transferred to Duke Hospital in Durham. The doctors in Fayetteville did not know what her problem was. As soon as she arrived at Duke her history was taken, she was given tests, and the doctor recognized the disease she had. She was there for three weeks.

Dave came to Durham and located a place for us to stay. Julie's husband Lynwood and I took turns staying at the hospital with Julie. Dave was back and forth between Durham and Simpsonville. I know she would do that for me. When family needs you, you come.

We are close enough to Sumter so that we could always be there for them. Your home is where your family is, and being with family is most important.

Joe Chandler Kirven

Selections from Joe's interview are interspersed with quotations from Joe's book of stories, *Living the Country Life,* along with comments and selections from letters given me by his wife, Sallie Munroe Kirven.

When I asked Joe what home meant to him, he showed me. He clasped his forearms with both his hands, making an arm-circle as if he were cradling a baby. His body swayed and rocked a little, and he gave me a look of complete earnestness.

Joe: "Home! It means the whole thing. If I could wrap it up like this [cradles his arms] . . . I've stayed here for a long time. Sally stayed here with me. I felt pretty good about it, I thought that I had got the right person. When I said, 'Sallie, will you marry me?' She said, 'Yeah!'"

Sallie: "What? I thought you'd never ask. We could have stayed in Dillon [75 miles northeast of Sumter], where Joe was teaching, and I was in Fairmont [20 miles further than Dillon], we could have stayed up there, but Joe felt that he'd worked this farm so long that he really wanted to come back here. His brothers were already in Sumter."

Joe and Sallie raised two now-prosperous children, Anne and Joseph, on land bought from his parents, near schools where they each taught and near the church they attended.

Yet "home" to Joe seems to mean not only his immediate family but also his extended family—his brothers and their families, and the family land. Joe always knew he would settle down close to The Farm. His cradling motion in response to the word "home" expresses Joe's heartfelt desire to hold all his family together—as if with his own hands—since he was a boy.

Joe's most piercing memories in his retirement were about two periods of crisis in the life of his extended family. First, after the bank foreclosed in 1933 on The Farm in Sumter, his parents and siblings had to migrate thirty miles west to Eastover and work rented land, as tenant farmers, from Joe's third year until he was thirteen. As soon as Joe was physically old enough to work, his boy's hands were much needed in that whole-family effort, as he writes in his book of family stories:

"In 1933 my father, my mother, and Grandmother Laura Kirven—as well as my older sister Ophelia, my older brother Tom, and I—all left for Eastover, South Carolina in a Model A Ford. I was three years old. My father's farm equipment consisted of two 2-horse wagons, one 1-horse wagon, an assortment of turn plows and harrows, and a reaping binder. There were also cotton planters, fertilizer distributors, and eight mules. Five tenant families, living in five tenant houses on the farm, supplied labor for planting, cultivating, and harvesting.

"Well before daybreak Dad was up, starting a fire in the kitchen stove. Tom and I had to milk six cows in time to catch the school bus by 7:30. Missing the bus meant walking the two miles to Eastover Elementary School, which offered grades one through seven. In later years we had to work with the field hands all day if we missed the bus to Lower Richland High, nineteen miles away.

"The field hands were also up before daylight. It was a common practice for dinner to be fixed and brought to work, especially when we were chopping or picking cotton. Dinner buckets were usually filled with rice and gravy and cornbread, and sometimes with rabbit, squirrel, or fatback. A quart jar of well water would complete this noon meal.

"All plowing, harvesting, and cultivating was done by the farm hands. Mules furnished the power. In 1938 Dad bought a John Deere model B tractor, a grain combine, and a disc harrow. This machinery could do the work of eight field hands.

"In 1941 the Japanese attack on Pearl Harbor brought us into the Second World War. We were left with only two farm workers living on the farm, and it was very difficult to keep crops planted, cultivated, and harvested. In 1943 Dad bought a second tractor. This made farming much easier for us and eliminated the need for mules. Prices for farm produce began to increase. Back debts were paid. Things began to look a little better financially for Dad. Since there were now seven children and another one on the way, it was a welcome development."

Mariann: When I read this passage from Joe's book of stories, I see Joe's own hands toiling away on a tractor-less, resistant farm—milking the cows in early morning, picking and chopping cotton with the field hands, toting a lunch bucket for sustenance during a hard day.

Then there was the boll weevil, which hit the South in the 1920s and proved deadly to the cotton crop. As Joe pitched in to farm 300 acres, mostly cotton, he remembers taking on that insect with his hands. He explained the battle in slicing gestures, as he set out to kill the boll weevil that threatened the family's livelihood.

Joe: "And the boll weevil, you ever heard of him? You know the thing was fixed in rows, like this far apart, and you could cut down the middle of them, turn round and come down, and cut the other way, you'd kill it. And if you didn't keep those things off of the cotton before they ate it up? Little bugs would get in that blossom and eat it off."

Mariann: Reading Joe's personal account, I am newly amazed by the fact that Joe would have been introduced to farm work in Eastover when he was three years old and continuing through primary school until he was close to thirteen years old. During Joe's elementary school years, he would have been performing sharecropper labor as a young and growing child.

And sometimes there were more dangerous tasks. Joe had to use his young hands again, along with all his strength and nerve, to keep the family operation together, as he writes in his stories:

Joe: "It seems that at least twice a year the mules would get out of their pasture. This would usually happen in the dark of night. We would be awakened by the sound of hoofbeats—mules running loose. Some twelve to fifteen animals would be running wild through the garden, clothesline, and front yard.

"All hands were summoned to key positions. In the dark, with only a kerosene lantern and some sort of stick, we would manage to get them subdued. You soon learned very quickly how to get behind a tree or climb the fence to keep from being trampled.

"Now, the bulls getting out of their pen—that was a different situation. Dad usually had two bulls and kept them in different pens. If one bull happened to break out of his pen, he would challenge the second bull. Soon both would be out of control, loose and fighting each other. When we were alerted, all hands fell out, usually around midnight. Armed with pitchforks, we surrounded the bellowing bulls and forced them back to their quarters. As the bulls turned their rear ends to you, you jabbed them with the pitchfork and forced them back into their pens . . . These episodes happened when I was ten to twelve years old. My brothers and I have often talked about how we ever survived them, particularly when they happened in the dead of night."

Mariann: In the fall of 1943 the family's fortunes grew worse. His father, Tom, was taken to the hospital, his back incapacitated. Joe and his brother Tom, at ages thirteen and fifteen, had to take over.

Joe: "I vividly remember the great change for me in the fall of 1943. I was supposed to begin eighth grade, but that was at Lower Richland High school, some nineteen miles away by bus. In October 1943, Dad was in the hospital with back problems. Tom and I had to drop out of school. We maintained the farm with the help of one farm hand, a tractor driver. Planting was difficult in the spring of 1944, but with no school to worry about, Tom and I got it all done. We milked six cows each morning and night, and we took care of the remaining chores with the help of Buddy DuBose, who was living with our family."

Mariann: The two older boys, having left school, became the main hands on the farm. They finished the spring 1944 planting, though. They felt they had prevailed. But then the final misfortune arrived. Worse than hard farming is having no land to farm. At the time of the fatal announcement, Joe was in his parents' bedroom, for his mother wanted Joe's hands-on help:

Joe: "Daddy wasn't doing too well [with the intense pain from crushed vertebrae and a subsequent back operation]. Mama was watching Daddy, and she asked me to move a cot into the room that they were in, so that if he needed attention for anything, I would be there. And Daddy was in the bed and Mama was in the bed and I was sleeping in the bed and I heard Daddy grunting and kind of carrying on in the middle of the night, and I got up and helped Mama.

"And the fellow [the man who had rented that land to Joe's family since 1933] came and knocked on the door. And Daddy was sick in there. And [the fellow] came in, and I was too nice about it. He said, 'I'd like to go in and talk to your Daddy,' and I said, 'Well, come on in,' and he said, 'Well, Mr. Kirven, I hate to tell you, but I can't rent this thing next year. You'll have to get out.'

"Yeah. Lost everything. Every-thing!"

Mariann: In that phrase, "I was too nice about it," Joe may be expressing his sense of desperation as a boy unable to safeguard his parents' well-being. He had to let that bad-news intruder into his sick father's bedroom. There was no help for it. The family had to leave by October, with no place to go. More than sixty years later, Joe can still remember the despair on his parents' faces, their frantic search for another farm to rent, and the arduous task of moving an entire farm.

It worked out, though, with the help of all hands. One of his father's friends discovered that August that The Farm in Sumter, their old homestead, was up for sale again. Crowds of his father's friends appeared with mules and wagons and trucks—even a chain gang dispatched by the county supervisor—to help the Kirvens take in the harvest and move furniture, farm supplies, equipment and machinery, cattle, chickens, "the 300 turkeys, the 150 pigs, the horses, the six dogs," the harvested crops, and a family with eight children.

It was a family triumph. Everything was lost, but then everything was found again.

Joe: "Daddy was going crazy, 'I don't know what I'm going to do.' They [the neighbors and friends] said, 'Don't worry, you tell us what you want to haul off, and we'll send it over there for you.' They caught all that stuff and brought it over to [Sumter]. Made them a place, took up everything else they could take up. My Daddy had put up some wire fences, pole in the ground here, pole in the ground there, he had them all around that place. He said, 'I'm not going to leave them a damn thing out here.' Took everything off."

Mariann: And Joe's own hands completed this coup. At thirteen years old, he drove the tractor and combine the whole thirty miles from Eastover to Sumter. Alone. It was a six-hour trip. He remembers his pride and his trepidation as if it were yesterday. Joe was chosen to drive the tractor-combine, he says, because he could *handle* it.

Joe: "The combine was as wide as from here to that window over there [Joe gestures about twenty feet] pulled behind the tractor. And I was driving that thing like anybody else, and I knew how to make it do this and do that and do the other. And Daddy who took care of everybody knew that I knew how to handle the doggone thing.

"And he said to me, 'I want you to take that combine, you reckon you can take it?'

"And I said, 'Well, I know where Sumter is.'

"'And he said, 'Well, we'll have Coit meet you at such & such,' which was right at the edge of town where you came into Sumter.

"I knew Highway 76. And I got up there, and I didn't know where to go. And Coit wasn't there."

Mariann: So what did you do?

Joe: "I stopped it on the side of the road, and somebody came by and said, 'Son?'

"And I said to them, 'The policeman [Coit] is supposed to be here, he belongs to me.'

"And he said, 'Well, I'll get him, I'll get him.' He sent somebody to tell me which turn would take me [out of town]. And I brought [the combine] on out to The Farm."

Mariann: So by the time Joe was thirteen, and the family had returned to The Farm, he had taken it in hand to drive the tractor and combine from Eastover to Sumter, with "no escort or companion," as he says, and re-discovered just how vital his hands were to the well-being of the family.

In the ensuing decades, Joe and his brothers put their shoulders and hands to farm work, as the family labored to support themselves on their regained farm. Joe drove the combine through the fields with all deliberate speed, while his brothers, and sometimes Perry, hurried to tie off the grain bags in back. Joe and Tom sold their labor to other farms, driving the tractor in twelve-hour shifts as a day-and-night tag team. They all sold turkeys at Thanksgiving and Christmas, melons in the summer.

Not that it was all grueling toil. Joe's hands, strengthened by all this work, made him a football star at Presbyterian College. And whenever they had time, the boys went hunting. In one of Joe's stories, "Big Buck Before Sunrise," Joe had a hands-on drama. It was November of 1951, at Lark's Creek in the Santee Swamp, after the last football game of the season. Joe and his four friends had hunted for a year. They were duck-hunting when a ten-point buck surprised them, no more than thirty yards away. Joe's friend E. M. whispered to Joe, "Shoot!"

Joe writes, "As the buck looked directly at me, I pulled the trigger. My aim had been right between his eyes . . . . That buck jumped six feet in the air, turned around, and ran directly towards us. I then knew that he was blinded by my shot. E. M. cut loose with two rounds of duck shot. The deer stumbled and then regained his footing.

"The deer came within ten feet of the two of us. He was not smelling us, and he surely had not seen us. As he struggled to get his footing, I reached out and grabbed his massive antlers. As he bucked and jumped, I managed to reach around a small sapling and grab him with both hands, thereby preventing him from using his antlers on me."

Mariann: Admittedly, Joe is a big man with big hands. That scene remains iconic in my mind, and probably in Joe's mind as well.

After college and a two-year stint in the Army as a paratrooper, Joe taught high school, coached football, and married Sallie Munroe. Back in Sumter, he was made principal of four schools from 1962 until 1989, when he retired.

As school principal, Joe took care of people in a hands-on manner. At retirement he was given a grand memorial quilt, eight by nine feet, with each one-foot square designed by a co-worker. The quilt hung over his fireplace. It made me imagine Joe wrapping his hands protectively around his colleagues, as if they were another family. Sallie's letter to me describes *ten* of the seventy-two squares.

Sallie writes in her letter, "I thought the teachers did an excellent job. The quilt tells stories from his life, and our lives, and they give us humor as well. The schools where Joe served as principal are the four corners of the quilt. They are Central Elementary, McLaurin Junior High, Bates Middle, and Millwood Elementary."

Here are Sallie's descriptions of ten of the squares:

[1] A teacher that belonged to our church cross-stitched First Presbyterian with the saying, 'What we are is God's gift to us, what we become is our gift to God.'

[2] We liked our house done by Anne Mathis. She had come to our house to measure for a new carpet. She told Joe she was working on her college degree. Joe told her to come and see him when she finished, and he would hire her. Two years later, he hired her.

[3] We like the school bus done by one of the teachers that did not care to do bus duty in the A. M. So Joe took bus duty each morning, with the understanding that the teachers would be ready for the students when the bell rang.

[4] We like Edisto Beach along with teacher Nancy McDuffie. She did an outline of South Carolina with palm trees denoting Edisto Beach.

[5] Double Dutch jump roping was started by Physical Education teacher Paul Shirah at Millwood. Double Dutch spread throughout the school district and state. The City of Sumter now sponsors a Double Dutch Jump Rope state tournament.

[6] The Popcorn Story began when eight buses would come to pick up elementary kids. They couldn't behave, so Joe taught the head custodian to make popcorn! That was her afternoon duty—and kids were rewarded with popcorn if they could catch the bus in an orderly

manner, preventing serious accidents. And yes, the Fabulous Four is on the quilt, with the names of the head custodian and other custodians.

[7]   A cousin-in-law, Cheryl Chandler, came to teach kindergarten at Millwood. She was chosen Teacher of the Year for the state PTA, and we accompanied Cheryl to receive these awards at the state convention.

[8]   We both like this saying done by Rose Simmons, "Age is a state of matter! If you don't mind, it don't matter."

[9]   The square I like best was done by the school nurse, Sandy Noonan. She did a nurse's cap. Joe had taught her in school. Later on, I was expecting a baby. When we got to the delivery room, Sandy was on duty. She knew Joe was anxious, so she slipped out of the delivery room to let Joe know he had a baby boy. But she swore him to secrecy and told him to act surprised when the doctor came to give him the news. Later on, she came to Millwood as the school nurse!

[10] I have to tell you about the square by Jean Mims. She was a member of the faculty at Millwood and she had graduated from Sumter high in 1968. Joe had been the sponsor for her class for three and a half years but left the school mid-year to assume a principal's job at another school. Jean did the square that had the dedication of her 1968 High School Annual, "Hi-Ways," that says, "To our most respected and cherished friend, Mr. Joe Kirven."

This quilt is a tribute to Joe, as a person who would like to cradle both friends and family in his hands. But not all of Joe's hands-on actions were without conflict. In high school he would paddle older boys when circumstances became difficult.

Joe: "I was at the high school, working in some heavy stuff up there, up through the twelfth grade. And I had to take care of all the ones who . . . the big boys didn't mess up with me. Back in those days, you could use a paddle. I didn't hurt any of them, but I knew, just like you're playing ping-pong, you take a paddle like that and crack him about three times on his butt, you don't have any trouble anymore."

Mariann: Joe saw his methods as "taking care" of the school. He himself had been whipped as a boy. He speaks of his corporal punishment by his father:

Joe: "Pull that belt out there like that and whack your butt, oh, about 15 times, and you couldn't stand still, you had to leave [laughs]. Not too much of that, though, but it happened, it happened."

Mariann: Today it is illegal in most states to strike children—big or small—in school. Joe's response to the new way suggests that he had paddled some "big boys" partly out of desperation. Probably using force made him uncomfortable, yet he didn't know what else to do.

Joe: "Then all of a sudden, you can't strike the child in school now. You can't do this and you can't do that, well, what can you do?"

Mariann: This same note of desperation marks Joe's words about the second extended family crisis, the one that began in the 1970s, when his parents died and The Farm slowly failed. What *could* he do?

In 1975 Joe's father died, and his mother passed away in 1977. His father Tom had taken over The Farm for his own dying father in 1921, and he no doubt wished that his five sons would do the same: Tom, Joe, Danny, Larry, and Rusty. The Farm was by then a dairy farm, and in the 1970s the dairy industry was in the middle of a long decline.

Joe and Larry had found their own jobs in the school system, for The Farm could no longer support the whole family. Eva thought that Tom and Rusty could manage the dairy business, while she and Danny set up an antique shop and a small restaurant in the house.

For a while, The Farm continued solvent.

After a time, though, Danny could not sustain a profit. He moved away and later died. Tom and Rusty found innovative ways to feed and milk the 150 cows. Yet the dairy business kept shifting its regulations and markets. As Joe says, "People that had taken milk from The Farm for ten or fifteen years could get it better somewhere else. Chasing the market, dairy farmers switched to Jersey cows." Change was constant.

Joe agonizes about the loss of The Farm. He worries that there must have been some way to save The Farm, and that he, Joe, should have found the right direction and led the family there.

Joe: "Mama did the best she could, and she just said, 'Here! You take care of this, Tom, and you take care of this, Rusty.' Tom was doing this, and somebody else was doing that. None of it went together, and it just went to pieces.

"But I got to the place where my God, if they don't do something right now, things are gone. Mama got sick, and she said, 'You all will have to take care of it from now on.' And I wanted to do one thing, and they wanted to do it another way, and things just didn't work out.

"I always felt, my God! If I don't go stop them from doing this, they won't have another nickel in the pot before long. And that's the way it worked out.

"My feeling was, I was trying to keep all of them on the right road together, and what it was had to be done we got to do it, and we can't sit down and hire somebody else to come do it for you, and pay them too.

"Danny thought he was going to set up the antique shop. We would go sometime, when they had a sale somewhere, and he'd want me to go in the trailer and go up there and buy this or that thing, and I helped him with that, but he had something nice going there for a while, but it didn't do. He never did get his money back that he put in there.

"Now you have to give Rusty some credit. He had some problems, and right along there he got married. Married again, and got two children, and when he turned around, his wife took the two children and ran off with them. He didn't know what to do, and I didn't know how to help him, and I couldn't go get them, and he couldn't go get them.

"It worked for a while [Tom and Rusty's method of running the dairy farm]. But all of a sudden—'We can't do right, this doesn't do right'—and I said, 'Well, I don't know what to tell you. I told you what I thought' . . ."

Sallie: "There were so many people, and all of them had different ideas. Like the silo. Joe wanted them just to get a medium-sized silo that he thought they could manage. But Mr. Kirven had so many people pulling on him, that he couldn't make ends meet, hardly, from the dairy."

Mariann: Joe's memory fastens on sequences of actions that he can see working, that he can imagine doing with his hands. Casting back to the past, he details how his father used common-sense strategies that made a profit.

Joe: "Daddy and this fellow Rhyttenberg, they used to sell hogs together. Daddy would find the little hogs all around in the pig places in the mountains that people were selling, you know, and this little fellow here would bring them up and sell them."

Mariann: Joe pictures human hands gathering pigs, or human hands setting out big milk containers.

Joe: "You know, the way it was, you had these big cans about this tall, and a small mouth on them like this, and you milk these cows and get a bucketful. You pour it in that big thing, and put the top back on it, and go on and get another one, and when you got 5 or 6 or 8 or 10, you put them out there on the edge of the road, and the people that were picking them up knew to come and get them [slaps his hands] as quick as they could. And they would take them and bring them uptown."

Mariann: When Joe helps Tom and Rusty with their dairy, he values the same kind of hands-on action. He likes to see his brothers' dreams being fulfilled. He likes to feel his own hands contributing to solve the problem. He admires his brothers' arrangement for milking cows while the cows feed.

Joe: "Well, I helped when I could. You see that big old thing down yonder? Silo, goes up there? There would be a flat piece about this wide, rolling back around—oh, it was sixty or seventy feet long. You cut the corn down, like it is right now, chop it up and throw it into that silo, and get it full. They were milking a lot of cows, about a hundred fifty for a while. They had plenty for them to eat. They had a track that would come out the bottom of the silo and go along the cement, about this wide, and the cows, when we were milking them, we had them lined up there, and they were sitting there looing.

"Somebody asked me about their hands. When I showed him my hands, he said, 'How you break up your hands?'

"And I said, 'Man, what's wrong with your hands?'"

"'I don't know.'"

"'Look at mine,' I said."

"'Oh, my God, what kind of hands you got?'"

"And I said, 'Well, that's how I got it. Milking cows.'

"Anyhow, Tom and Rusty had all those cows, 120 cows, feeding them through that silo. You put the corn things that are left over, still green, and you chop them up and blow them up there, it comes out of the bottom, down a run. And while you're milking them, they're sitting there eating."

Mariann: Joe does not blame anyone in his family. Yet he can't shake the wish that he himself might have been able to do something. He may wonder why—since he used his hands and his wits to help his family for so many years—why he could not save them this one last time. I imagine he would like to cradle them all in his own hands, both the people and the land. If Joe feels strangely powerless in this turn of events that was no one's fault, he shares that kind of anxiety with many others on this earth. It is one of the most painful feelings in the world.

Joe dispenses kindness with his big hands. I asked him whether he had built his own house on the site where the family's old house had burned down in 1915. His response was typically generous.

Sallie: "That old house was further up that way, I think. Joe found some bricks up there not long ago."

Joe: "I've picked up some bricks that—when they played across there, cocked a brick up, I picked up a bunch of them. Like a dozen or so. I've got some stuck out there. If I could get out there and see them, I'll give you one of them."

Mariann: Joe took me out behind his workshop and showed me the bricks he suspected were from the old house. They seemed a lighter red, with a more spongey texture than bricks I've seen in modern structures. They had yellow protuberances, as if caulk had stuck to them. Joe offered to let me take one of those bricks home.

Joe loves to give away good things—figs from his enormous fig tree, cantaloupes and watermelons from the garden he shares with Larry. He gave me a serving tray that he made himself from pinewood. During the period when the family moved back from Eastover, Joe was the chief cook and bottle-washer who baked biscuits in the Eastover fireplace and sent them home with family members traveling to Sumter.

Barbecue is another food Joe likes to give. He rehearses the way his father's Jewish friend, Harry Rhyttenberg, taught the family to barbecue. Joe's hand gestures serve as words:

Joe: "We would cut a place almost as big as that sofa over there, down in the ground, put all the charcoal down there and get it all fixed up and get a screen, and put that old hog down on it. And lay it out like this—we had already cleaned him out—and we got him and cooked up and you cut off this, and you cut off that, and man, you have some good eating. And you got a lot of lard. You want to save that lard."

Mariann: Did you make pies with that lard?

Joe: "Yeah. Cook that lard and everything else."

Mariann: "Everything tastes good."

Joe: [Throws his hands up] "You have the history of my soul.".

Joe has a giving soul. And that is the end of our interview.

www.ingramcontent.com/pod-product-compliance
Lightning Source LLC
LaVergne TN
LVHW010200070526
838199LV00062B/4435